FOREX
TRADING
FOR BEGINNERS

3 BOOKS IN 1

The Best Strategies & Tactis to Make Money, Day
Trade to Make a Living, Master Crypto Investing, Plus
the Ultimate Money Management Guide

FOREX TRADING

CRYPTOCURRENCY INVESTING

DAY TRADING

FOREX TRADING

Make Money Today

The Ultimate Guide With The Best Secrets, Strategies
And Psychological Attitudes To Become A
Successful Trader In Forex Market

INTRODUCTION

There are people who, thanks to trading, have changed their lives and that of many people who have believed in them. It is enough to mention the name of Warren Buffet or George Soros because dreams and visions begin to start in the heads of many traders.

Trading success is achieved by staying very down to earth.

Starting from this belief, I wrote this manual in a simple way with the aim of helping newbies to find the right way to be successful, but above all to find the right methods to avoid losing money, very often, saved with many sacrifices.

Trading is not synonymous with gambling. Trading on the financial markets is neither a game nor a hobby. Your approach must be extremely serious and disciplined, especially your attention must be paid to safeguarding the capital you decide to invest. Knowing your character, your fears, your goals, knowing how to use all this to your advantage, is certainly an added weapon.

CHAPTER ONE
THE FOREX MARKET

What is the Forex Market

The stock and bond markets are not the only ones that allow you to invest in the hope of being able to grow your capital and thus earn money.

Alongside these markets that are more known to the general public, there are lesser-known markets which, however, also offer excellent opportunities in terms of returns and earnings. The Forex market, for example, is the market where currencies are traded and the value of a currency is quoted. The way Forex works is not too dissimilar compared to the stock market. In the latter, investors and traders seek to take advantage of changes in the share price of listed companies; in the Forex market, traders will seek to take advantage of fluctuations in the prices of various monetary currencies and increase the value of their investment portfolio.

Forex is the abbreviation of Forex Exchange, which is the currency market, where currencies are traded with each other. These operations in the Forex market create fluctuations in the price of currencies, which the Forex trader will seek to exploit to increase the value of his investment and thus create profit.

The Forex market is a global market, the second largest in terms of trading volume after the interest rate market. A market that does not stop growing all over the world.

Trading is nothing more than the purchase and sale of financial assets to take advantage of the increase or decrease in their prices. The trader, on the other hand, is the "market operator" who makes purchases and sales on markets of various kinds: from the stock market to the bond market, passing through government bonds and, obviously, currencies.

Unlike a "classic" investor who buys a product and waits for its value to increase over time before reselling it, a trader usually adopts a more dynamic approach, with transactions that can last a few days, minutes or even seconds. This is a potentially more lucrative but also riskier approach.

Forex trading, therefore, consists of buying or selling currency pairs on Forex, trying to predict which direction the pair will take in the following days or minutes. Forex trading can be risky, so you should try to be well prepared and make sure you understand the risks before investing your money.

The basic principle of the operation of the Forex market passes from the concept of "couple". While in the stock market we operate and invest on the shares of individual companies, in the Forex market we operate on currency pairs. This means that the value of one currency is expressed not in an absolute sense, but in relation to that of another currency.

Forex, from its Origins to Today

The currency trading market from which Forex is born has very ancient origins, but it has evolved especially in the last few centuries, hand in hand with the financial innovations of the markets.

Background

The modern foreign exchange market was born in 1971 when exchange rates were allowed to float. Before 1971, in fact, the currencies were regulated by an international agreement called the "Bretton Woods Agreement", with which the participating nations had decided to keep the value of their currencies within a narrow margin of exchange with the Dollar. On the same day of August 1971, the Nixon Administration unilaterally interrupted the convertibility of the Dollar with gold and started the era of free fluctuations of currencies of which Forex is a child. In the eighties the international movements of capital accelerated after the arrival of personal computers that led Forex to be a continuous market.

According to a 2018 Reuters study, London has established itself as the leading global currency center, with the amount of currency trading recently exceeding 40% of the average daily value, growing since Britain voted to leave the European Union. A sign that London will likely continue to be one of the world's two leading financial centers for currency trading even after Brexit.

According to a study by the Bank for International Settlements (BIS), the Forex market reached $6.6 trillion a day in April 2019, up from $5.1 trillion three years earlier.

Forex: the turning point

The system of fixed rates began to falter as early as the 1950s and 1960s. In 1971 the Bretton Woods agreements were abandoned, thus leading to the opening of a new phase of Forex. From this date, the era of the Gold Standard ended and the era of flexible exchange rates began. Since 1973, the currencies of the various countries have freely begun to float again and thanks to this, the market for buying and selling currencies was born, the Forex.

From the Eighties onwards, with the advent of computers and the internet, the spread of Forex has had an extraordinary acceleration, because the market has taken on a global dimension. London has represented and currently represents the center of the Forex market. The British capital also has a dominant position within the Euromarket. Today Forex is the largest market in the world and it is expected that in the next few years the volumes of the Foreign Exchange Market will further increase considerably also thanks to the success of online Forex operations, which is making this market very popular even among private investors.

Forex Market Operators

Banks and Funds

When we talk about the Forex market, like it or not, we are talking about the interbank market, the market in which banks and credit institutions operate. In the interbank market, banks in excess of liquidity offer excess capital to banks in need of liquidity through deposits made by one bank with another for a specified period of time at a given interest rate. The interbank market or even the residual money market is the fulcrum of the currency exchange market, in this regard, just think that the prices viewed on the online trading platforms are precisely the result of the negotiations conducted on this market.

The protagonists of the Forex market

With a minimum lot of one million units of the base currency (one million euros for the EUR/USD pair or one million Dollars for the USD/JPY pair) lots of 10 million to 100 million Dollars are routine for this market, a market that still remains to all intents and purposes an over-the-counter (OTC) market or a market whose transactions are concluded directly by the parties outside the official stock exchanges, it is therefore an unregulated market.

The interbank market is made up of a network of international banks that carry out trading operations aimed at increasing their capital or the one of their customers through electronic brokerage services (EBS) or more commonly electronic trading platforms. However, with the contribution of new trading technologies, the "monopoly" of banking institutions has disappeared, new financial companies have entered the Forex market and in a few years the trading volumes produced by Hedge Funds, pension funds and mutual funds of investment have far exceeded those of the interbank market although the latter undoubtedly remains the primary source of liquidity.

Financial operators and speculators

Now given the above premise, Forex market players typically fall into two categories: financial traders and speculators. Financial operators operate on the Forex market purely as a function of their financial activity without necessarily implying some lucrative purpose, on the contrary, speculators operate on the foreign exchange market exclusively for profit.

Although financial operators account for a significantly lower daily trading volume than speculators, who alone make up 90% of the FX market volumes, their transactions play an important role for several reasons:

- the amount of their transactions is often large enough to exceed one billion;

- their transactions are usually a circumscribed event that does not tend to repeat itself;

- their transactions do not tend to take account of price fluctuations and their purpose is not to maximize profits.

For all the aforementioned reasons, financial operators are able to produce counter-trend fluctuations which, if exploited in the appropriate way, can often constitute excellent profit opportunities.

Speculators, needless to say, operate on the markets with the sole aim of making the maximum possible profit from price fluctuations. Speculators, as already announced, account for 90% of the volumes of the FX market and generally tend to operate in the form of Hedge Funds or Speculative Funds, mutual funds managed with speculative criteria that use the financial leverage offered by derivatives to maximize their profits thereby exposing themselves to the risk of large losses.

Financial investors

Among the Forex market operators, a significant component

is undoubtedly given by financial investors. The latter category is mostly made up of international companies engaged in mergers and acquisitions.

Trader

This is undoubtedly the category to which we will ascribe ourselves and most of our readers. Due to their nature as daily traders, traders tend to focus on market variations between 20 and 30 pips, fully constituting the primary source of short-term fluctuations. With the contribution of new trading technologies, retail traders have gradually managed to conquer an increasingly important slice of the Forex market, so much that they have reached a daily incidence of 10%, a figure which, moreover, seems to be able to boast an annual growth of 37%.

> *Pip: abbreviation of percentage in point or price interest point, it is the smallest numerical price movement of an asset (stock, index, currency pair, etc.). Generally when a price changes on the stock exchange it refers to a change in pips.*

> *Since most pairs are priced up to the fourth decimal place (€ 0.0001), the smallest variation refers to the last digit after the decimal point, for example € 0.0001, which is the 1 shown in the example. While a pip refers to the fourth decimal place, a pipette refers to the fifth decimal place.*

> *For most pairs, a pip equals 0.01% or one hundredth part of 1%; this value is also commonly known as BPS. A basis point (BPS) refers to a common unit of measurement of interest rates and financial percentages. A BPS equals 1/100 of 1% or 0.01%*

(0.0001) and denotes the percentage change in the exchange rate.

Governments and Central Banks

Governments and central banks are undoubtedly extremely active players on the Forex market and if on the one hand a large part of their transactions is attributable to the daily routine of payments, particular importance in relation to the foreign exchange market is covered by the management of foreign exchange reserves: currency stocks and government bonds in currencies other than its own managed and held by a central bank in order to operate on international markets, to protect the value of its own currency. Depending on the policy deemed most useful in a given historical period, a country's central bank manages its foreign exchange reserves to protect its currency by "manipulating" its exchange rate downwards or upwards against the currencies of its major trading partners. In this sense, according to data from the International Monetary Fund in 2010, the U.S. Dollar accounted for 62% of global currency reserves, the euro for 37%, while sterling and Yen for 3% and 4% respectively.

How to Trade on Forex

For many, not used to operating in the Financial Trading sector, it may seem difficult to operate in the Forex sector. This is absolutely not the case, all it takes is some knowledge, even minimal, of the Forex jargon and a desire to learn.

Forex is based on trading currencies, buying or selling a currency with the hope that the market for that currency will follow the desired trend. Before investing, it is necessary to make a technical and detailed analysis on the price trend of a specific currency pair; normally these currency pairs have a consolidated trend over time.

There are two types of Forex positions:

Long: this type of position is taken at the very moment of the purchase of a currency, with the hope that its price trend is increasing, thus generating profits thanks to its resale.

Short: this type of position allows the investor to speculate on the sale of a currency and then buy it at a lower price.

The term Day-Trading indicates those operations that begin and end on the same day, considered a short-term investment.

In Forex you will always invest in a currency pair, for example USD/EUR.

To the left of the slash ("/"), we find the base currency, while on the right the quoted currency.

For some years this type of synthesis of the name of currencies has been adopted, to allow all users, who speak any language, to immediately understand which currencies are being talked about.

To do trading it is essential to rely on a good broker

The Broker is that online platform that allows you to invest your money in buying and selling currency pairs.

When you decide to trade on a currency pair, for example EUR/USD, the broker we turned to provides us with the sale price and the purchase price. The selling price is also called

ASK, while the buying price is BID. Spread is the difference between the two prices.

Prices are expressed in decimal numbers, the PIP is the smaller unit between the prices of the two currencies.

The Main Currencies of the Forex Market

The Forex market is the financial market where the currencies of various countries (or groups of countries, considered the euro) are exchanged between them. But which are the most traded? And why are they being traded? Understanding how the market works is fundamental, which is why we see together a review of the main Forex currencies, classified according to the volume of business they generate on Forex in accordance with the official surveys of the Bank for International Settlements. The sum of the percentages of 200 because when you operate on the currency market, remember, you always operate with a pair of currencies (therefore two at a time).

Symbols of euro, Dollar, Yen and Pound, major currencies of the Forex market.

The symbols of Euro, Dollar, Yen and Pound, the top 4 currencies by number of trades on the Forex market.

Dollar (USD)

It is the currency of the United States of America and is the one that generates the majority of all market transactions, reaching 86.3%. In practice, almost all Forex transactions involve the Dollar which is exchanged against another currency... And this should not surprise us, since the U.S. currency is used for the trade of important raw materials, starting with oil, and it is also the basis for the foreign exchange reserves of all countries in the world. In some countries the Dollar is used as the official currency, in others such as Argentina between 1991 and 2002, there is a 1:1 exchange rate with the local currency. In any case, in most Third World countries, the Dollar is usually a reference currency also for daily exchanges, given the very little confidence that the population has towards local currencies. The U.S. currency also has very strong speculative appeal, as most Forex traders usually trade currency pairs involving the Dollar.

The single European currency is the second for transactions on the Forex market.

The euro is the second largest currency in Forex trading volumes.

Euro (EUR)

The single European currency ranks second, with a good 37%. In fact, this value is primarily due to the economic strength of Europe which, although declining, is still significant worldwide. Furthermore, the euro is used as a reserve currency although to a much lesser extent than the Dollar.

Japanese Yen (JPY)

The Yen ranks third in the ranking of the most traded currencies on Forex, with 17% of transactions. In fact, Japan is the second largest economy in the world and can count on an export of high added value technological products. The currency is strong, despite the fact that the Japanese public budget situation is not ideal. The government and the Bank of Japan have recently attempted to diminish the strength of the currency with monetary operations.

In any case, the Yen is also important as a reserve currency and is often used for typically speculative trading. Furthermore, before the Fed implemented a monetary policy of zero interest rates, there were also very strong speculative movements of carry trading, with international investors borrowing Yen in Japan at very low rates and then changing them into Dollars to invest them in the USA (where rates were significantly higher), for example on the stock market.

British Pound (GBP)

Before the Second World War, the Pound sterling occupied the place that today is the Dollar, the reference currency of the whole world. Currently it has lost almost all its appeal, but it still holds the fourth place in the ranking, with a good 15% of total Forex trades. The fact is that London is still one of the financial centers in the world even if, lately, in addition to the competition from New York, which has always been its rival, it must also suffer the very tough competition of emerging Asian markets (Chinese for example) which have better operating conditions of those in Europe and therefore are destined to grow at incredible rates.

Swiss Franc (CHF)

Switzerland is a very important economic power on the international scene, not only because it has a strong economy capable of high value-added exports, but also because the proverbial quality of its financial system has made its currency a safe haven asset par excellence. This is why the Swiss Franc still manages to total 6.8% of total transactions on the Forex market.

Australian Dollar (AUD)

The Australian Dollar is following the Swiss Franc in the ranking of the most traded currencies, with a more than decent 6.7%. This value is mainly determined by the country's great ability to export raw materials (for example minerals). Furthermore, the currency is particularly appreciated by traders who operate for speculative reasons.

Other currencies

The other currencies occupy an unimportant place after all. Among them we can however remember the Canadian Dollar (CAD) with 4.1% of total exchanges, the Swedish Krona (SEK) with 2.8%, the Hong Kong Dollar (HKD) always with 2.8%, the Norwegian Krone (NOK) with 2.2%, the New Zealand Dollar (NZD) with 1.9%, the Mexican Peso (MXN) with 1.3%, the Singapore Dollar (SGD) with 1.2% and the Korean Won (KRW) with 1.1%. All other currencies in the world, added up, come in at 14.5%.

Currencies for trading

Why is it convenient to operate with the most traded currencies? For several reasons, but above all for a reason of transparency: the more popular a uniform is, the more reports and information about it there are. For example, we can know everything about the Dollar, there are thousands of analysts who churn out more or less interesting reports every day. But how many analysts follow the Norwegian Krone instead? Furthermore, as far as small traders are concerned, often the brokers used, even if they are the best Forex brokers, do not support the trading of all currencies, but only the main ones.

CHAPTER TWO
HOW DOES FOREX WORK

How Does it Work

The main trading centers

The Forex market is open 24 hours a day from Monday to Friday. Despite the presence of different time zones, the Forex market is accessible five days a week.

The intimate nature of Forex is in fact Over the counter, i.e. it lacks those standardization and transparency mechanisms typical of regulated markets such as Borsa Italiana or the Nyse on Wall Street. When the Chicago Mercantile Exchange and Reuters attempted to impose a regulated central market with a clearinghouse in 2006, they failed miserably. In practice, contracts are traded directly between parties without a trading platform that standardizes the contracts themselves, guarantees prices and counterparty risk.

Forex trading

Trading on the Forex market involves the simultaneous purchase of one currency and the sale of another. In fact, we speak of "currency pairs", where the currency used as a reference is called the "base currency" and the other currency, quoted in relation to the base one, is called the "quoted currency".

The most traded currency pairs are called "Major" and represent over 80% of the total trades that take place on the

Forex market. The high liquidity makes the trading conditions of these pairs particularly advantageous, with relatively low spreads compared to other less traded pairs or so-called "exotic" pairs, i.e. relating to emerging markets.

Major currency pairs:

EUR/USD Euro - US Dollar (EuroDollar);

GBP/USD British Pound - US Dollar (cable);

USD/JPY US Dollar - Japanese Yen (gopher);

USD/CHF US Dollar - Swiss Franc (swissie);

USD/CAD US Dollar - Canadian Dollar (loonie);

AUD/USD Australian Dollar - US Dollar (aussie);

NZD/USD New Zealand Dollar - US Dollar (kiwi).

Minor currency pairs:

EUR/CHF Euro - Swiss Franc;

EUR/NZD Euro - New Zealand Dollar;

GBP/AUD British Pound - Australian Dollar;

GBP/JPY British Pound - Japanese Yen;

CAD/JPY Canadian Dollar - Japanese Yen.

Exotic currency pairs:

USD/TRY US Dollar - Turkish Lira;

USD/MXN US Dollar - Mexican Peso;

USD/ZAR US Dollar - South African Rand.

Characteristics of exchange contracts

The most common type of trading is the Foreign Exchange

Swap which records daily trades for 3,201 billion Dollars. This is followed by spot contracts (i.e. with settlement of the two-day contract or on the next working day) which oppose futures contracts typically with a three-month maturity. This "immediate" market alone covers 1990 billion Dollars of exchanges per day on the total 6,600 billion of Forex. At a distance come the outright forwards ($ 1 billion) and the options category and other products ($ 294 billion). Finally, currency swaps remain, amounting to 108 billion Dollars of contracts traded daily (Source: BIS Triennial Central Bank Survey 2019).

Exchange rate fluctuations between currencies respond to a highly articulated series of variables, including the macroeconomic factors of countries with a market in the currency in question (for example gross domestic product, balance of payments, public debt and more) or even monetary policy factors (a rise in interest rates practiced by a central bank should make the currency issued by the central bank appreciate, according to the theory of interest rate parity).

Characteristics of market prices

The quotes are expressed with two reference prices, where the one on the left indicates the "bid" price and the right price indicates the "ask price". Between the two prices there is always a difference which is called "spread". For example, if EUR/USD is quoted at 1,1142/1,1144, the differential is equal to 0,0002 and is generally indicated as 2 "pips" (point in price or percentage in point).

Forex

A pip indicates the smallest movement in the price of a currency pair. Since most currency pairs are priced up to the fourth decimal place, the smallest variation refers to the last digit after the decimal point.

What Moves the Currency Market

Currency pairs move for fundamental reasons in the long run, for technical reasons in the medium and short term and for emotional reasons in the short term.

The fundamentals and the long run

Fundamentals have a long-term effect because it takes time for the change in certain economic forces to have a real effect on the country's economy.

Basically the fundamentals are grouped into two broad sub-categories: Trade Flows and Capital Flows.

Trade Flows: Trade in goods and services between one country and another generate capital flows between the two states. If a US company buys $ 1 million worth of technology equipment from a Japanese company, it will first have to exchange the million Dollars into Yen to buy the desired goods. This transaction takes place in the currency market and will increase the demand for the Yen and the supply of Dollars. This shift in the balance between supply and demand will cause the price of the Yen to rise against the Dollar.

Capital Flows: Concept similar to the previous one where capital flows are moved not to buy goods or services, but to invest in countries where the return on investment rate is higher. In particular, reference is made to the Bond market and the Shares. If, for example, the US economy is healthy and offering above-average returns, there will be an inflow of capital from foreign investors who want to get higher returns than in their own country. To buy US Bonds and Stocks, investors need to exchange their currency for US Dollars. This will have the effect of increasing demand for the Dollar and therefore its price will rise.

Technical reasons in the medium and short term

Even if technical motivations play a fundamental role also in the long term, they tend to be recognized more as the cause of medium and short term movements.

In fact, prices seem to obey particular market geometries and respect certain levels of support and resistance. Due to the fact that many traders know and use technical analysis is a self- sustaining technique in the sense that if most traders observe the same price conformation and operate together other traders this will cause a market movement.

Emotional reasons in the short term

The market is made up of people who, when it comes to money, are distinguished by two conflicting feelings: fear and greed.

In certain market situations, especially following some important event or news, sudden movements may follow without being caused by a real cause other than the perception of risk and price value by market operators.

CHAPTER THREE
VOLATILITY

Financial markets never stand still, they are in constant motion. To understand this, just look at the chart of any financial instrument: prices are rising or falling and very often they are traded sideways. To assess market activity and price dynamics, there is an indicator called volatility.

Volatility is a range of movements in the price of the financial instrument over a specified period of time (day, week, month, etc.). In other words, volatility shows how high or low the price of the financial instrument can rise or fall in a given time. Volatility can be calculated as a percentage or as points (the minimum value of price movements).

The stock market is believed to be one of the most volatile and the price changes of different companies are often measured as a percentage. For example, if a stock costs $100 at the start of a trading session and added (or lost) $10 during the day, then its volatility is 10%. Shares of large companies usually have daily volatility of around 5-10%, mid-cap and low-liquidity stocks - 20%, 50% or even more than 100%.

How to use volatility in trading

First of all, volatility is used to evaluate the opportunities to trade a given financial instrument. Traders make money on price movements, which is why instruments with high volatility are more preferable for trading. The more actively a financial instrument moves, the greater opportunities traders have to make a profit on this move.

Long-term investors are more volatility conscious because they usually trade without stop-loss, while high volatility implies high risk. Consequently, they prefer a balanced approach, when choosing an instrument with moderate volatility but which has a powerful fundamental or technical background for long-term movements.

On exchanges, volatility can be traded directly through futures and options. For this, many different volatility indices have been developed with VIX being one of the most famous. This index is calculated on the basis of the US S&P 500 stock index. The VIX is sometimes called the fear index at the moment of panic increases and at the moment of calm - vice versa.

When trading Forex by volatility assessment, you can choose a suitable indicator. In my opinion, the average daily volatility offers three main recommendations for trading:

Expected movement - guide for Take Profit in pips.

Risk limitation - guide for Stop Loss in pips.

Rising volatility - confirmation of the start of a new trend.

Indicators for trading that uses volatility

To calculate and use volatility in trading, many technical indicators were created. Let's check out three of them, which are quite popular among traders.

ATR (Average True Range)

ATR indicator is famous for volatility assessment, created in 1978 by J. Welles Wilder. ATR's main objective is to calculate the current volatility of a financial instrument. Pips volatility is calculated by averaging the highest and lowest price values over a specified time period.

The ATR indicator is built in a separate window below the price chart and consists of a main line, which only shows positive values starting from 0. Average True Range shows changes in volatility, it will grow equally as volatility increases both in ascending and descending tendencies. The higher the market volatility, the higher the indicator value.

Bollinger bands

Bollinger Bands is a trend indicator created in 1984 by John Bollinger. However, the main objective of the Bollinger Bands is not to define the volatility of a financial instrument but to look for new impulses and signals that suggest a possible trend reversal. However, the indicator helps traders to see changes in volatility on the chart.

The upper and lower bands of the indicator are forming a kind of channel in which the price chart moves. These price channel boundaries provide information on current market volatility. When the boundaries shrink, volatility reduces and the price slows down. As the boundaries widen, volatility increases and the price can start a new movement.

ADX (Average Directional Movement Index)

The ADX indicator was also created by J. Welles Wilder. ADX is a trend indicator, which evaluates the strength of the actual trend by comparing the highest and lowest prices over a specified time period (defaults use 14). The indicator consists of three lines: two directional, + DI and -DI, and the main one, ADX.

Basically, ADX shows the current market volatility: if the ADX starts to go down, it means volatility is decreasing, the actual trend is slowing and may reverse.

If the ADX starts to rise, it means that volatility is increasing and indicates the start of a new trend.

CHAPTER FOUR
BENEFITS OF FOREX

Trading Fees

The first clarification to make, before talking about commissions, concerns the difference between the different types of brokers, market makers and ECNs.

The market makers are those brokers who do not charge any commissions on trading but keep their profit on spreads, while the ECNs are those brokers who offer the real market quotes and charge a commission on each trade.

ECN brokers therefore have the advantage of offering the real market prices and the lowest spreads, while market makers have the advantage of being able to trade freely without limits. In both cases, however, the commission is paid, the brokers are intermediaries and they have to earn somewhere, trading at no cost does not exist. For a more complete overview, see the list of top market maker brokers and the one of the best ECN brokers.

Having said that, the most solid and reliable brokers able to offer the lowest trading commissions but also the best conditions, are: XTB, Capital.com, AVATRADE and XM.COM among the market makers, IC Markets and Pepperstone among the ECNs.

Always remember that cost is not the one and only parameter to be evaluated, regulation, training, assistance, stable platforms and punctuality in deposit and withdrawal operations are even more decisive aspects.

The intermediaries indicated here were therefore selected by our experts taking into account all this and chosen on the basis of the best quality/price/service ratio.

XTB

XTB is one of the most competitive brokers, with extremely affordable commissions and different account types with fixed and variable spreads. XTB is one of the best STP brokers in the world by trading volume and operating levels, offers 2 platforms, the proprietary xStation and the standard MetaTrader 4, does not require a minimum deposit and is among the most complete in terms of training, able to provide truly reliable analyzes and reports. A recommended choice for investors of all experience levels, from individuals to professionals.

IC Markets

In addition to being one of the most respected brokers in the industry, IC Markets is among the best brokers in terms of trading conditions.

Used by investors of all levels, from small savers to professionals, IC Markets is now one of the largest ECN brokers in the world, becoming popular for its scrupulous compliance with the rules and high level of expertise.

IC Markets offers 3 trading platforms and different types of accounts both in market maker and no dealing desk mode, therefore specific for different investment profiles and styles, advanced tools and a large number of assets on which to trade between currencies, metals and shares, with extremely competitive and transparent commissions.

ASIC regulated and based in Australia, IC Markets is a broker in business since 2007 and suitable for all types of investors, individuals, companies and institutions, able to guarantee high operational standards and an undoubtedly high level trading experience.

Capital.com

Capital.com offers one of the best combinations of trading conditions and quality of services. It offers extremely competitive spreads, among the lowest we have found among brokers with zero commissions, good quality training material and a complete and intuitive trading platform, fast (therefore also ideal for scalping) and with various integrated useful tools, including market news and trade sentiment.

Capital.com has a minimum deposit of $20 and also offers weekly updates with analysis and reports and a fast support service. A reliable choice to evaluate for both private and professional traders.

Avantrade

Avantrade is one of the largest brokers when it comes to trading on Forex, CFDs, ETFs, indices, stocks, precious metals and commodities. Different platforms to choose from, professional training and assistance and the possibility to choose between fixed and variable spreads. AVATRADE is another top-tier, secure and regulated broker market maker, with a minimum deposit of $100 for opening an account and numerous deposit bonuses.

Pepperstone

Pepperstone is one of the largest ECN brokers in the world, ASIC regulated and able to guarantee very high operating standards. It allows you to trade currencies, stocks, indices and commodities through 11 platforms, 4 types of accounts, very low spreads and very competitive trading conditions.

Pepperstone is an Australian-based broker with an excellent reputation among investors, able to meet the most stringent security requirements and offer one of the most complete and professional trading environments available today.

XM

Among market makers, XM is one of the best brokers for beginners and intermediate traders, offering extremely low commissions, tight spreads and very advantageous trading conditions. All this combined with high-level assistance and training, the MetaTrader 4 platform and a large variety of assets to trade on. Xm has a minimum deposit of $5, and offers a $25 no deposit welcome bonus.

The Forex Market is Open 24 Hours a Day

The Forex market is the largest financial market in the world. Forex trading is not done in one central location, but is conducted between participants by telephone and electronic communications networks (ECNs) in various markets around the world.

The market is open 24 hours a day in different parts of the world, from 5pm EST on Sunday until 4pm EST on Friday. At any given time, there is at least one market open, and there are a few hours of overlap between the market closing of one region and the opening of another. The international reach of currency trading means that there are always traders all over the world who make and meet the demands of a particular currency.

The currency is also needed worldwide for international trade, central banks and global businesses. Central banks have particularly relied on foreign exchange markets since 1971, when fixed currency markets ceased to exist due to the fall of the gold standard. Since then, most international currencies have been "floating" rather than linked to the value of gold.

The reasoning behind 24/7 trading

The Forex market's ability to trade over a 24-hour period is due in part to the different international time zones, and the fact that trading is conducted on a computer network rather than any physical exchange that closes at any given time. For example, when you hear that the US Dollar closed at a certain rate, it simply means that it was the closing rate of the New York market. This is because the currency continues to trade around the world long after the close of New York, unlike stocks.

Securities such as domestic stocks, bonds and commodities are not so relevant or necessary on the international stage and therefore are not required to trade beyond the standard business day in the issuer's home country. The demand for trading in these markets is not high enough to warrant the 24-hour opening due to the focus on the domestic market, which means that few stocks are likely to be trading at 3am in the

USA.

Europe is made up of major financial centers such as London, Paris, Frankfurt and Zurich. Banks, institutions and dealers all conduct Forex trading for themselves and their clients in each of these markets.

Each day of Forex trading begins with the opening of the Australasia area, followed by Europe and then North America. As the markets of one region close another opens, or has already opened, and continues trading on the Forex market. These markets often overlap for a few hours, providing some of the most active periods of Forex trading.

For example, if a Forex trader in Australia wakes up at 3 in the morning and wants to trade currency, he will not be able to do so through the Forex dealers located in Australasia, but he will be able to carry out all the operations he wishes through European or North American dealers.

Understanding the Forex market hours

The international currency markets are made up of banks, trading companies, central banks, investment management companies, hedge funds, as well as retail Forex brokers and investors around the world. As this market operates in multiple time zones, it can be accessed at any time except for the weekend break.

The international currency market is not dominated by a single exchange market, but involves a global network of exchanges and brokers around the world. Forex trading hours are based on when trading is open in each participating country. While the time zones overlap, the generally accepted time zones for each region are as follows:

New York from 8 am to 5pm EST (from 1pm to 10pm UTC)

Tokyo from 7pm to 4am EST (from 12m to 9am UTC)

Sydney 5pm to 2am EST (10pm to 7am UTC)

London 3am-12noon EST (8pm-5pm UTC)

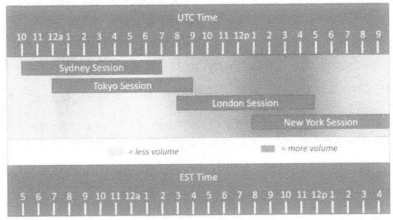

Forex Market Hours.

The two most popular time zones are London and New York. The period in which these two trading sessions overlap (London afternoon and New York morning) is the busiest period and accounts for most of the volumes traded in the market of $6 trillion per day.

It is during this period that the Reuters/WMR reference spot exchange rate is determined. The rate, which is set at 4pm London time, is used for valuation and daily pricing for many money managers and pension funds.

While the Forex market is a 24 hour market, some currencies in various emerging markets are not traded around the clock. The seven most traded currencies in the world are the US

Dollar, the euro, the Japanese Yen, the British Pound, the Australian Dollar, the Canadian Dollar and the New Zealand Dollar, all traded continuously while the Forex market is open.

Speculators usually trade in pairs that cross these seven currencies from any country in the world, although they favor times with heavier volumes. When trading volumes are heavier, Forex brokers provide tighter spreads (bid and ask prices closer to each other), which reduces transaction costs for traders. Similarly, institutional traders also favor times with higher trading volumes, although they can accept wider spreads for the opportunity to trade as soon as possible in response to new information they have.

Despite the highly decentralized nature of the Forex market, it remains an efficient transfer mechanism for all participants and a far-reaching entry mechanism for those wishing to speculate from anywhere in the world.

Price fluctuations in Forex

Economic and political instability and endless other continuous changes also affect the currency markets. Central banks seek to stabilize their country's currency by trading it on the open market and maintaining relative value to other world currencies. Firms operating in multiple countries seek to mitigate the risks of operating in foreign markets and to hedge currency risk.

Companies enter into currency swaps to hedge risk, which gives them the right, but not necessarily the obligation, to buy a certain amount of foreign currency for a certain price in another currency at a future date. Through this strategy, firms limit their exposure to sharp fluctuations in currency valuations.

The bottom line

Currency is a global necessity for central banks, international trade, and global businesses, and therefore requires a 24-hour market to meet the need for transactions across various time zones. In summary, it is safe to assume that it does not make sense during the trading week that a participant in the Forex market is potentially unable to make a currency trade.

Market Liquidity

When we talk about liquidity in any financial area, we refer to the ease and speed with which we can buy or sell a certain asset at a more or less stable price. If we talk about our daily life, a person or company will be considered liquid if they have the ability to meet their most immediate financial obligations.

The ability to pay in the long run is called creditworthiness.

If we talk about the liquidity of the market, this will largely depend on the number of buyers and sellers that are present there.

Logically, the more participants there are, the easier it will be to 'position' our assets. And the more liquidity an asset has, the faster we can sell it.

In light of this, we can say that cash is the most liquid asset because we can exchange it at any time for any product or service. Conversely, a home and a car are illiquid assets because they are not easy to trade, they require time, price calculations and, almost always, bureaucracy and intermediaries.

Why liquidity is important in trading

When we decide to make the leap into the world of trading is very important for our capital to take into account the liquidity of the market in which we want to operate. Why?

First of all because the more liquid the market is, the less risk we will run. This is due to the fact that there will always be someone willing to buy or sell.

Secondly, the more liquid the market is, the more participants it will attract, which will make it easier and easier to open different trades, depending on our interests.

Additionally, in trading, liquidity can directly affect the spread we pay to the broker to trade a particular instrument. A market that is automatically liquid has many daily trades and is made up of many active traders.

This will cause the difference between the buy (ask) and sell (bid) prices of a certain financial asset to decrease and therefore the spread is narrower.

If we trade the most liquid currency pair, the Euro Dollar EUR/USD, the typical spread with Admiral Markets UK Ltd is 0.6 pips, with no additional fees. However, if you trade a less liquid asset like stocks, the cost will be a little higher. In the IBEX35 for example, the Telefonica stock is one of the most liquid: with Admiral Markets you can invest in its shares paying a commission of 2 euros and with a typical spread of 2 pips.

When we choose to operate in a market that is considered very liquid, we must also take into account the trading hours. The reason is that there will not be the same number of participants at one time. For example, the Forex market is considered to be one of the most liquid markets, however, if we trade the euro-Pound pair it will not be as liquid during the European period as it is during the Asian period or during the holiday periods.

 Moreover, when sellers outnumber buyers or vice versa, trading can become more complicated and we may not be able to successfully close our position.

One of the reasons why the last financial crisis broke out in 2008 was the lack of liquidity of the so-called subprime mortgages. Although the current environment is very different, in early 2020 the European Securities and Markets Authority (ESMA) warned against liquidity risk in the real estate and funds sector. "Many of the real estate funds offer liquidity on a daily basis, indicating a risk of structural vulnerability, as they invest in illiquid assets but allow investors to trade their shares in a short period of time."

Forex- The Most Liquid Market in the World

Forex (Foreign Exchange Market) is the market in which currencies from all over the world are exchanged through an exchange rate, that is the mechanism that allows to know the value of one currency in terms of another.

Forex involves millions of investors from all over the world every day: from banks to companies to small savers. In fact, any economic transaction carried out by operators of different nationalities must necessarily go through the purchase and sale of a currency. For example, if a European citizen intends to buy an American product, he will have to sell euros and at the same time buy US Dollars to pay for it.

Forex's ability to attract capital makes it the most liquid market in the world, much more than all the American stock markets combined! In fact, the daily turnover is now around 4 trillion Dollars, even if the transactions are increasing every day. It must be said that of this incredible amount of volumes, 90% is purely speculative.

Forex is essentially an over-the-counter market, that is, it cannot be precisely located in a particular financial center. There is no regulated market or clearing house: transactions take place directly between two counterparties, which are banks and brokers. This Forex feature means that there are no official prices.

However, everyone can know the trend of an exchange rate at any moment as transactions are recorded and communicated to the whole world thanks to the main international information circuits, such as Reuters and Bloomberg. Spot (i.e. cash), forwards (forward exchange rates), swaps and options are traded on the OTC market. It is a market dominated by large investment banks, which trade on their own account or on behalf of their customers: we are talking about banks of the caliber of Deutsche Bank, UBS, Barclays Capital, Royal Bank of Scotland and Citigroup, just to mention the main banks that move capital on this market. Next to the

OTC market there is also a sort of parallel market, that is the regulated one, in which futures and options on currencies are traded. In this case there is the market filter through a clearing house, which will take care of the respect of contractual obligations. The quotes are official and cannot differ from one broker to another, like on the OTC. Furthermore, the contracts are standardized.

In addition to banks and broker-dealers, we find other operators who on Forex may have interests ranging from hedging to speculation, but also macroeconomic objectives: central banks, companies, investors, speculators.

Central banks have the task of guaranteeing the stability of an exchange rate in order to limit its volatility, but also to pursue specific monetary policy objectives. For example, in the case of the earthquake in Japan of 11 March 2011, a few days after the earthquake, the Bank of Japan (i.e. the Japanese Central Bank) organized an intervention in open markets - together with the other major world banks - to avoid a excessive strengthening of the Yen following a quick repatriation of capital by companies and insurance companies. The concerted action of the various central banks, in the hundreds and hundreds of billions of Dollars, has pushed the Yen lower and convinced investors to sell the Japanese currency on the expectations of new interventions in open markets. Not always, however, a central bank intervention can be fruitful in relation to its objectives. This is the case of the Swiss National Bank, that is the Swiss Central Bank, which in 2009 and 2010 tried several times to stop the formidable race of the Swiss Franc against the main world currencies but without success. In the end, the SNB paid a very steep bill: tens of billions of

Swiss Francs to be entered in the balance sheet among operating losses.

Multinational companies, also labeled as "commercials" on Forex, are by nature subject to foreign exchange transactions. These companies pursue hedging objectives in order to lock in an affordable price for the next weeks or months and to have an easily estimated capital flow in the business forecasting processes. The objective, therefore, is to eliminate the exchange rate risk.

Investors are those who apply for foreign currency to buy foreign securities or to make direct investments abroad (usually in companies). There is also a more sophisticated category of investors who exclusively pursue short-medium term profit objectives through speculative exchange rate operations. These are the so-called large traders, i.e. all institutional investors who manage masses of hundreds of billions of Dollars for speculative purposes such as hedge funds and proprietary traders. Finally, again among the investors, we find small savers classified as small speculators. This is the so-called "ox park", i.e. private traders who have a few thousand (sometimes only hundreds) of euros, almost always in clear difficulty in competing on the market with highly capitalized traders. On the other hand, the statistics speak for themselves: 90% of small traders lose money.

CHAPTER FIVE
TECHNICAL AND FUNDAMENTAL ANALYSIS

Fundamental Analysis

The main premise of Forex fundamental analysis, as well as in other financial markets, is that the price of an asset can differ from its value. For this reason, various markets can sometimes "get it wrong" in the price of an asset, overstating or undervaluing it in the short term. Forex fundamental analysts argue that although the price may be wrong in the short term, assets will always return to the correct price in the long run. The ultimate goal of fundamental analysis is to find out the true value of an asset, compare it with the current price and then identify a trading opportunity.

This clearly shows the basic difference between technical analysis and fundamental analysis. While technical analysis basically pays attention to the current price, fundamental analysis looks for everything but the current price. While fundamental analysis may not be the best tool for a short-term trader in everyday markets, it is the fundamental factors of Forex and how they are analyzed that respond to what happens in the long term.

Fundamental analysis of the Forex market: methodology

Forex fundamental analysis is not just about comparing the current data of individual economic indicators with previous data. There are a large number of economic theories surrounding Forex fundamental analysis, which seek to contextualize various economic data, to make them comparable.

The parity condition is based on the most widespread economic theories in fundamental currency analysis - a price condition for which currencies should be traded when adjusted, based on their local economic factors, such as inflation and rates of interest.

Fundamental trading analysis: good and bad news

You have probably noticed that, from the practical point of view of an average Forex trader, it is the economic news that then produces the movements in the markets. How and why does all this happen? There are several economic indicators that can provide insights into the health of a given economy that financial experts observe.

These indicators are often reported in the news and newspapers. Some are published weekly, most monthly and some quarterly. You can follow these announcements and developments through our Forex calendar.

But now let's compare technical analysis and fundamental analysis based on the frequency of data updates.

Technical and fundamental analysis

Technical analysis and fundamental analysis, what are the main differences? In the case of fundamental analysis of currency trading, new data comes in every second in the form of a price quote, while fundamental indicators are published at most once a week. Capital flows gradually from countries where it accumulates at a potentially slower rate, compared to countries where it could accumulate at a potentially faster rate.

This has mainly to do with the strength of an economy. If an economy is expected to remain strong over time, it will appear as an attractive country for foreign investment, as it is more likely to produce higher returns on financial markets.

Following this thought, to invest, investors will first have to convert their capital into the currency of the country in question. Buying more of that currency will push demand up and force the currency to appreciate. Unfortunately, economy is not that simple, which is why the examples of healthy economies showing weakening currencies are not entirely unknown to history. In fact, currencies are not like company stocks that directly reflect the health of the economy.

Currencies are also tools that can be manipulated by political actors - such as central banks and even private traders such as George Soros.

When economic reports are published, traders and investors study the signs of strengths or weaknesses in different economies. If before a news or press release is released, market sentiment leans in a specific direction, changing the price before release is known as a "market price". In fact, this practice often causes a bit of confusion when the data is released.

Conversely, when the market is uncertain, or the results of the data vary from what is expected, severe market volatility can occur. This is why novice Forex traders are generally advised to avoid trading based on this type of news when practicing fundamental analysis.

Fundamental analysis indicators

Economic data can provide us with suggestions on changes in a country's economic situation.

Let's find out below the main economic indicators in the Forex fundamental analysis to be taken into account.

Interest rates

Interest rates are an important indicator of Forex analysis. There are many types of interest rates, but in this article we will focus on the nominal or base interest rates set by central banks. The ECB and other central banks create money, which is then borrowed by private banks. The percentage or principle under which private banks pay central banks to borrow currencies is called the base interest rate or nominal interest rate. Whenever the expression "interest rates" is heard, people usually refer to this concept.

The manipulation of interest rates, an important part of national monetary or fiscal policy, is one of the primary functions of central banks. This is because interest rates are a great leveler of the economy. Interest rates are perhaps stronger than any other factor, and they affect currency values. They can have an impact on inflation, investment, trade, production and unemployment.

Here's how it works:

Central banks generally want to boost the economy and reach

a government-set level of inflation, so they lower interest rates. This stimulates the indebtedness of both private banks and individuals themselves, as well as stimulating consumption, production and the economy in general. Low interest rates can be a good tactic, but not an effective strategy.

In the long run, low interest rates can over-inflate the economy with liquidity and can create economic bubbles which, as we know, will sooner or later trigger a chain reaction of overthrowing the entire economy, if not entire economies.

To avoid this, central banks can also consider raising interest rates, thus reducing interest rates and leaving less money to banks, businesses and individuals. From a Forex fundamental analysis perspective, the best place to start looking for trading opportunities is in changing interest rates.

Inflation

Inflation news reports the fluctuations in the cost of goods over a specified period of time. Note that every economy has a level of what is considered "healthy inflation". Over a long period of time, as the economy grows, so should the amount of money in circulation, which is the definition of inflation. The logic behind all this is that governments and central banks balance themselves to a level of self-satisfaction.

Too high inflation turns the balance between supply and demand in favor of supply, and the currency depreciates because there is simply more of it than is required. The flip side of inflation is deflation. During deflation, the value of the currency increases as goods and services become cheaper.

In the short run it can be a good thing, but for the economy in the long run it can be a bad thing. Money is fuel for the economy. Less fuel equals less movement. At some point, deflation can have a drastic impact on a country, to the point where there will hardly be enough money to keep the economy going, let alone grow it.

GDP

Gross domestic product (GDP) is the measure of all the goods and services that a country generates in a given period. GDP is believed to be the best overall economic indicator of the health of an economy. This may sound strange, especially when you consider that GDP is basically a measure of the supply of goods and services, but it has nothing to do with the demand for these goods and services.

The general idea is that it would take a great deal of knowledge of both supply and demand to make reasonable and accurate estimates. It would be unwise to believe that GDP reflects both sides of the market. Therefore, an increase in GDP without a corresponding increase in the demand for gross domestic product or affordability, is the exact opposite of a healthy economy, from the point of view of a fundamental Forex analysis.

Interest rates, inflation and GDP are the three main economic indicators used by the Forex fundamental analysis. They are unmatched in the magnitude of the economic impact they can generate, compared to other factors such as retail sales, capital flow, trade balance, bond prices and numerous other additional macroeconomic and geopolitical factors. Furthermore, economic indicators are not only measured against each other over time, but some of them also relate cross-cutting and cross-border disciplines.

It is important to understand that there is a lot of economic data available which has a significant impact on the Forex market. Whether you like it or not, learning how to do Forex fundamental analysis is certainly an important part of your trading strategy in order to predict market movements.

How to do the fundamental analysis of a company

There are many different ways to perform fundamental analysis of a company, each trader has their own method. In this article we have chosen a top-down method, i.e. from general to particular, highlighting the most important indicators and ratios that serve as the basis for any fundamental analysis. To these main points, you can add as many as you deem necessary. Let's start!

Fundamental macroeconomic analysis

Macroeconomic analysis refers to the general situation of the economy, its strengths and weaknesses. This type of information, necessary to carry out fundamental analysis, can be found in the economic news of the media and in official communications of various public organizations, both national and international. To know the date of the publications, the forecast of each of them and the previous data, we can consult the economic calendar and select the data we are looking for.

The most important macroeconomic indicators for carrying out a fundamental analysis are interest rates, inflation, gross domestic product (GDP), employment rates and, in the case of a company linked to the financial sector or construction housing, it can also be interesting to be updated with Euribor data.

Gross domestic product (GDP)

Gross Domestic Product (GDP) measures a country's wealth production over a specified period of time, usually over a year. Although some analysts consider it incomplete as it does not include elements that are difficult to quantify, such as the shadow economy, GDP remains the most used indicator to measure the health of an economy.

The statistical offices of each country usually publish the evolution of GDP on a regular basis. In the USA it is the Government's Economic Analysis Office, in the case of the Eurozone it is Eurostat. In addition, global organizations such as the IMF usually make estimates of the GDP evolution of major economies.

The most interesting data for traders who do a fundamental analysis of a company is not the GDP in absolute terms but its evolution quarter after quarter and year after year. A growth rate above 0% means that the production of wealth has increased and therefore the national economy is developing positively.

Experts often interpret an economy as having entered recession when it has two consecutive quarters of negative rates (bear market).

Interest rates

Interest rates are basically the price you pay for the money you borrow. The percentage or rate that private banks pay central banks for lending money is called base or nominal interest rate, a macroeconomic indicator consulted by long-term traders because it affects many areas, from inflation to consumption.

Why? Because an increase or decrease in rates by central banks will strengthen or weaken the reference currency. A rise in rates causes the currency to appreciate due to a lack of money in circulation. Similarly, when interest rates fall, loans rise and the currency loses value.

Central banks use increases or decreases in interest rates to regulate the economy, control inflation and stimulate economic growth.

It is important to keep interest rates in mind, as they affect many sectors of the economy, such as inflation and consumption. A rise or fall in interest rates will tend to strengthen or weaken the currency in question. If the company being analyzed is a large importer or exporter, these changes in the currency will have a direct impact on the company's costs and revenues.

Central banks use interest rates as a tool to regulate the economy, control inflation and stimulate economic growth.

The lowering of rates increases consumption. An increase in interest rates deteriorates it.

Lower interest rates increase consumption and vice versa.

This is one of the reasons why a decline in interest rates tends to be good for equities.

Euribor: how they affect fundamental analysis

Euribor is the acronym of Euro Interbank Offered Rate and is the average interest rate at which the main european banks grant each other loans. There are 5 Euribor rates, each one with a different duration (1 week, 1 month, 3 months, 6 months, 12 months).

This rate is important because banks use 12-month Euribor as a benchmark interest rate for mortgage loans. If the Euribor rises, mortgage payments will rise.

Inflation: how it affects the fundamental analysis

The prices of goods and services rise and fall according to economic factors, we speak of inflation when the prices of these goods and services rise. It is calculated on the basis of the average consumption of households, the so-called "shopping basket", with some items having a greater weight than others, for example the price of electricity higher than the price of sugar.

Countries determine the healthy inflation rate based on the needs of their economy. For example, developed economies seek inflation levels of around 2%, while developing countries can seek levels of up to 7% without scaring investors.

Too high inflation skews the supply-demand balance in favor of supply, and the currency depreciates because there is simply more of it than is required.

The opposite side is deflation. In a deflationary situation, the value of money increases as goods and services become cheaper. Deflation is much more dangerous for the economy than inflation, even if it is more difficult to provoke. Deflation negatively affects activity and employment and leads to an increase in interest rates, which damages demand and slows the recovery of the economy.

Work: how it affects the fundamental analysis

Employment reports are also very important in any fundamental analysis: if the percentage of the unemployed population is very high, consumption will be significantly affected and the number of people dependent on public aid will increase. If an economy develops favorably, it will create jobs and encourage consumption, and money will then circulate.

From a trading or investing perspective, if unemployment rises significantly, there will be a shock for the markets. One of the employment reports that has the greatest effect on market price developments is Nonfarm Payroll (NFP), which reflects the total number of wage earners in the United States, with the exception of agricultural employees, those who work for the government, and non-profit organizations (NGOs).

Fundamental sectoral analysis

When we do an analysis of the sector to which the company we want to analyze belongs, there are many factors that we need to study:

Regulatory environment. The policies of different

governments in the economic field are decisive when it comes to maintaining investor confidence in a particular sector. For example, if we talk about the automotive sector and the government wants to penalize diesel, the sector could suffer.

Growth potential - is this an industry that still has growth potential? Is it a new sector?

Main threats and opportunities in the sector to which the company belongs.

Fundamental analysis ratios

Once we know the macroeconomic context and have studied the strengths and weaknesses of the sector, we must study the accounts of companies, their income, their margins, their solvency, their profitability, etc. To do this, we will look at what are the key relationships we need to know within the fundamental analysis of a publicly traded company.

Company results:

From an investor's perspective, the most compelling performance reports are those submitted by companies on a quarterly and annual basis. The most important indicators of these performance ratios include the following:

Revenue

This term refers to a company's profits from its activities that increase the company's equity.

EBITDA

This term refers to the gross operating result before taxes, interest, depreciation and write-downs. The goal of this indicator is to be able to measure the cash flow of a company.

Net benefits

The net profit of a company is the result of the subtraction of costs (taxes, depreciation, interest) from the income realized in a given period of time. In other words, it measures the result of the firm's business after deduction of tax costs.

There are many other interesting indicators within a company's income statement, but these three are essential for getting a general idea of the company's financial situation.

Debt

We must also take into account the company's debt: it may have profits in the millions, but even if its debt is in the millions it may have serious profitability problems. We cannot expect him to have "zero" debt because debt is necessary, but it must never exceed or come close to income, it must be balanced.

Profitability indices - Fundamental analysis

EPS or Earnings Per Share

Earnings per share (EPS) is one of the most important indicators in analyzing a company, as it measures the profitability of the stock. It is calculated by dividing the net profit by the number of shares in the company.

ROE

ROE (Return on Equity) is the return on equity and is calculated by dividing net profit by equity. In short, it is the company's ability to generate profits for its shareholders, hence its importance. If, for example, a company's ROE is 12%, it means that for every 100 euros invested, it generates 12 euros in profit.

ROA

ROA (Return On Assets) or ROI (Return on Investments) calculates the profitability of a company's assets. How? Dividing EBITDA by total assets and multiply it by 100.

Dividend yield

The dividend yield is the difference between the cost of our stock investment and what we get back by receiving the dividend. To calculate this important ratio, we need to divide the value of the dividend charged per share by the price at which the stock is quoted on the market and then multiply it by 100.

This indicator is used, for example, by traders practicing the Dogs of the Dow strategy, based on the shares with the highest annual dividend yield among the Dow Jones 30 shares.

Valuation indices - Fundamental analysis

PER

PER stands for Price-to-Earnings Ratio. This indicator compares the price of a company's stock with the profits recorded over a given period of time.

How is it calculated? PER is the result of dividing the current price of a share by the earnings per share (PPS). If the result is a low PER, it could mean that the company's stock price is undervalued. This report is very useful when comparing it to the PER of other companies in the same industry, so that if it is below the industry average, it means it is undervalued.

EV/Ebitda

EV/EBITDA compares the value of a company (Enterprise Value) with gross profit before interest, taxes, depreciation and write-downs. When we talk about the value of a company we mean what we would have to pay if we wanted to buy it. When calculating EV, the market capitalization, the number of shares outstanding, the share price and the debt are basically taken into account.

Price to Book Value (PVC)

The price-to-book ratio is used to measure the price of a company's shares in relation to their book value, i.e. the value of its assets minus its liabilities, divided by the total number of shares issued. In this way, the investor will know how much money he would get if the company was liquidated.

PEG

The Price-to-Earnings-to-Growth (PEG) ratio compares the PER to the company's expected future growth, usually over the next five years. Investors can then estimate the company's growth potential.

To calculate the PEG, we must divide the PER by the estimated annual growth rate of earnings per share.

Pay out

Pay out is the ratio that reflects the percentage of profits that a company allocates to the remuneration of its shareholders, in the form of dividends. Logically, the higher the remuneration, the higher the remuneration offered to its shareholders, so it is an indicator to be taken into account in the fundamental analysis of a company.

Cash flow

Cash flow is also a very important indicator when analyzing a publicly traded company. It refers to a company's ability to generate cash to meet its payments. It is also called cash flow.

To calculate it, we need to add net income, commissions and depreciation.

Ratio SOTP

If the publicly traded company we are studying is part of a holding company, it is convenient to know a ratio called the 'Sum of the parts' or SOTP ratio. It is a process of evaluating the parts of the holding to find out how much they would be worth if they were spun off or sold to another company.

To find out which are the richest listed companies in the world, which have presented the best results compared to the indexes listed above, have a look at this article about the 10 richest companies in the world.

Technical Analysis

In any type of financial market, technical analysis is a recognized and widely used method to anticipate or predict price trends, while keeping an eye on macro aspects.

Technical analysis, as the name reveals, is based on the technical aspect of the market, using graphs and historical data. In particular are analyzed:

- Prices;

- Volumes traded;

- Temporal bands.

For technical analysis, traders use mathematical, statistical and graphical indicators. The signals and suggestions derived from these tools guide traders in their decisions regarding the opening and closing of trading positions.

In the Forex market, as in any other financial market, technical analysis is a method of predicting prices based on historical data.

In the Forex market it is possible to obtain five basic historical data on currency pairs:

- Opening price;

- Maximum price;

- Minimum price;

- Closing price.

The fifth is volume, which can be problematic in the Forex CFD market because it cannot be measured in the same way as in stocks, commodities or currency futures.

Trading technical analysis - The origins

Technical analysis was born together with supply and demand oriented markets. The first known historical records date back to around the 17th century by Dutch traders and around the 18th century by Japanese rice growers.

Throughout history and for most of the 20th century, technical analysis of financial markets has been limited to charting, as it has not been possible to perform statistical calculations with large amounts of information.

Technical analysis and fundamental analysis of financial markets have never traveled on the same wavelength. Technical analysis for Forex and other financial markets requires a lot of statistical calculations, which until a few decades ago, without computers and digital tools, were unlikely.

In the digital age we can consider that technical analysis is in its golden age!

Trading technical analysis - Advantages and disadvantages

Advantages of technical analysis:

Real-time Forex technical analysis requires little basic data and uses only currency chart data.

Technical analysis allows you to accurately predict the best entry and exit points on the market.

Disadvantages of technical analysis:

Due to its widespread use, real-time Forex technical analysis can lead to very abrupt market movements in the event that many traders reach the same conclusions. This phenomenon is called "direction of travel", as they all go in the same direction.

To be relevant and sustainable, technical analysis must always be combined with fundamental analysis.

Technical analysis uses several tools to determine the probability of price movements.

Trading technical analysis - Methodology

For many traders who base their trades on technical analysis, once the instrument is chosen, it is necessary to determine whether the market is trending or in range.

If the market is trending we need to determine the trend in terms of direction, i.e. :

- Bullish trend;

- Bearish trend.

The ideal would be to be able to measure the duration of the trend.

If the trend is within a range, it is best to do nothing if you are not familiar with these consolidation moves. If not, taking advantage of the support and resistance levels is usually a good way to trade the product.

To determine the trend, technical analysis uses several tools, including charts.

Charts try to identify patterns: whether they are trend, reversal or range.

To identify these patterns, traders have developed and refined a series of charting tools for analysis. These tools start with the support and resistance lines, or channels that understand the price and allow you to determine the meaning and price levels to consider. This analysis can be refined with a series of technical indicators that are applied to the charts in real time.

Trading technical analysis - Indicators

Technical indicators are complements programmed on the basis of statistics from trading platforms that mathematically analyze the relationships of the various elements to try to predict the price of a financial product.

Both novice and experienced traders can use technical analysis. This technical analysis uses charts to make forecasts and take trading positions.

For this it is enough to study the simplest indicators, which deal with:

- indicate the possible market trend;

- support and resistance levels indicated;

- identify the patterns/patterns.

In general, there are four groups of technical indicators. The most popular are:

Trend indicators:

- Moving average: certainly the best known trend indicator;

- ADX: is another technical analysis indicator that tries to predict the strength of the trend and is based on the EMA (exponential moving average) of the + DI and -DI indicators;

- DI (directional indicators): calculate the relationship between the highs, lows and the daily close of the current day with the previous day.

Other popular trend indicators are:

- MACD;

- Parabolic SAR;

- Ichimoku Kinko Hyo.

Pulse indicators

Pulse indicators are used to indicate whether an instrument is overbought or oversold. They measure the speed and magnitude of price movements. The impulse represents the rate of change in the price.

The main ones are:

- Relative Strength Index (RSI);

- Stochastic;

- ATR (as an indicator of volatility) or Bollinger Bands.

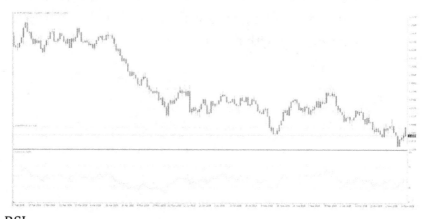

RSI

Volume indicators

There is no doubt that technical analysis of total volumes traded is very useful for traders of stocks, futures, commodities and other products. For example, the most commonly used indicators in this area are the following:

- The technical indicator of monetary flow;

- The technical indicator of distribution.

Among the volatility indicators we find:

- ATR true midrange;

- Bollinger bands.

Trading technical analysis - The principles

The price action

The logical framework and the justification of technical analysis derives from one of the postulates of Dow's theory that price accurately reflects all the information about it.

Therefore, any factor that has an impact on supply and demand (the main forces that determine prices) will inevitably end up in the charts.

Traders who are more attentive to price action believe that data relating to major events or economic calendar publications are mostly useless because they are not quantifiable and reliable.

For this reason, the difference between technical and fundamental analysis is that the latter is based on the principles that underpin the activity, while the former is based solely on its historical prices.

Prices move in trends

Technical analysts defend the fact that the market moves in technical trends or patterns - another nod to Dow's theory.

Markets can move in bullish trends - a rising market continually reaching new important highs and lows while in general the price appears to be bouncing on an upward path.

Similar market behavior, but characterized by descending lows and highs, is a downward trend.

A horizontal trend is also called a secondary market or range and is not exactly a trader's preferred environment. This is due to the fact that during lateral interval periods, there is very little certainty of what will happen in the future. A secondary market indicates that buyers and sellers have similar power and neither side is strong enough to form a trend to prevail over the other.

Markets are on the side for about 60% of the time, so it is very important to know how to identify trends. It is worth mentioning that real-time Forex technical analysis does not particularly deal with the reasons that lead to a given chart situation.

For example, asking "why is a trend occurring" is more reasonable, but for a technical analysis trader it is completely irrelevant as he would not know how to quantify it. To him, the existence of trends is an empirically proven fact and this is all that interests him and catches his attention.

History repeats itself

To talk about the third basic premise of Forex technical analysis, let's not to go too much into the philosophical or psychological field. Nor will we try to prove or disprove that human beings work according to patterns.

Technical traders agree that investors work following a number of patterns. Because of this behavior, it is believed to be able to identify patterns and open highly profitable operations; all that is needed is a small statistical advantage multiplied by repetitions and leverage.

But it's not a good idea to use only Forex technical analysis. Ideally, this analysis should be used in combination with fundamental analysis or market sentiment. Although people who use technical analysis are adept at identifying and confirming trends, it is the fundamental factors that create the conditions for these trends to develop.

One last thing to consider is the backtesting method also known as historical verification, where traders use past data to test a particular trading strategy. This procedure can only be done with the technical analysis of currencies.

However, like other statistical results in other spheres of the human area, past data does not guarantee the repetition of a pattern. It is just a tool.

Additionally, backtesting requires knowledge of exact market conditions to establish entry and exit points.

Trading technical analysis - Efficiency

As we have commented, technical analysis in trading can be applied to any market, but it is a method that favors Forex traders:

- Scalping: times less than 1 day;

- Intraday Trading: 1 day time frames;

- Swing trading: time horizons longer than 1 day.

There are some Forex traders who doubt the effectiveness of technical analysis as they find prices difficult to predict. These traders believe fundamental analysis is more effective. They make their decisions on the basis of announcements relating to central bank monetary policy.

Trading technical analysis - Charts

Currency charts represent the fluctuation in the prices of currencies. The information contained in these charts allows the development of trading signals that will be related to the activity of a currency.

In MetaTrader we can find three types of charts:

- Linear graphs;

- Bar charts;

- Candlestick charts.

***MetaTrader** is a software commonly used by Forex traders. In particular, the Meta Trader offers a communication channel between the currency trading systems and the trader's computer or mobile device. Accessing online markets is simple and free if you use AvaTrade and the Meta Trader platform. There are two versions of MetaTrader:*

MetaTrader 4 - Available on desktop, mobile and web

MetaTrader 5 - Available on desktop, mobile and web

With both versions you can use different platforms without any delay on your server or PC. The software requires few resources and will not overload the system, allowing you to trade quickly, with immediate executions, a real "must" when trading in volatile markets

These are the most common charts used by traders and the best known within the currency community.

The profitability of your Forex trading operations will depend on your ability to make the right decisions at the right time. When an imbalance occurs in the market, charts are essential to determine when is the best time to trade and minimize losses.

Inline (or linear) charts

Line graph is a very simple type of graph that displays information in the form of a series of points connected by straight line segments. By extending the scatter plot, the chart is widely used to visualize a trend over time intervals. Therefore, its line is often drawn chronologically.

The effectiveness of the chart lies in its simplicity: it allows you to easily view the closing prices of a currency pair at a specific time. These are the easiest charts to understand: in a line chart, prices are shown sideways and dates below.

The line chart does not show price increases, decreases and market prices. Offering less detail than Japanese candlesticks, this type of chart is often used by contemporary traders

Advantages of the Forex linear chart:

- It is the simplest tool for traders;

- It allows you to obtain crucial information;

- Easy and neat to read;

- Excellent analysis tool for beginners;

- A faithful synthesis of past trends.

Disadvantages of the line graph:

- It only represents a currency pair;

- Offers very limited information.

Bar charts

This chart allows you to see at a glance how the price changes in a day. It indicates the volatility of the trading session, the opening price and the closing price.

In bar charts, vertical bars are used to show the price level for a given day.

These charts allow traders to see four prices per day, i.e. the lowest price, the highest price and the price levels at closing and opening. They allow you to track and anticipate price trends.

The bar chart consists of four elements:

Opening: the opening price of the market. It is symbolized by a horizontal line to the left of the vertical bar.

- Maximum: the highest point of the vertical bar;

- Minimum: the low point of the vertical bar;

- Closing: the closing price of the market. It is symbolized by a small horizontal line to the right of the vertical bar.

In bar charts, the length of each vertical bar or line indicates the price spread over a given trading period or range for a given currency pair.

Advantages of the Forex bar chart:

- It shows 4 prices within a single bar;

- Provides more in-depth analysis than linear charts.

<u>Charts with Japanese candles</u>

There are many different types of charts. Probably the most popular and most used type of chart among traders around the world is the Japanese candlestick chart.

What do they represent? Candles represent the movement of prices in a predetermined time.

Usable with different time units, candles provide four key information about the period in question:

- the level of opening and closing;

- the maximum and minimum points.

In Forex, candlestick charts are often used in technical analysis to analyze the price levels of currencies.

Trading technical analysis - Candlestick chart

Japanese candlestick charts are the most popular charts for currency traders, and for good reason: they provide complete, safe and accurate information on market developments.

The Japanese candlestick chart represents the difference between the opening and closing of the market.

If the opening price is lower than the closing price, the period implies a profit and the Japanese candle is blue. So let's say that if the candle's body is blue, the session is bullish.

Otherwise, if the opening price is higher than the closing price, the Japanese candle turns red. So, if the body of the candle is red, the session is bearish.

In addition, when the market moves above the opening and closing prices, bull highlights will appear at the ends of the Japanese candlestick body.

What candlestick charts represent

As stated above, candles have the function of presenting the price action in a given unit of time. Furthermore, they can provide useful information, such as market sentiment, or possible trend reversals through specific figures. Understanding this is a great start to using candles in trading.

While trading, especially in Forex, you will analyze price charts to observe market movements. If we compare the line and candlestick charts, there are very noticeable differences.

The line chart is a very simple method of showing price trends. Displays information on a single line using a series of points. This is the kind of chart you might be used to seeing in different magazines and newspapers, showing market sentiment and the performance of a product.

To understand candlestick charts, you need to know what price movement is, not just a line, but a series of candles.

Forex traders prefer candlestick charts because they show much more information than a line chart and can be much more useful for making informed and informed trading decisions.

Candlestick charts are used in different time units. Specifically, if we view a candlestick chart over a period of 30 minutes, each candle will take 30 minutes to form. Similarly, if the chart is set to a 15 minute period, the formation of a candle will last 15 minutes.

Let's give a concrete example:

Imagine that we have two charts showing the price action for the EUR/USD pair if we consider an hourly range of one hour:

The first graph shows a 30 minute time frame, so after an hour, you will see two candles of 30 minutes each.

The second graph shows a 5 minute time frame, so after an hour, you will see 12 candles of 5 minutes each.

Trading technical analysis - Structure of candlestick charts

The body:

The rectangular figure is called the candle body. It is the widest part of the sail.

It is the first step in reading the graph. It shows the opening and closing price for a given period.

<u>The wicks:</u>

The low and high wicks of the candle represent the lowest and highest price reached during the set time period.

A chart that shows the opening price, closing price and the highest and lowest price is called the OHLC Forex chart.

<u>Candle colors:</u>

Different body colors indicate if the candle is bullish (i.e. the closing price is higher than the opening price) or bearish (the closing price is lower than the opening price).

Trading technical analysis - Trends and charts

Logically, if the candle is bullish, the opening price is lower than the closing price, if the candle is bearish, the opening price is higher than the closing price.

The use of different colors allows you to immediately know if the candles are going up or down.

Let's give another example:

Imagine the candle is bullish (blue or green). This tells us that over a 1 day period the price of the EUR/USD pair has risen.

It also means there were more buyers than sellers during this time. The price at the end of this hour is much higher than when it opened. For example, the price at the beginning of the hour is 1.3009, at the end of the hour the price is 1.3171.

Even during this time period, the highlights indicate the highest and lowest pair of the EUR/USD pair.

Using the previous example, you can switch from the time unit 1 day to the time unit 1 hour, for example.

The 1-hour chart will then show more candles and more details on the evolution of prices during this session. If you want even more detailed information on price trends, you can switch to a 15 minute or 5 minute unit.

Trading technical analysis - The best chart

Choosing between the line chart, the bar chart and the Japanese candlestick chart is not easy. In fact, each type of chart provides particular information, and most of the time it will be necessary to consult different types of charts to optimize the chances of making profits with the Forex market.

Generally, experienced traders use Forex candlestick charts which provide them with technical and accurate information on currency pairs.

However, we recommend that you try all available technical analysis tools to find the one that best suits your needs.

To develop an effective trading strategy and achieve your financial goals, nothing better than trying to interpret different charts.

Trading technical analysis - Patterns

Graphic technical analysis is based on the identification of figures called "patterns" that announce the trend reversal or its continuation.

<u>What is a pattern</u>

A pattern is a repetitive template that allows you to predict the evolution of the price of a stock, a prediction that is safer than a random position.

Predicting the evolution of prices through charts is a very ancient technique that forms the basis of foreign exchange operations.

If there are a multitude of possible charts in the stock market, we will present graphical figures that offer the best trading opportunities.

<u>The "shoulder head shoulder" figure (head & shoulders)</u>

This figure prevents a possible reversal of the downward trend. It is formed with a first fairly high point (the left shoulder) of a correction, a low point, then a slight correction and finally an additional top located above. This new vertex will be the head, and the second part will appear symmetrical.

This is a setup that provides good trading signals, and currency trading volumes tend to be higher on the first shoulder and then gradually decrease on the head and then on the second shoulder.

To observe the shoulders of the figure, it is important to check the evolution of the path.

For example, the volume of the slope that rises near the head must imperatively be less than the volume found during the constitution of the path of the left shoulder.

All models of this type are similar in construction as there are four main parts of this graphic model, namely two shoulders, a head and a clavicular line.

These patterns are confirmed when the clavicle line that serves as a support/resistance level is interrupted.

Once the trend change figure is confirmed, we have two price targets.

Depending on our risk management we can use the right shoulder width as the main target, where we could make a partial profit to secure a part and leave part of the order open until the main order is fulfilled. This is an option that should be evaluated based on the strength of the market. And move our stop loss to breakeven point.

The main focus is the width of the head. This is where we should place the take profit and exit the market.

The triangles

Like the previous figure, the triangle is a graphic figure widely used by Forex traders. Triangles are made up of what is called support or resistance, as well as a trend line to set a target price.

These data are observed in markets that do not have a clear trend and more particularly in times of uncertainty. These graphic figures start in an area where prices are moving a lot. Market participants are waiting for a signal to make a decision.

Triangles are high-performance tools: they allow you to anticipate the direction of the price by the market or a security in a very precise way. To confirm the trend, exits from the triangle occur with large volumes in the case of small transactions.

The figure of the "double ceiling" or "double roof"

Thanks to the double ceiling it is possible to predict a bearish market reversal. This Forex figure is represented by a single vertex which is touched not once but twice.

A sell signal is emitted at the lowest point of the descending path of the second ceiling. During the formation of the first ceiling, we can observe a sharp increase in volumes. These volumes decrease over time as data is plotted. The double ceiling figure gives a good indication of when to close a buy position.

The figure of the "double floor"

Unlike the double roof, the double floor is a good indication to close a sale. Very useful for predicting a bearish market decline, the double floor represents the same low that will be hit twice. During the formation of the first "floor", the volumes increase and then decrease sharply once the central peak is created. From the moment the second channel ends, the volumes increase strongly.

The figure of the "diamond"

The diamond figure is a very rare Forex graphic figure, but with serious consequences. Characterized by a very volatile construction, it is difficult to analyze, even for the most experienced traders.

It is relatively easy to detect due to its original diamond shape. Moreover, the first half of the figure is enlarged. Faced with such an extensive formation, volatility increases and supports/resistance diverges. As this extended formation shrinks, it is necessary to wait for the diamond to exit for the trend to settle.

It is possible to observe a diamond in an ascending or descending trend. In this area where the trend is not yet established, sellers and buyers come together to try to raise or lower the stock.

"Flag" figure

Bullish figure of the flag

Both flags (in the canal) and small flags (triangle) imply that the current movements are sustainable. This figure is nothing more than a transitional balance between the forces that push to buy and the forces that push to sell.

Very similar to symmetrical triangles, flags and pennants are considered as continuation patterns in currency tables. They have a short duration and are usually formed as a result of a large abrupt movement.

The figure of the "rectangle"

The rectangle is arguably the most recognizable of all the patterns. Of course, the consolidation of the figure can lead to the continuity of the initial movement or, on the contrary, to a reversal of the trend.

In a rectangle, the prices of currencies vary within a

horizontal channel that indicates the equality between the forces of supply and demand. From the moment the price breaks through the resistance or support, the figure ends.

Trading technical analysis - The time frame

Multi-time analysis is part of technical analysis. This analysis consists of the graphical study of a currency pair over different time periods.

Traders who specialize in momentum, intraday, risk-by-event or breakout strategies may not pay attention to signals that anticipate long-term trends. This will make them lose information about obvious support and resistance levels and good opportunities to enter and exit the market. For this reason we find it interesting to explain the Forex analysis with various time frames.

Trading technical analysis - MTFA definition

The analysis of multiple time frames in Forex Trading involves, firstly, the monitoring of the same currency pair during different frames, i.e. in different time frames.

MTFA stands for Multiple Time Frame Analysis.

There is no real maximum of frequencies that can be monitored simultaneously, or a selection of the best to choose from. However, there are some general guidelines, which are followed by most traders regarding this issue.

The use of three different periods is usually sufficient to obtain a broad and complete reading of the market situation.

Using fewer than three periods can result in substantial data loss, while a larger number of periods could provide irrelevant analysis and cause some clutter.

Trading technical analysis - The rule of MTFA

When choosing three time slots, a simple strategy is to follow the rule of four.

This rule implies in the first place the identification of a medium term period which will represent the duration of the operation. Once this period has been established, a shorter time period will be selected, at least one quarter of the average period.

For example,

A short time span of 15 minutes

An average time span of 60 minutes

If we follow the same logic, the long-term time frame must be at least four times longer than the medium term. That means:

Long term of 240 minutes (or 4 hours)

Choosing the right times is essential.

A long-term Forex trader who holds positions for months will find no use in the 15, 60 and 240 minute ranges.

Conversely, an intraday trader who holds positions for hours, and rarely for more than a day, would benefit little from daily, weekly or monthly plans.

Long term trading technical analysis - MTFA

We have covered the basics of analyzing multiple time periods in Forex, so we will now examine how to apply it directly to the market.

In this type of technical chart analysis, it is always a good idea to start with a long-term time frame and gradually lower the frequency.

Looking at a long-term time horizon, it is possible to establish the prevailing trend. And remember what is often said in long-term trading "the trend is your friend".

Orders should not be executed in this time frame, but open trades should be in line with the direction of the trend.

This does not mean that you cannot trade against the long-term trend, but the odds of success will be lower. In other words, the profits will be lower than they would have been if you had traded in the direction of the trend.

In the Forex markets, when the long-term time horizon has different periods (daily, weekly, monthly Forex technical analysis) the news has a substantial impact on the direction.

Therefore, the Forex Trader should always be up to date with economic news, while monitoring the overall market trend over that time frame.

Regardless of the current economic news and events, the trader must follow what has happened to understand the direction of the price. This is one of the main multiple time analysis techniques.

Another aspect to keep in mind for the long run is the interest rate. Interest rates are used as a reflection of economic health and have a direct impact on exchange rates. In most cases, the principal will flow into the currency with the highest interest rate in a pair, as this refers to much higher investment returns. This leads to an increase in investment returns.

Technical technical analysis -MTFA medium term

Let's now move on to the next framework for analyzing the different time periods in the Forex market. We will look at the average time frame with minor moves within the broader trend. This is the most flexible of the three frequencies, because from this level you can acquire a sense of time, both long and short term. In fact, this time frame is the most commonly used to trade.

Trading technical analysis - Short term MTFA

There are some operations that need to be done in the short term. As minor fluctuations in price action become clearer, a Forex Trader will be able to better select an attractive entry for a position whose direction has already been identified by the faster charts.

Perhaps another consideration to reiterate for this period is that once again the news substantially affects the price action in these charts, albeit in a very different way than in longer time frames.

Fundamental trends are no longer visible when charts are less than four hours in frequency.

When applying an analysis to multiple time periods the short term will respond with greater volatility to Forex trend market indicators.

In most cases, sudden movements are short-lived and are sometimes described as "noise". However, a Forex Trader will normally avoid trading during these temporary imbalances, as they monitor the progression of the other time periods.

Trading technical analysis - MTFA combined

When all three time slots are combined to value a currency pair, the Forex Trader can easily increase the chances of success of his trades. Top-down analysis encourages trading with relatively broader trends. Indeed, this only reduces the risk because there is a greater chance that price action will eventually continue in the longer trend.

When using this theory, the level of trust in a business should be evaluated based on the alignment of different time periods. For example, if the general trend is increasing, but short and medium-term trends are decreasing, cautious measures must be taken to achieve rational profits, such as in the case of stop losses.

Alternatively, the Forex Trader can wait for a bearish wave to execute its direction on the low frequency charts and hint at a satisfactory level when the three time frames are aligned again.

Another benefit of integrating multiple time frames into Forex technical analysis is the ability to see supports and resistances and strong entry and exit levels. The odds of a trade's success increase when it's tracked by a short-term chart. This helps traders to optimize their market entry, avoid inappropriate targets or stop losses.

CHAPTER SIX
FOREX SWING TRADING

The market never moves according to a linear trend, but makes continuous fluctuations. This trend occurs not only during phases of uncertainty, but also during more sustained and solid trends.

The Swing trading strategy precisely aims to profit from market fluctuations, entering when the corrections of a trend make a pullback and immediately afterwards the trend push starts again.

Basically when a strong trend makes a temporary deviation from its course, the trader straightens the antennas and then takes action when a counter-deviation occurs (a "swing", as in the image below) that puts the price back on trend.

The greater the new momentum of the trend, the greater the gain you will from this strategy.

Technically speaking, when it comes to swing trading it would be more correct to speak of trading style, rather than strategy. In any case, the essential element remains the one of grasping the temporary change of direction of the market and then riding the new wave, doing it for a period of time that is not too short (because it would limit earnings), but not too long to risk a reversal.

Given its characteristic features, Swing Trading is an intermediate methodology between short-term trading and position trading. In the first one, in fact, the aim is to obtain "hit and run" gains in a single day, while in the second, the aim is to obtain big gains by riding a trend for very long periods.

Swing trading, on the other hand, is in the middle, since each investment ranges from a couple of days up to a few weeks at the most (however, if you use 1H timeframes, certain swing trades can also close within the same day, but they are exceptions).

Even clearer is the difference compared to scalping, where the operations last even a few minutes.

This represents one of the great advantages of Swing trading, because its "pace" is ideal: there is no excessive stress typical of short-term trading (or worse still of scalping), but neither is the excessive slowness (sometimes boredom) which characterizes position trading.

For this reason it can also be managed as a part-time activity, because it can be organized on a few hours of work per day.

Let's clarify: managing it in a few hours does not mean that you can trade in a good way! It means that accurate analyzes will always be needed, but these can be done without rushing and in reasonable time frames.

Timeframe swing trade

Since at the base of swing trading there are the concepts of trends and trend corrections, we cannot think of applying this strategy at very low timeframes, where those concepts would lose their effectiveness.

Usually the minimum recommended timeframe is 1H, but the majority prefer a 4H chart which is already larger. There are not many who, instead, take advantage of the "daily", probably because it involves too sparse operations and therefore similar to position trading.

In any case, except for too short timeframes, the Swing trading strategy can be adopted on all other time horizons.

For this investment method, Forex is undoubtedly an ideal hunting ground. In fact it is a very volatile and extremely liquid market. The trend of currency pairs in fact proceeds with continuous fluctuations, which generate many opportunities for swing traders.

However, this technique is very versatile and can be conducted effectively in all other markets, including the stock market.

Regardless of the type of market in which you operate, it is essential to carefully select the asset on which to operate.

In fact, it is necessary to select only those situations in which - due to the dynamics that are having prices and the market - in the face of the possibility of success, the risk seems very low. In other words, this type of trader scans the markets very well in search of the best opportunities.

The three weapons of the swing trader

When you decide to adopt a swing trading strategy, you have three "weapons" with which you define your inputs. Any trader before venturing into the market should be able to "handle" these three weapons with sufficient ease.

Here they are:

1) Technical analysis: it can help us to identify the moment in which a corrective movement can end, and therefore a trend can resume the race The swing trader therefore tends to look for graphic patterns such as "head and shoulders", "flags", "wedges", "triangles". But inversion candlestick patterns such as hammer, falling stars, etc. are also exploited.

2) Prevailing macroeconomic themes. News such as rate decisions, macro reports, geopolitical situations, etc. can create volatility in the market and generate excellent swing trade opportunities, considering that often the events that occur around us help us to evaluate the sentiment in different financial markets.

For example, let's think how much the outbreak of tension in the Middle East can suddenly affect the price of oil, perhaps modifying an ongoing trend or dampening a correction.

3) Price analysis. Thanks to the analysis of candles we can understand the recent history of the "battle between buyers and sellers", and therefore check if a trend is running out or restarting.

Through the three weapons we have just seen, a trader aiming to take advantage of the "swings" should be able to identify the moment when the trend correction is about to end and the price surge will start again.

The concrete techniques that are used are very personal and change from trader to trader, since everyone has their own ideas of the market and operates according to them.

However we can identify three "basic" ways to "catch" Swing, let's see them:

1) Continuation figures

One of the ways to capture swings is to identify if there are "continuation figures" (flags, wedges, rectangles, triangles etc). When the price correction occurs with the formation of these figures, then we have a good signal.

2) Test on the maximum and minimum levels

Another way to find market entrances in swing trading is by taking advantage of the minimums or maximums already tested several times by the market (the greater the number of times, the more reliable they are). These points are possible levels of price bounce or market turn.

This technique can be performed both on the basis of static supports/resistances, and on dynamic levels.

3) First pullback, after a breakout

Another favorable situation to trigger a swing trade occurs when 4 very specific phases occur during a trend:

1. the price of an asset enters a congestion zone after a

trend;

2. makes a breakout resuming the march towards the trend;

3. then a new pullback occurs, with prices going against the trend (return move);

4. 4)finally as a result of this trend - especially if this phase is accompained by a reduction of the range (body of the candles) - a swing is often generated with the subsequent resumption of the trend.

The reliability of the swing

Not all swings are created equal. In fact, their reliability must be evaluated on the basis of various factors, which can make it more or less "safe" to trade.

1. The% retracement (viewed via Fibonacci levels) should remain in the range of 38 to 62%. Beyond this level, in fact, the possibility that this is not a simple correction of the trend, but a real inversion, begins to be very concrete.

2. The strength of prices. If prices are approaching a support/resistance level quickly (i.e. with a few large body candles) it is believed that the chances of a bounce on support/resistance are increased.

3. The impulse/correction ratio. The number of candles that make up the trend correction should never exceed the number of candles of the last impulse (i.e. the last push received from the trend).

The size of the trade and the overnight risk

As we have said, actual swing trading involves multi-day operations, i.e. positions are held open overnight (unlike day trading where positions are closed before the market closes). This raises the danger of running into a price gap/lap, or sudden jumps in prices. This is why "swing trades" are usually done with a smaller position size than day trading.

Furthermore, strict discipline is required for the management of positions, with appropriate stop-loss orders to protect the allocated capital.

Countertrend swing trading

Some swing traders tend to trade swings even against trends. Even if we don't agree very much, technically nothing prevents us from doing so. However, much more accurate analysis skills and a "multi-timeframe" approach are required. In practice, a trader does not analyze a single time interval on the chart but makes his decisions based on the analysis of multiple intervals.

The logic is this: if on a daily chart we grasp the existence of an uptrend and therefore swing lows could form, on a lower timeframe (type H1) there could instead be a short-term bearish movement where swing highs could form. In this case the trader knows that even if the long term trend is up, he can still make profits in the short or medium term by making use of the signals generated by the shorter time frames.

Swing trading is a very common methodology among traders, because it allows you to keep positions open for several days and therefore not worry about having to constantly check the position (if it remains within the stop). It also allows for larger profits on average than in day trading and generally the operating rules provide for tight Stop Losses, so the risk of losses is usually reduced for each operation.

This requires a certain amount of care in planning your trades, and also greater frustration if things don't go as hoped. In fact, it is clear that reversals do not always occur and sometimes a retracement can continue for a long time, ending up triggering one or more stop losses that throw us out of the market making us lose money and patience.

CHAPTER SEVEN
DAY TRADING FOREX

An experienced day trader can make large profits trading Forex, but day trading can be extremely dangerous for less experienced traders. In this article, you can find out what day trading is and the best way to try it. It is advisable to practice opening a demo account and ensure constant profitability for a few months before opening a real money account with the best Forex brokers best suited to day trading.

Day trading

What does Forex day trading mean? We could define it as the act of sitting in front of a trading screen for an extended period of time, carrying out operations that should essentially be closed when the trader turns off his computer and interrupts the session.

Day trading is defined as buying and selling instruments on a single trading day but can generally apply to slightly longer maturities. Typically, day traders use high amounts of leverage and short-term trading strategies to capitalize on small price movements, with the aim of making a small but not insignificant profit. There is a lot of misinformation and controversy surrounding day trading - with the false promises of rich quick earnings schemes and negative media representation - but as long as reasonable risk management is applied, day trading can be an exciting and profitable source of income.

A day trader could use a strategy called scalping, which is to

89

try to place orders quickly to earn profits of around 10 pips, or he can use swing trading, where he will try to spot a daily movement for around 200 pips for example. Both methods can be done in day trading, if the positions are opened and closed within a single session.

The pros and cons of day trading

There are potential pros and cons of choosing to be a day trader.

The main advantage of day trading over long-term trading is probably the same for most people: that day trader usually closes their trades at the end of the daily trading session, shuts down and forgets the market until the next session.

Many are drawn to the peace of mind this can offer, especially on weekends when the Forex markets are closed, although there are now some brokers that offer Forex trading on the weekend, not to mention cryptocurrencies that also trade on weekends. Day traders can also enjoy the benefit of not having to pay overnight swap fees if they don't leave any positions open after 5pm New York time when swaps are usually paid or debited.

Perhaps the most important thing is that a successful day trader can earn more money than he would using a long-term trading style.

The main drawback of day trading is that it is very demanding and, for less experienced traders, tends to be less profitable than long-term trading styles.

The challenge of day trading

The intraday Forex strategy is extremely difficult, both from a technical and psychological point of view. There are so many elements that have to balance in order to systematically make profits, that it is easy to lose your investment. Most traders who trade this way are unsuccessful. This does not mean that it may be your case, but you simply have to be competent, organized and emotionally stable in order to have a good chance of earning.

For new traders it is not advisable to enter this world with day trading. Forex day trading is very popular because it is exciting, there can be a lot of movement and it is easy to see the price swing throughout the day and think you can convert it into profits. An experienced trader might be capable of this, but it's never as simple as it sounds. We advise new traders to start with a position and/or swing trading, which is a much easier way to make money with the market and develop technical skills at the same time. Once you have become competent enough, you can move to day trading if you want.

If you wish to invest with the intraday Forex strategy, you will need to have an organized and systematic approach.

A plan for day trading

First of all, decide at what times you want to operate. Find a place where you won't be interrupted or disturbed, where you feel comfortable. When trading day trading, it is essential to enter and exit positions quickly, so you need to protect yourself from external problems or distractions.

Before you start investing, check the economic calendar to see if any important data will be released regarding the pair you want to trade. Keep in mind that you will have stop-losses at only 10 or 40 pips, and unexpected economic data could also suddenly turn a large trade into a huge loss. Is it really worth being exposed so much to any stop-loss, so that the investment becomes a gamble? Probably not, so get out of positions near stop losses before major news releases.

It is probably a good idea to be prepared to trade one of the three major currency pairs: EUR/USD, GBP/USD or USD/JPY. Before you start trading, you should look at a long-term chart and mark the key trend lines and support and resistance levels that are anywhere near the current price. If there is a couple that has been more active and directional than the others lately, then this is the one to focus on, especially if there is high impact news scheduled for one or ideally both sides of the couple.

Secondly, depending on the time of day you are trading, it is a good idea to mark lines on the chart to identify the highs and lows of the previous session, especially those that really stand out as turning points. Some traders also like to mark the opening of a session, but I personally believe they are much less important.

A good day trading strategy will involve being flexible and leveraging your continuous presence in front of the screen to quickly identify low risk entry points with tight stop losses. Another aspect of your day trading strategy will consist of always being ready to quickly exit a trade if at a loss, but without being overly hasty in doing so.

Real example of a daily operation.

For example, have a look at the chart below. I was thinking of investing with the GBP/USD pair and start at the opening of London. In the course of my preparations, I marked the high and low of the previous Asian session (Tokyo) with pink lines:

An unusually wide Asian session range is usually a sign that it will be difficult to break out of the Asian range, so a profitable day trading strategy here was to try to vanish the pink lines. Looking at the latter, it can be seen that the lower pink line seems more solid than the upper one, as it was respected three times during the Asian session. Another thing that made it interesting is the fact that it was just 10 pips above the key long-term support at 1.5750, a key psychological level because it is also a round number. For all these reasons it was logical to look for a price reversal at that point for a possible long trade.

A little over an hour after the London opening, the price had reached the low of the Asian session, reversing quickly and providing a good chance to go long. Note that the candle in the 5-minute chart below was easily identifiable, as it bounced quickly and strongly from the lows.

It was the first strong bullish candle after the entire bearish move.

It did not touch any of the moving average lines, suggesting that the price was extending too much, then quickly recovering in the long direction.

I took a new long position when the price broke above the candle high. This trade offered a maximum of 38 pips per 7 pips risk, which is a good risk-reward ratio. It is the ability to trade with this type of relationship that makes day trading fruitful.

A profitable day trading strategy that works

Creating a good day trading strategy is quite simple - take any trading strategy that works on higher time frames such as the daily time frame and use shorter time frames to catch entries that have already been reported.

For example, a trading strategy that has a very good track

record for many years is the 50 day breakout trading on the EUR/USD and USD/JPY currency pairs, using a stop loss equal to the average real range of one day in the last 15 days or so.

You can apply this to day trading, for example, waiting for the EUR/USD pair to finish the New York session for a maximum of 50 days, then opening a day trading session the next day and looking for a long trade.

The closing of the EUR/USD currency pair must be completed within the maximum 50 days.

You already know that the daily chart and long term trend tell you the odds are in favor of a long trade, so just look for a long trade. The great thing about day trading like this is that if you take the turn that day, you may be able to catch a 200 pip profit move if you leave the trade open for several days, but only using a 20 pip loss stop instead of maybe 80 pip stop loss you would need when trading this strategy on a daily chart.

I mentioned earlier that day traders close all their positions at the end of a day trading session, but there is no rule that tells you that you have to do so, as long as you make sure there is a reasonable rigid stop loss order in place, before turning off. If the price is trending strongly, why not let at least part of your floating profit winning trade run overnight?

The real secret of day trading is that it allows you to make bigger profits through the use of relatively tight stop losses. In the example above, if you succeeded with a 20 pip stop instead of an 80 pip stop, you would multiply your profit, your reward/risk ratio, by a factor of four.

The reality is that Forex trading is pretty straightforward.

Think about it: make a trade and either it goes in your favor or not. Each trade you make has a roughly 50-50 chance of working, maybe up to 60-40 if you do really well. Markets will go higher or lower. You can help shift the odds a little more in your favor if you can find tighter spreads. The spread is essentially the same thing a casino does on a roulette wheel, with those two green numbers making sure that the red and black players don't automatically win half of their earnings each. The casino acts as a market maker, keeping everything hitting those two green numbers while the red and black players throw money back and forth at each other. This is essentially the way most Forex platforms work. This is why I say there is "about a 50-50 chance to train". Due to the spreads and other trading fees, it's probably a little closer to 49%.

In the end, an exchange works or doesn't. If you have some trading acumen, you can tilt the odds further in your favor. Or maybe you have the ability to hold on to earnings much longer than the average trader, and therefore your profits are much larger. In the end, there is no specific magical strategy. This doesn't mean there aren't some things you can do to increase your profitability and the likelihood that you will become a profitable trader.

The importance of money management in day trading

I will use two words that many traders around the world hate to hear: money management. I know it sounds like a very boring topic, but in the end it's the only one that really matters. I know that most of you have probably read articles about how risking just 1% on a trade is much better than

10%, mainly because it allows you to take a series of losses, which is sure to happen eventually.

How would you feel knowing that professional traders very rarely risk more than 1% and often risk much less? I can feel you roll your eyes. However, this is the reality of professional trading and most professional trading shops won't allow you to lose more than a couple of percent per day. There is a reason for this: you need to be able to preserve your trading capital to stay in the game. Even a good trader can lose five trades in a row. Think how brutal it will be if you lose 10% of your capital every time you make a bad trade. It will take you a long time to get it back, even under the best of circumstances. Most traders fail at that point and then do something truly desperate, increasing their true leverage and losing the rest.

Money management is by far the most important part of success in this trading world. I know you've heard it before, and I also know you're probably tired of hearing it. However, there's a reason you've heard it more than once.

The importance of backtesting in day trading

There are a multitude of trading systems that are available for free to try on the internet. It can be a simple moving average crossover system, or something as simple as buying a hammer or selling a shooting star at a large, round and psychologically significant number like 1.20 on a chart. It doesn't necessarily matter what your system is, but you need to give everything you're doing the opportunity to work overtime.

If you are unwilling to demo trade on any system for a

significant period of time, you are simply looking to play. The stats won't lie given a large enough sample, and so you'll know if something works. Once it is proven that something works in the long run, it is ready to be published. However, this is where psychology comes in, so you need to learn to trust your system. If it really works over a long period of time covering a wide range of market conditions in a Forex demo account, it should do the same in real markets. If we have a sample of 1,000 demo trades with 61% success rate, if you try 1,000 live trades, your success rate should be close to the same 61%.

The real question you will come across is whether you can believe and trust your system. I truly believe that trading psychology is a poorly served part of anyone's system. Unfortunately, this is something most people will ignore. They are too worried about being right on the market and not listening. This is why most would-be traders will fail.

Successful day trading is all about looking at the big picture and being flexible, then identifying opportunities where, for a risk of 10 pips or less, there is an opportunity to win maybe 30 to 40 pips at least. Taking the low or high turn in the day at the start of an important session for a Forex pair can be a good way to achieve this entering right in front of a small, low-risk, turning candle with the stop loss only the other side of it.

CHAPTER EIGHT
MARGIN TRADING

The trading margin or simply margin is the minimum amount necessary to guarantee the opening of the trade. For this reason, margin trading is one of the most important concepts in trading.

However, many novice traders do not fully understand the meaning or otherwise misinterpret the term. This could lead to making a series of mistakes and generating losses, precisely because the basic definitions relating to the Forex margin are not fully understood.

Margin trading

Forex margin is, in a nutshell, a deposit required to maintain open positions. This margin is not a commission or cost per transaction, it is simply a portion of the capital in your account that is set aside and allocated as a deposit. Margin trading is a percentage of the total amount of the chosen position.

Trading on margin can have important consequences: it can affect the results of your trades both positively and negatively.

In summary: the initial margin in trading is the minimum amount you need to have in your trading account in order to open a position in the stock markets.

Currency brokers take the initial margin to place orders on the market. Margin is a client promise that he can deal with the possible losses of a trading position. A margin is often expressed as a percentage of the nominal value of the chosen contract.

Most Forex margin requirements are estimated at: 2%, 1%, 0.5%, 0.25%. These percentages represent the equity to be considered as a percentage of the trading position. The higher the trading position, the greater the margin will be if you maintain the same leverage.

Based on the margin required by your broker, you can calculate the maximum leverage you can have with your current trading account.

Forex Leverage and Margin - Forex Margin Calculator

Let's see now an example of Forex margin calculation:

Instrument: EURUSD

Leverage: up to 1: 30 for retail traders and 1: 500 for professional traders.

Forex contract size: $ 100,000 = 1 lot

Margin trading 0.2% = 0.2% * 100,000 = $ 200 for professional traders. Or 100,000 / 500 (leverage) = $ 200

Margin trading 3.33% = 3.33% * 100,000 = $3,333.33 for retail traders. OR 100,000 / 30 (leverage) = $ 3,333.33 R.

This means that a professional trader with 1: 500 leverage will need to have $ 200 in their trading account to open a 1 lot position in euro Dollar.

On the other hand, a 1:30 leverage trader will need to have $ 3,333.33 in their trading account to open the same position.

Apply margin on MT4

Would you like to know how to apply margin on MetaTrader 4? Start logging into your account on the MT4 trading platform

As we explained in the previous section, if you open a euro batch trade, the margin retained with 1: 500 leverage will be $200.

You can see it in the MT4 and MT5 toolbox at the bottom of the platform.

What is free margin

Forex free margin is the amount of money that is not initially used to open more positions later.

Another way to define or calculate it is as follows:

- Free margin is the difference between equity and margin.

If the open positions are beneficial, then your capital or net worth will be higher and your free margin will increase accordingly.

On the other hand, if you lose positions, your available margin decreases.

Then there is still a topic to discuss. There may be a situation where you will have open positions and also some pending orders at the same time and the pending order may not be activated or it would be automatically canceled.

In this case, the trader may think that his broker has failed to execute the order and has not released his orders to the market, and therefore the broker is unreliable. Of course, in this case, that statement is incorrect, as you simply have no margin available to open a new position.

If we go back to the data of the previous example:

Retained Margin for Professionals: $200

Retained Margin for Resellers: $3,333.33

Let's suppose your trading account balance is $1500 and the Forex trader initiates a 1 lot trade in EURUSD:

The free margin or available margin on your trading account will be $1,300 (1,500 - 200 = $1,300) for a professional trader.

The margin required for a 1 lot EURUSD position is $3,333.33. This amount is higher than the amount in the trading account, so the trader will need to make an additional deposit of $1833.33 to open this position.

The level of the Forex margin

To better understanding Forex trading, we need to know all about Forex margin. This is why we also want you to familiarize yourself with the term "Forex margin level".

The margin level in Forex is the percentage value based on the equity of the account compared to the used or retained margin. In other words, it is calculated as follows:

Margin Level = (Equity/Retained Margin) x 100

The broker uses the margin level as a tool to detect whether the trader can open new trades or not. According to the broker, the limit for the margin level can vary, but the majority sets it to 100% before the margin call jumps, a concept we'll explain later.

The margin level in trading is not a constant percentage. Depending on whether it is a buy or sell transaction and whether the price rises or falls, the free or available margin will vary.

It is therefore essential to have a good business background to try to avoid these situations.

How to calculate the level

Before we proceed with the example, we have some good news, which is that there is no need to manually calculate the margin level. The MetaTrader platform includes a margin calculator.

So let's use an example to answer this question. Imagine you have an account of $10,000 and you have a losing position with a retained margin of $1,000.

If your position goes against you and reaches losses of $9,000, then the principal or principal will be $1,000.

Example: 10,000 - 9,000 = 1,000 = which equals the margin

So the margin level will be 100%. Again, if the margin level reaches the rate of 100%, no new positions can be placed, unless the market suddenly turns in your favor and your equity becomes larger than the established margin.

Let's imagine the market is holding up against you. In this case, the broker will have no choice but to close all losing positions.

Negative trading margin

Margin in trading is not always positive.

In principle, yes, but sometimes it can happen that the margin is negative. Margin is the fixed amount to open a position. When losses exceed the initial margin, it is called a negative margin. A trading account that has a negative margin means that the margin level is less than 100%.

We can have a negative margin when an account has a margin level of less than 100% on your trading platform, we are talking about a negative trading margin. In this case it means that the trader does not have enough money in his account to hold his position.

If the trader has an equity of $800 in his account and the trading margin withheld for a euro contract is $1000, the trader's account has a negative margin of $200.

Margin call trading

Margin call (or margin call trading) is perhaps one of the biggest nightmares Forex traders can have.

Technically, a 100% Forex margin call level means that when your account margin level reaches 100%, you can still close your positions, but you cannot open new ones.

As is evident, a 100% margin call level occurs when the equity of your account equals the margin. This happens when you lose positions and the market is quickly and steadily against you.

When your account equity equals margin, you will not be able to open any new positions.

The trading platform notifies you when you reach that margin level. The problem occurs when you are notified and the market keeps moving quickly against you or it is not possible to act at that time.

In this case, if your account's equity is within margin requirements, your broker may close some or all of your positions, as we'll see in the next section.

How to avoid this unpleasant surprise:

- Margin call trading can be avoided by closely monitoring the account balance on a regular basis and using stop-loss orders on each position to minimize risk. There is no point in keeping open losing positions in the portfolio in the hope that the market will turn in your favor. It is better to suffer small losses than a call finance margin;

- Adding funds to the account when the margin level is dangerously close to 100%;

- Closing of a transaction to free up the retained margin trading. Why? More open trades means more funds are used to hold trading positions, so you have less margin available to avoid margin calls in trading;

- Apply strict money management. Many Forex traders don't know how to protect themselves. It is not possible to trade currencies without using risk management. The first step is to make sure you don't invest more than you are willing to lose;

- Use the appropriate leverage. The most successful traders invest around 2.5% to 5% of their capital. A demo account can help you to better understand margin call mechanisms.

This can currently help to prevent your account from having a negative balance due to closing operations.

Forex margins are questionable. Some traders argue that having too much margin is very dangerous. However, it all depends on the personality and the amount of trading experience you can have.

If you are planning to trade in a margin or leverage account, it is important to know the policies your broker offers in margin accounts and you need to understand them and feel comfortable enough with the risks.

Now it is important to keep one fact in mind. Most brokers require high margin on weekends. In fact, this can take the form of a 1% margin during the week, and if you want to hold the position over the weekend, it can go up to 2% or more.

Stop out and margin trading

Forex stop out or Forex stop out level is the level or percentage, set by the broker, at which the platform will automatically close your positions.

For example, if the broker sets the stop out at 50%, the platform will close your positions when your margin level is 50%. This will prevent your trading account balance from being negative.

It is important to note that it starts closing from the position with the highest losses. If the other positions continue to lose and the margin level reaches 50% again, the system will close another losing position.

You may be wondering why brokers do this. Well, the reason is that brokers close positions when the margin level reaches the stop out level because they cannot allow traders to lose more money than they have deposited into their trading account. The market may continue against the trader's position and the broker does not want to bear his losses.

How to calculate the losses we can face before the operations are closed to us?

Retained margin * Stop out level = Equity

Trading account balance = $2000

Retained Margin = $1000

Stop out level = 30%

1000 euros x 0.3 = 300 Dollars of equity

This means that the losses should be = 2000 - 300 = $1700

Finally, after seeing concepts such as "inheritance", "balance", "margin" and it is possible that they are sometimes confused, we will see the differences between them.

Differences between balance and equity

Let's start with the definition of balance.

Margin Trading - Definition of balance

Balance = initial trading account amount or amount with all trades closed.

The balance is the initial amount the Trader contributes or the resulting amount once the trades are closed and the losses or benefits are consolidated.

Here we have introduced an important term, "profit and loss consolidation" and that is, until a transaction is closed, we cannot consider profits or losses as such.

And from here and through the concept of consolidation, the concept of Heritage comes into play.

Definition of equity

The value of the equity and therefore its definition will depend on whether the trader has open positions or not.

If there are open positions:

Equity = used margin + free margin + unconsolidated profit or loss

Equity = Balance + Unassociated Profit or Loss

If there are no open positions

Equity = free margin = account balance

Equity is actually the capital that traders hold in their accounts, which involves adding or subtracting the capital that traders have when all open positions have been completed. If the market undergoes a change in trajectory and there is a decrease in the degree of losses, then more margin will actually be freed up and equity will again exceed that margin. There is a second situation. If the market continues to move against you, equity will drop to a level where it will be below margin, making it virtually impossible to support open trades.

Loss positions should be closed to balance trade and protect the rest of the capital.

As previously explained in this article, the broker sets the stop out levels. Once these levels are reached, the broker will close the position with losses, starting with the one with the highest variable loss.

If the trader deposits more capital, this can be added to the margin and thus be able to keep the position open. Which is not a good idea, as the market may continue to counter it and consequently lose even more capital.

Forex margin final thoughts

As you know by now, trading margin or Forex margin is one of the aspects of trading that should not be overlooked, as this could lead to unpleasant results and risk generating significant losses.

To avoid the margin call and all that it entails, you need to understand the theory of margins, levels and call margins and apply trading experience to create a viable Forex strategy.

Without a doubt, understanding Forex margin and its consequences can save you a lot of trouble.

Margin trading is a moot topic. Some traders find margin trading very dangerous, others, such as currency speculators, find it particularly useful for trading short-term strategies that can pay off with a small initial investment.

It all depends on your trading experience and your goals.

Once you have practiced everything you learned about Forex margin today in the demo account and are confident in your knowledge, you can take the step to the real account.

CHAPTER NINE
FOREX SCALPING

Scalping is a trading technique which consists of buying and selling financial products in very short periods of time. The Scalper thus only gets a handful of points on the market.

Scalping trading is often done on derivatives and with significant leverage. The investment return on each position is modest compared to the risk taken, but the advantage lies in the number of positions successfully completed at the end of the session.

A Dax 30 scalper, for example, is a person who scales the stock market. The gains made per position with strategic scalping are relatively low due to the small movement sought, which is why the scalper multiplies the number of his trades and uses greater leverage than the swing trader. When trading in the very short term, we try to take advantage of the smallest market fluctuations on the stock exchange. A single scalping trade means little because the trader will execute a relatively large number of trades.

It is also the fastest way to trade after high frequency trading. Of these two trading techniques, scalping is actually the only one available to the individual trader, as high frequency trading requires expensive professional equipment and an extra fast priority internet connection.

Scalpers do not follow the classic money management rules, such as the 2% capital risk per trade rule.

Once you start gaining experience in currency trading, you

understand the role and importance your Forex strategy has in trading success.

Valid trading strategies are different, here we will focus on scalping and in particular we will address more than one scalping strategy and several indicators at the end of this article.

Definition of scalping trading

Forex scalping is a style of trading with high volumes and a very short duration in position. The scalping method is used by those who wish to become trader with a short term strategy.

Short-term currency trading is a form of algorithmic trading.

The average gain on short-term trades is around 5 pips maximum. Very short-term equity market investments are often made with strong leverage effects to speculate on the stock markets for larger changes in the euro.

But the definition of scalping doesn't stop there.

More specifically:

Scalping is not only a style but also a short term trading strategy. As you know, Forex is the most liquid and volatile stock market in the world. The volatility of currency pairs allows Forex traders to earn money with movements from 100 to 200 pips.

Scalping is also known to represent very active Forex traders and scalpers: orders are opened and closed very quickly, very often even by Forex scalping robots who will try to recover any point on the currency market. In other words, it allows you to make small gains on Forex speculating on the very short-term exchange rate.

Scalping trading strategies are very popular among professional traders, as they allow you to limit market exposure over time while taking limited risk. Exchange rate scalpers seek to benefit from small moves on Forex pairs and have chosen Forex scalping, as it offers many short term opportunities.

A scalper aims to earn no more than 10 pips on average per trade and takes a maximum risk of 20 pips. The volumes destined to the market must be high and the brokerage fees must be as low as possible to ensure that the profits are optimized.

The best short-term indicators

Scalping is clearly a trading strategy based on technical analysis and price action. Fundamental analysis is only marginally relevant when making this type of investment in financial derivative instruments. Technical indicators are very often used in scalping, but you never know which indicator is better to choose!

Let's go through some possible choices together to get you started on the right foot in Forex scalping.

The Ichimoku 1 Minute Scalping Indicator is a very popular technical indicator and is at the top of our list of the most commonly used indicators in Forex Scalping. Whether or not this is the best indicator for Forex scalping is entirely up to you. Some say it's the best indicator for scalping, while others don't even consider using it. Trading is very personal and is closely tied to your personality and your vision of the market.

Other free trading indicators available on MetaTrader 4 and 5 often include oscillators.

Below you can find listed some of the most used technical indicators in Forex scalping:

Ichimoku;

Bollinger bands;

Heiken Ashi;

Renko;

CSR;

Moving average;

MACD;

Support and resistance;

Fibonacci.

This list is not complete.

Other scalping indicators can be used on a simple scalping strategy, such as moving averages, MACD, Renko, Parabolic Sar, etc.

How to do Forex scalping

In general, most Forex traders look at charts in the 1 minute, 5 minute or 15 minute time frames.

You can't scalp without using the shorter time units. You can try all time scales below the 15 minute chart or even charts that do not depend on time but only on movement using the MetaTrader 4 and MetaTrader 5 Supreme Edition tools available at Admiral Markets.

This will allow you to decide which approach is best for you with which you can make long-term gains.

You may be wondering: why are we talking about the long term when scalping is based on the very short term? This is a good question that we will answer immediately!

The question is really simple: both in trading, as in any other investment or business, for a style or an approach, the actual results can only be assessed over time, and therefore, in the long term. It is possible, for a beginner or a professional, to have one or even five good consecutive sessions of:

- Scalping in Forex, with for example the EURUSD pair;

- Scalping RSI with indices such as CAC 40 or DAX 30;

- Scalping of cryptocurrencies such as Bitcoin or Ripple;

- Scalping with ichimoku.

But eventually, inevitably, you will also have negative sessions in which you will lose money. And until you have a complete idea of the structure of your scalping strategy, across several good and bad times, you won't be able to objectively judge whether this method is the best for your trading or approach to this discipline.

The gains and losses you are aiming for also depend on the

time unit you decide to use.

Let's give an example:

If you trade on a 1 minute euro Dollar chart, you will want to earn 5 pips rather than 10 points.

If you are trading on a very short Renko chart you may be looking for even less than 5 pips of profit.

The smaller the time unit, the smaller the potential movements will be. For this, it makes sense to adjust the expected profits based on the MetaTrader trading chart you are working on.

The so-called technical scalping trading techniques are performed on the smallest units of time available:

- 5 min;

- 1 min;

- Seconds;

- Ticks.

Bars Range

Renko bars

Renko and Range bars eliminate "noise" from the trading chart and are widely used with Bollinger Bands and the MT4 MACD scalping indicator. These bars allow you to trade the breakouts themselves.

On the other hand, Renko and Range candles require you to

know how they are formed and the size needed in relation to the financial products you want to market, because each product will have a different corresponding size.

This is a more professional approach which is a real advantage in the CFD markets because it is recognized that scalping with Ranges and Renko bars is much better than scalping on a time chart.

How to trade Forex scalping

The first step to becoming a pro scalper is to learn the basics of Forex scalping and then evaluate if this approach suits you. A demo account allows you to do it in real conditions but without risking your capital.

Scalping also depends on how much time you intend to spend developing your currency strategy and whether you are genuinely interested in Forex scalping. Since it is a method that requires a lot of time and attention, both for money management and for the management of stock market orders it is essential that you are aware that this style will require a lot of your time and especially your maximum concentration.

Scalping the DAX 30 or short-term trading on the CAC 40 for example requires continuous analysis and monitoring of the stock market. When it is possible to start scalping the order book, trading hours are limited: this short-term trading strategy requires high financial market liquidity and low spreads. The trader scalper needs to be responsive and close orders quickly to redeem his winnings.

Here is a simple explanation on how to scalp the DAX:

When scalping a CFD index, you try to make the most of a minimum number of points. This is why many online traders use tick charts to better see price movements. The Forex scalper EA also does a lot of round trips during the day, meaning it opens and closes a lot of positions. All these operations are performed in very short times, a few seconds, 1 minute, 5 minutes and must be precise and accurate.

Forex scalping guide: 5 Steps

- Identify market conditions (low or high volatility);

- Identify on which instrument it is advantageous to enter scalping;

- Identify the trend: uptrend, downtrend or range trend;

- Identify key support and resistance levels across multiple time units;

- Take trading positions in the market according to your own scalping strategy, money management and well-developed and studied trading plan.

Each pro scalper has their own method of analyzing the stock market or foreign exchange market, but there are many trading scalpers who also observe:

The key levels of the day

- The economic calendar, especially for a Forex news scalping strategy;

- The supports and resistors before entering the position;

- Forex Scalping: The Best Products.

You can trade with a short term trading strategy on all financial assets. However, some of them will allow you to optimize your results!

Here is an overview of the categories of tools available to you:

- Stock market indices;

- Futures;

- Forex;

- Raw materials;

- Bonds;

- CFD.

In order to take advantage of technical scalping trading, you need to have volatility in the desired market, but also sufficient liquidity. That's why it's best to use assets like currencies and indices for scalping. Among the commodities it is possible to do scalping on gold (GOLD) and oil (WTI or Brent). Other commodities are less attractive because the spread is too high.

Each stock market has its own particularities, but scalping, in each market, generally takes place on the most liquid instruments or with the lowest brokerage fees: for example on stocks like Apple or Google in the stock market, on the euro Dollar of Forex or on the DAX 30 in futures contracts.

The scalper often tries to win small trades - which is why most scalpers trade on a single market. Doing a good trading does not mean diversifying the risks in this case, but above all knowing very, very well your reference market. This is the reason why there are fewer actions to be realized in stocks than in currencies. Short-term trading requires liquidity on the underlying market with the possibility of short selling. Not all markets offer this chance and often the most liquid financial instruments are ultimately the most used in high frequency trading.

Are you scalping the DAX 30?

If your answer is yes, you probably know that it is not a very easy index to predict and that you need to follow it closely to know what the price action of the index is, the maximum and minimum in the different periods and, of course, the levels of support and resistance. A good idea is to monitor the tick charts and the correlation of the German stock market index with other financial assets (e.g. US indices) available on the MT4 Supreme Edition platform.

There are of course other trading strategies that can be used in 1 minute of Forex scalping: you can use a Forex robot scalper, a software scalper, or a scalping expert advisor for a profitable DAX scalping strategy. It's up to you to apply yourself and find the strategy that interests you the most.

Forex scalping is volatility-based trading. To make money with scalping you need to choose a fairly volatile currency pair with minimal brokerage fees. For example, we can't scale the Chinese currency, the yuan, because the exchange rate hardly ever changes.

Another example of a currency pair that is difficult to scalp is that of exotic exchange rates: the Russian ruble, the Brazilian real, the Mexican pesos, the Romanian leu, the Polish zloty or the Turkish lira are unsuitable Forex products for scalping.

Exotic pairs can have high volatility, but not regularly distributed, so the risks are much higher than in other currencies. The movements can be very large and with these currency pairs and exiting the position can sometimes be difficult.

If you choose a currency pair with too low volatility, it may take a long time for the exchange rate to move, thus losing the goal of trading in the short term.

The best Forex scalping techniques

You are already aware that there are many scalping trading techniques.

But in reality, every trader has a personal scalping strategy. Most of the time, the best scalping strategy for a trader starting out as a pro is a basic and simple strategy.

You will probably think that if a simple Forex scalping strategy worked so well, everyone would know and use it. Well no, most of the time, the trading expectations are too high and the trader's lack of personal work with historical tests (also called backtests) prevents the investor from pursuing the long-term strategy and thus enjoying its efficiency.

Later in this article we will look at some of these simple and effective scalping strategies in detail.

Stop Loss and Take Profit

How do you manage the stop loss in scalping?

To develop a profitable scalping method, it is important to think about two essential concepts:

- Where to place an order to protect my capital, or the Stop Loss;

- Where to profit if the scenario moves in favor, i.e. set a Take Profit.

A Stop Loss, as well as one or more Take Profits, is essential, but not necessarily time-consuming for Forex or equity index scalping orders. Indeed, in the time to set and calculate the risk, the price movement could anticipate us and the position could be lost.

Quickly calculate the number of lots for your Stop Loss based on a number of pips or points and a fixed risk in USD.

Take a position with a predefined Stop Loss and Take Profit and position yourself in the market for better execution in case of very fast movements.

Also keep in mind that if you are scalping Forex with the economic calendar or trading on multiple exchange rates at the same time, using pre-built order templates will greatly facilitate the use of your day trading scalping strategy.

Let's see now how to choose a good Forex broker to invest in the short term and do Forex scalping.

The best broker for Forex Scalping

If you are looking for the best broker for scalping, you need to find a solution that can satisfy several conditions. The Broker must:

- be regulated by a recognized and competent financial authority, such as the London FCA;

- ensure the safety of funds with a reputable bank and with segregated account deposits;

- offer speed of execution thanks to cutting-edge technological tools;

- provide its clients with competitive spreads and transparent commissions

- offer advanced trading platforms such as MT4 and MT5 Supreme Edition;

- be able to provide training material and organize events or webinars for free training on scalping and on all topics related to trading and financial products offered.

If you decide to become, or already are, a scalper - you need to apply for the best trading conditions, because it is very difficult to make long term profits if the spreads are very high and your broker does not guarantee you the best working environment to achieve success. The choice of the broker for scalping is very important. It is not possible to do "quality" scalping without the conditions listed above.

When it comes to choosing the best regulated Forex broker for your scalping strategy, you should first discard all online brokers who do not allow this style of trading. Oh yeah!

Because not all Forex brokers allow their clients the freedom to choose the trading style they prefer, and some have banned scalping.

Now that you have a small list of regulated Forex brokers that allow scalping, you should start looking at the available trading tools and the corresponding spreads. Many brokers charge commissions on the operation, others have no commissions but report higher spreads: it is necessary to make an accurate assessment and calculation.

The absence of commissions on entry and exit in trading scalping offers greater potential profitability for you. However, price shouldn't be the only issue that matters when choosing the right broker for your scalping.

Scalping is based on taking many trading positions during a trading session or day. To make sure you can withdraw your winnings, you need to verify that you have opened a trading account with a regulated broker in Europe, even better if in the UK.

The most suitable Forex trading accounts and CFD indices for scalping are found in Forex STP accounts. On these accounts, you will have access to the interbank spread and generally there will also be a commission per contract:

The fundamental factor SPREAD

In summary, for a Forex scalping strategy to be profitable, the financial scalper must pay attention to the following elements:

- The scalping spread;

- The quality of order execution.

As we have already said, when scalping, you have to choose a broker with very low costs.

If we open a trade to earn 3 pips for example and our spread is 1 point, the price of the stock must move 4 points so that the scalper can close his position with the target gain.

Equally important is the quality of order execution, i.e. whether the broker has several liquidity providers and can execute orders as quickly as possible and under the best conditions. A Forex scalping or manual scalper EA does not like referrals and wants their orders to be filled as much as possible at the asking price.

The execution of the order

Having the best spreads displayed is always a good place to start, but very fast execution is better. There is no point in working with a Forex broker who offers the best spreads if order execution is not available!

Some brokers are very transparent in their execution and publish order execution statistics. For further information on our order execution statistics, please visit the Order Execution Quality page.

Another important aspect for a successful Forex day trader is the choice of the execution system. It can be difficult to be successful in Forex scalping if the order execution system is flawed.

What does it all mean?

In other words, a good broker is someone who has hardly any revaluation and is able to pass your scalping orders in the shortest time possible.

It is a shame to find good opportunities on the foreign exchange market or CFD indices and not be able to take advantage of them because the broker makes the transaction at a different and less attractive price than desired. That's why it's only you who can see the quality of an order execution and only on a real account.

Using a demo account to test the quality of order execution is a mistake, as very often the broker demo accounts do not work on the same trading servers as the real accounts. It is recommended to use two real accounts:

A low deposit account to test the broker's execution

An account with your standard deposit once you have evaluated the proposed service

scalping Forex mt4

Scalping trading tools

Forex trading scalping is one of the most sophisticated trading techniques and is the short term trading method that requires the most powerful technical tools.

In order to position himself well in the market, the professional speculator must be able to carry out an excellent graphical analysis. Stock market chart analysis is the basis of scalping trading, since we are not talking at all about medium-term trading or long-term equity investing which could be based on fundamental analysis.

The Robots

The Forex robot scalper is a computer product that is developing more and more. An MT4 scalping robot attracts the attention of retail and professional clients, with undeniable advantages:

- Forex scalping robot is not prone to fatigue or tiredness;

- It can remain operational 24 hours a day;

- It has a faster execution speed than the human trader;

- Calculate in an instant the risk to be respected based on the Stop Loss recorded in the scalping trading strategy.

In short, you will have realized that automatic or semi-automatic trading is a significant advantage, but it is often misperceived due to the sale of overly optimized EA scalpers on the internet that promise huge gains in a very short time. This does not reflect the reality of trading.

MT4 and MT5 scalping trading platform

For scalping pro, the trading platform is much more important than for a day trader or swing trader. A platform installed on your computer is often more responsive than an online platform on a web browser. For a scalping trader, the platform must have some essential factors:

- Excellent order processing speed;

- Professional-grade features;

- Intuitive and reliable operation;

- Robustness;

- The ability to backtest.

Live trading scalping techniques

Many FX market professionals try to make a living from trading. In particular, there are many beginners in trading who want to make a regular income using a scalping trading strategy.

Even if it is possible, know that live scalping takes time to master and most of all experience. If you have time to devote to this activity, you will be able to have a good understanding of technical indicators, learn to make quick decisions and quickly interpret incoming and outgoing signals.

CFD scalping techniques

Stock market scalping is often linked to CFDs.

Why?

The reason is the following: by definition, trading scalping refers to the search for small movements in the financial markets, with orders of a few points. If you earn some points with a small number of lots, the result of the operation will be measured in cents - it is not worth it.

Very often scalping traders use high leverage to multiply the value by one point. This is a risky strategy, and it is also the reason why scalping is not a strategy for novice traders.

CFDs allow:

- To speculate on the upside;

- To speculate on the downside;

- To use the financial leverage so that small movements in the financial markets can multiply into large losses or large gains.

CFD or Futures

Futures contracts and CFDs are two types of financial assets on which intraday speculation can be made. More than one Forex broker offers competitive leverage and spreads.

Dax CFD contracts are easily accessible, it is in fact possible to start with little capital to take advantage of a DAX scalping technique, unlike futures contracts. It is true that in general, future scalping techniques are developed by professional traders with large capital.

However, we note that the leverage effects on futures are much lower than the trading levers offered by CFD brokers.

For example, there are CFD regulated brokers that offer a leverage of 1: 500.

CHAPTER TEN
TRADING PSYCHOLOGY

The world of financial investments is often compared to a casino: emotions, passions, bets... When a trader starts his career it is really easy to get into the vortex of his passions and emotions, only an experienced professional can manage these components, often typical of this practice. Keep in mind that every trader feels emotions when he loses or when he wins, but the pros stand out for their spartan endurance and control of their feelings and emotional reactions.

There is an unwritten law valid for all those who wish to trade:

The higher the level of emotionality, the lower the work efficiency

It seems like a simple thing: controlling your feelings. However, the mechanisms for suppressing all our emotions and experiences are very complicated to apply. In the initial stage, it can be nearly impossible to refrain from the joy of winning or the worry of failure, but if you learn to reduce your emotionality it will be much easier to achieve success as a trader. This is the psychology of trading. Otherwise you run the risk of adding to the sad statistics of those who have abandoned halfway.

It is important to remember that unlike in a casino, where everything depends on luck, in trading you have to keep a cool head at all times as we have to decide the course of trading, stop it completely or double the investment. If these decisions are made quickly and without thinking, then it will become a game of luck, nothing more.

Our job is to make a profit, not to win a prize. Being lucky at any given moment is undoubtedly a pleasant prospect, but too ephemeral and too illusory. This is why it is important to answer several questions before starting to trade: How do we feel about trading? If we want to earn money consistently then we should abandon the idea of playing the market.

Of course, we shouldn't expect all traders to become newsboys, waving their arms in the markets as we often see in movies and even on the news. But it is a good image for us to have an idea of how emotions behave within us. The main difficulty in defeating the enemy is identifying him.

The main emotions of the trader

The trader's main enemies are his own emotions. Traditionally there are four emotional manifestations related to trading, they are:

- Fear;

- Greed;

- Hope;

- Euphoria.

Surprisingly and unlike other contexts in life, positive emotions do not help the trader and lead to "stupid things", taking actions that he had not even remotely planned to do.

<u>Fear</u>

To understand why it's so bad to be dominated by feelings, let's take a look at the main situations, with typical examples that almost all traders encounter. We will also see how to deal with these circumstances.

The feeling of fear is usually the first of the emotions manifested by a person who starts trading on the Forex or stock market. Fear can be classified into two types: primary fear and secondary fear.

Primary fear. Stages in trading psychology

At the start: this fear appears early on, before the first trade. When you study the charts, you look at the quotes and an inexplicable fear begins that the first trade may not be profitable.

Uncertainty: you decide that you are ready for the first trade but immediately a sense of uncertainty arises. What if it doesn't work? What if I'm not ready?

Doubt: doubt is a psychological phenomenon, a result of critical thinking. In decision making in any life situation, everything is analyzed from different perspectives, weighing the pros and cons, and emotions enter the evaluation process.

Chronic fear. In some cases, the fear of the first transaction can become almost chronic: when a person, who has not done anything yet, is afraid to enter the market for weeks (or longer). In the general case, the primary fear is overcome quite quickly, but some people are included in the "risk group", i.e. in the category of traders who are, in fact, afraid of becoming investors.

Here are the main factors that predispose to fear, so that a person who has never traded in the financial markets is able to understand if he is facing a primary fear:

Tendency to excessively long and unproductive analysis of situations. It consists of "walking in circles" around the same aspects of the problem.

Uncertainty in the decision made (even when the work is done, there is concern).

Habit of checking everything several times (if the iron is off, if the child has done all the homework, etc;)

High rigor and a high degree of responsibility towards others.

What to do? How to overcome fear in trading? This can only be done if you understand the reason and mechanism for the appearance of a particular feeling. These are the most common excuses to delay trading practice due to primary fear and possible solutions in each case:

"I will lose money" - Open the first trade with a small amount. It is not necessary to plan a large-scale or long-term trade to conquer the market. Even if the first transaction is not profitable, assume the loss of this small amount of money as an investment in the business, which will bring good results in the future.

"I don't have enough knowledge. I still have to learn" - If a trader does not have results, positive or negative, it is impossible to truly understand if you have enough knowledge or not. It is possible to verify its quality only by analyzing the results of the operations carried out.

"If I lose the first trade, then it's fate. It's not for me ..." - Fatalism is not the best helper. Operating with destiny in mind is not productive. Don't stop thinking that your first transaction is a litmus test of general success or failure.

"If I lose money, then I am a bad trader" - You will be able to know if you are good or not, after at least 7-10 transactions have been completed. A consistent analysis of the results will help to identify any errors and correct them.

"I'm afraid and I can't help it": That's not true, for example,

1. Choose one of the low volatility instruments (for example the EUR/USD exchange rate).

2. Prepare a trading plan. It is desirable that it is short-term.

3. Just click on the corresponding "BUY" or "SELL" button in the trading platform, and don't forget to open reduced positions.

4. As a general rule, in the first few seconds, the heart jumps out of the chest, but almost immediately the pulse returns to normal rhythms.

5. Don't worry, 99.9% of the time the world stays the same, the computer keeps running, the quotes keep flashing and the market won't backfire on your position within seconds.

Secondary fear. Stages in trading psychology

Operations failed. It appears after experiencing failed transactions. Sometimes a small unprofitable position is enough, sometimes fear appears after several failed trades.

Impotence. Secondary fear is stronger than primary fear because it is based on "proven" failure facts: a wrong prediction, a wrong analysis, a wrong interpretation of the fundamental data and, consequently, a loss. Unlike primary fear, secondary fear can make even a very self-confident person fall into that spirit. If the primary fear is experienced as a feeling of anxiety and doubt about the success of the trade, the secondary fear inspires a feeling of helplessness and demoralization and, above all, overshadows the ability to correctly analyze the market. Therefore, secondary fear affects not only a person's emotional state, but also his intellectual abilities.

Why does fear arise? The emergence of a secondary fear is always due to the negative experience and not to irrational ideas about one's own abilities. Therefore, it is more difficult to deal with than the primary fear. This situation is comparable to swimming. If a person has never swam before, they will be afraid of entering the water for the first time. But this fear is more easily to overcome than in the case of a person who has nearly drowned in the past. However, each of us realizes that it is much better to know how to swim than not to be able to swim at all. And even if in the second case it will be more difficult to overcome fear, it is still worth doing so, in order not to repeat the mistakes of the past.

The same psychological mechanisms apply to the financial markets. However, here, unlike the swimming example, no one forces a trader to dive into the depths of the market from the very first minutes. It is best to go progressively, in small steps. It's not that scary. However, if mistakes are made and the fear of their possible repetition is established, then it is essential not to succumb to them, everything is repairable.

There is always a risk. Absolutely all traders go through this stage of personal development. Since there are no investors who do not make mistakes, it is impossible to overcome the secondary fear phase, which can only be overcome with varying degrees of effectiveness. Therefore, the "risk group" includes anyone who decides to participate in the financial market.

What to do? To neutralize doubts, it is necessary to understand their essence. Therefore, it is necessary to find out why mistakes were made that led to an unsatisfactory result.

You can determine what has become the cause using the following method:

Take some time to practice analyzing the market. A trader should write all his thoughts and predictions in detail in a trading journal for at least two weeks.

From the results of the trading diary, the trader should conclude: how many transactions would have been profitable if they were completed, and how many would not have been. If according to the forecasts positive results prevail, the mistakes made will be the result of an exclusively emotional impact (e.g. failure to comply with the trading plan). If the ratio is 50/50, or the number of negative forecasts is greater than the positive ones, then it is necessary to analyze each trade to understand where the error is.

As a general rule, in these cases, poor performance is due to a lack of specific knowledge. For example, if all negative trades are characterized by steady but small losses, then perhaps the key will be incorrectly set to stop loss orders that the market 'eats' because they are too close to the entry point. Or, perhaps, the trader misinterprets signals from technical or chart indicators. In this case it is necessary to fill the lack of information with the necessary knowledge and find out what are the criteria used and how to set a stop loss or what a shoulder-head-shoulder reversal is.

Trader emotions and typical situations

"I do a market analysis, I make a trading plan, but when I enter the market I lose control and I don't follow the plan. I get a negative result because I don't stick to the trading plan."

This situation is the most common. As soon as trading starts, emotions are activated automatically and everything that happens on the market is not objectively evaluated.

First of all, technical signals start to appear and a lot of importance is given to unnecessary information. Secondly, the trader believes that it is possible to "control" the operation intervening on its course (unplanned changes in the trading plan). To avoid this, spend more time working out your trading plan, writing down in advance everything you plan to do when in the market and what you cannot do under any circumstances.

"I close open trades early because it is unbearable to observe a loss. I prefer a small stop loss to waiting for the price to reach the previously set level."

This option is another of the most common forms of fear. A trader has a tendency to close losing trades as soon as the price goes negative.

When deciding where to set a stop-loss order, use not two or three criteria, but at least four or five. Then the stop loss will be more reliable and correct. You will have more confidence that the risks will be proportional.

"I close the trade early as soon as I make a small profit, even though my trading plan is written correctly and tells me otherwise."

In this case, in general, after closing the trade and observing that the market follows the direction we predicted in the trading plan, we reopen it again. After reopening the position, it closes early. Let's say that, of the 150 points of profit initially planned, the trader reaches 30-50 points. Fear can be fought in the following way: as soon as the transaction starts generating income, instead of closing it with minimal profit, transfer the stop loss to the break-even point.

If profits rise even more and break out of the next resistance level, the stop-loss will move even further. Therefore, without closing the position, you will protect your trading activity from any kind of loss.

Greed

Another emotion that commonly affects the trader is greed. Generally, greed and fear in trading psychology are opposite emotions and a trader who feels fear is unlikely to feel greed at the same time. Indeed, in the first case, the trader is afraid to enter the market, while in the second case he has an unrealistic view of the market and, consequently, loses money due to his own ambitions. Perhaps the only relationship between fear and greed is that both of these drives can be controlled by a trading plan.

At the beginning greed appears in two cases: the trader has a predisposition from the very beginning or appears later following several successful trades.

"I could earn more". The first thought that gives rise to greed is the idea that "I could earn more". Self-confidence increases, you think that you can control the market and the desire to use aggressive strategies arises.

Why does this thought arise? The desire to make more money often arises after several successful transactions and the belief that you could have risked more on them.

High risk. Greed is often a feature of successful business and life, of confident leaders. A trader also exposes himself to a high risk if his temperament type is choleric.

What to do? It is clear that you cannot change your temperament, but you can learn to control it and organize your work in an appropriate way. Here too the trading plan is indispensable, as in the case of fear. Greed is perhaps the most damaging feeling, because when it appears it inhibits the need for caution.

In short, if the manifestation of fear threatens potential gains, greed increases potential losses. Here are some typical situations in which this feeling is fully revealed:

Forex Trading Psychology - Typical Situations

"As soon as I start analyzing the market, I look at the chart and I understand that a strong movement has begun. The thought is born: you have to act quickly, otherwise I will lose a great moment. The result flies to the market at full speed and only then I understand that it does not was worth".

It is a very common situation, typical of recruits. Even those with an initial bias towards stable and quiet trading, as soon as they see the price movement "live", are eager to do something immediately.

This can be compared to everyday situations in life. If you arrive at a bus stop and see that the bus has left without you, has moved away from the stop and has accelerated, are you running after it? It probably doesn't make sense: trying to catch something that moves faster than you. It is much safer and wiser to wait for the next bus.

With the financial markets the situation is similar, except that you are not late at all, so there is no reason to chase a bus. To cope with an unbearable desire we need to control our emotions, analyze and elaborate the trading plan. To do this, carefully look at all the charts. Your task is to choose the most suitable opportunity. And for this it takes some time to study the market situation.

Another way to combat the urge to "do something now" is to listen to your inner common sense.

"I have the patience to analyze the market and come up with a trading plan, but as soon as I open a trade and the price starts going in my direction, I immediately understand that I have invested very little money and that the profits could be many more, so I increase the volume of the operation even if it was not planned ".

In this case, the mistake made is a violation of the risk

management rules. The initial idea of "I will open a few more lots" usually does not take into account the fact that, along with this, all risks increase exactly as many times as there are lots added to the market. In addition, there are also unplanned risks.

For some reason, when there is a sudden desire to add something to an open position, it just seems like there will be more profits, and few think the losses will grow in exactly the same proportion.

"When I am in the market and the price is close to my profit level, I begin to doubt that I have set it correctly. As a result, I move it to earn more, because I feel that the movement is not over yet and that I can take advantage of it to earn more money".

This case of greed is less common than the previous two. It is usually combined with the second option. Traders who are faced with such a desire to hold their position for as long as possible do not know the feeling of fear described above.

A different pattern of behavior is characteristic here, and it differs from the behavior of "impatient greed". The trader falls into this mistake because:

The market is still moving in his direction;

There is no sign confirming the reversal;

The extra ten points won't change anything.

The Dow Jones Principle states that price movements are subject to trends: the trend cannot end suddenly, etc.

Forex Trading for Beginners

To be convinced of the wrongness of this position, it is enough to ask: where to transfer the take profit level? where is the most favorable limit? The most likely answer to this question will be "when I get a signal confirming a market reversal, then I will close".

Real reversal signals are unlikely to be seen as the trader is dominated by emotions. A frequent end to such greed is the search for signs that confirm the resumption of movement in the right direction and, consequently, the loss of money.

The hope

It may seem that hope is a positive, useful and important feeling in human life. How can it harm a trader? Very simple. When a person decides they want to invest, they do so with an optimistic outlook on the future. In fact, whenever we commit to studying something new and interesting, we approach it with a certain positive attitude, otherwise it would not make sense to start something new.

However, as soon as a person starts trading, hope can turn against, shifting from healthy optimism to utopian expectations and belief in miracles. One way or another, it is important to understand what the trader's level of hope is at any given time. A person who does not believe in himself and his success simply has no interest in being on the market, but he cannot even think that success depends on a miracle or fate. So what is hope and why is its excess so dangerous?

When is it born? Hope always arises at the same time, exactly when the transaction starts generating losses.

How do we feel? This feeling is experienced in various ways: a trader who prays to all the gods, mentally talks to the market and does other strange things. The most important negative quality of hope is that it completely captures a person and blocks all possibilities of finally trying to save the situation with the help of mental activity.

The reasons. An open position in the market (or multiple positions) that causes losses. The paradox is that the greater the extent of the loss, the more the feeling of hope shines through and the greater the trader's tendency to believe in a miracle and not in his own strength and intellect.

High risk. One way or another, everyone experiences hope, but for some people it is out of control, just like their trading. It is important to be able to control this emotion.

What to do? In general, a hopeful situation can get out of control if you don't adhere to a trading plan categorically or if you don't have one at all. If the trading plan is followed to the letter, the trader will not be faced with such a state of hope that he can only count on a miracle. However, if the trading plan is not followed and the circumstances are not favorable to the position, then hope will be inevitable. If that happens, we need to be prepared and take control of the situation and take action.

Typical situations of hope

"I had a trading plan but I was greedy and I didn't close the trade with profits, so I sit and wait for the price to come back, but everything goes against my position... but I wait and wait..."

If the trader is not strong enough to correct the mistake and close the trade with less profit and continues to wait for the market to reach its new target, then the situation will reach a tipping point, i.e. it may end up going in the opposite direction.

At the same time, the further the market moves away from gains, the greater the hope. In this state, it is typical for the trader not only to believe desperately that this will happen, but also to look for supporting factors. Below are some examples of classic arguments for keeping an open position in the market in the hope that it will change:

The Dow Principle says that price movements repeat themselves, which means that sooner or later the market must return to its previous values.

The signals from technical analysis say that the market will definitely go in my direction.

Success only comes to those who can wait.

Later, if the transaction remains "negative", the most typical arguments may appear:

It can't be that everything is going so badly

I will not close the trade until the market returns to its previous values

Sooner or later I'll have to be lucky.

All these arguments are completely useless and dangerous, as half of them resort to ephemeral things like luck and fate, which have nothing to do with the normal job of a trader. And the other half is based on a subjective analysis, on the search for confirmation of his own thesis.

"I've been losing money for a long time, but right now the market is starting to change, so I'm opening another position to regain and hedge the existing one. So, I'll win again."

The situation described has a proper name among traders: "tactic to add loss". This tactic is the fastest way to become an unsuccessful trader. The biggest mistake a person can make is trying to recover in this way.

Imagine watching a football match and one of the two teams is losing badly: who would you bet your money on? It is really unlikely that you will decide to bet on the losing team. This same reasoning also applies to the aforementioned tactic. In addition to all the other arguments described in the previous paragraph about hope, there is also a part of fatalism about the desire to win back.

It is difficult to fight against this sentiment, because for a trader to close a trade at a loss is to admit his failure. Oddly, most traders are much angrier about this than the loss of money. However, in any case, it is worth remembering that only fools persist in their mistakes, and only fools make no mistakes.

"I have been losing money for some time, but now the situation seems to be improving. I want to wait for the market to reach zero, the break-even level, and then close the position. As soon as the market gives me the chance to go back to the starting point, I will close the trade immediately.

The hope that the market will get to the point where it all started is utopian, if only because there is no such point. The equilibrium point is a subjective concept that has nothing to do with the real market. The error, based on the fact that, being the market a dynamic system, sooner or later it must return to its original position, is obviously false because the concept of 'zero point', 'status quo', in this case, is the value where the loss position becomes neutral. But for the entire market, the "zero point" is a zero price, and nothing else.

Euphoria

Euphoria, the excessive joy, often arises suddenly, resulting in many positive experiences. The main disadvantage of euphoria is that of falling into uncontrolled joy and, consequently, causing a negative impact on the quality of the analysis.

In any emotional state, the trader's efficiency decreases: as emotions grow, the quality of his mental abilities decreases. Not to mention the loss of the sense of risk and, consequently, the decrease in control over operations. In this case, euphoria, unlike, for example, fear or hope, can be felt by any trader, not only by a beginner, but also by a fairly experienced trader.

When is it born? Euphoria usually occurs after a series of successful operations.

How does it feel? High mood, joy, pride, the feeling that everything is working and will continue to work. With every successful transaction, trust builds.

The reasons. Every euphoria begins with the joy of a successful transaction. In this case, it is best to assume right away that joy should be expressed as a feeling of satisfaction with your work, in a moderate way.

The benefit is your salary. This dynamic should be treated this way. Otherwise, for everyone, even a slight fit of joy will gradually turn into euphoria. And several successful transactions in a row will lead to the fact that the trader will fall into a state of uncontrolled cheerfulness and self-confidence. Control the joy and it won't turn into an illness called euphoria.

High risk. Any trader who has completed more than five successful trades in a row or who has increased the size of his deposit several times in an extremely short time is automatically in danger of falling into euphoria. The only solution is to use special psychological methods to cushion it.

What to do? First of all, learn to approach work with minimal emotion. Secondly, learn to determine when joy appears and to control it. Thirdly, deal with the typical situations outlined below.

Trading Psychology - Typical Euphoria Situations

"Whenever I make money, I feel great joy. Sometimes it's out of proportion to the profits made."

Positive emotions are important in strengthening the trader's confidence. It would be strange and wrong if a positive response did not generate positive emotions (dissatisfaction with a positive result is a clear sign of greed). Caution should be exercised when:

A feeling of joy appears after a more or less positive result, even without following the trading plan

The feeling of joy lasts more than half an hour

Joy manifests itself in a very violent and excited way.

You can approach the issue in the following way. To enjoy the success of an operation, it takes some time, about 20 minutes after it is closed. After this time, never open new operations. It is recommended that at least several hours (if it is an intraday position) or at least several days (if it is a medium or long term position) pass between a successful trade and the next opening position.

A break from work is a good technique for inhibiting the chemical and hormonal processes that work when a person thinks with his heart or mind. After waiting for a certain amount of time, don't rush to explore new market opportunities immediately. First of all, analyze your success. What was the result of the profit? Did you plan it or was it a coincidence? Did the result meet your expectations? Did you expect more from the market? Did it go as you expected or did you deviate from the plan?

The essence of the analysis, in the end, must be summed up in one question: are you happy that your trading plan worked or were you just lucky? If luck has smiled at you, then, in general, there is nothing to be happy about.

"I make money because I always know when to enter the market and when it is time to close the position. I believe this is my method. In the end, intuition is also important!"

This example is much more dangerous than the previous one because intuition is unlikely to lead to real success, which in principle can appear only after six months of stable work on the market.

If the investor is lucky, he may be happy, of course, but he can hardly become happy. In a situation where nothing depends on the trader, we cannot say that we control the market.

"Often I enter the market immediately after a successful transaction, because I want to strike while the iron is hot. I have had a wave of success and I cannot let it slip away. Destiny always favors me when I act decisively.

This topic is similar to the previous one. The difference is that this case is even more problematic because it refers to ephemeral situations such as success or destiny. Furthermore, the danger is that seizing the moment means losing focus on risk management and planning. In fact, in this state of euphoria, the feeling of fear is minimal, the risks are not calculated. On the other hand, if we fail, it is likely that we will attribute it to bad luck.

As in all the cases we have talked about in this article, the most sensible thing is always to have a good trading plan and stick to it. We may not make a profit in the first few days, but it will probably help us not to lose too much money and be successful in the long run.

Intuition

The concept of intuition is sometimes overrated and sometimes completely ignored. Let's try to clarify this term, find out what it is and find the best way to use it in trading.

The trader's intuition is nothing more than a subconscious 'file' with all the market information previously made and reproduced by heart at some point. To understand how intuition manifests itself, let's look at how memory mechanisms work. We do this with the following example.

The relationship between intuition and memory

The explanation of this perception and the ability to "see the future" has nothing to do with mysticism. It is scientifically proven that a person does not forget anything he has heard or seen at least once. Human memory stores absolutely all the information that is obtained in the life process. The same goes for the information that the trader receives from his trading.

All information and knowledge that are irrelevant at the moment are stored in the subconscious, but when a similar situation occurs it can return in the form of a preview of events. For this to happen, sometimes a clue, a similar or identical moment is enough. Therefore, the fundamental point is experience.

The principle of technical analysis according to Dow that "history repeats itself" is based on this phenomenon of human memory and on the phenomenon of the psychology of the multitude (the mental mechanisms of memory are the same in all people).

To develop intuition, a good technique is, at least once a week, to open a clean chart, without trend lines, without supports or resistances, without indicators, and assess the situation as a whole, visually. There is no need to look for a pattern. Intuition usually appears after 5-10 seconds of study, or does not appear at all. However, we must have operated for at least six months before doing this exercise.

If you analyze the graph for more than 10-15 seconds, the subconscious stops dominating and the conscious mind takes over. We close the chart and move on to the normal work area, to the standard analysis schemes. Repeating this exercise with different tools once a week can be very helpful.

But overestimating the importance of intuition is not the best way to approach trading. If a trader already has a system to work with, only technical signals, i.e. only objective data, should be a priority in making the decision to enter or exit the market. Intuition as a method can only be used as a 'filter'.

To summarize all of the above, let's highlight the main points:

- Do not enter the market when you are in one of the emotional states we have mentioned;
- Emotions progress when a trader constantly looks at the charts. Avoid it. After you open a position and have established take profit and stop loss, go do other things;
- It is very useful to leave the monitor once in a while or turn off the computer completely;
- Don't panic, don't rush into action;
- Remember that the trader's main enemy are his emotions;
- Always follow a trading plan;
- Do not participate in trading when you are sick or in a bad personal situation: this also implies a decrease in the quality of your work;
- Don't listen to the advice of others when you are in the market;
- If you've had a leak, don't worry, it's normal. There are no foolproof traders;
- The surest way to hone your skills and learn to control your emotions is to trade on a demo account until you feel completely confident that you are ready to switch to a real account.

CHAPTER ELEVEN
TRADING PLAN

If you want to be successful in the Forex and cfd market, a great way to start is to create an efficient and effective trading journal that accompanies you day by day in your investment activities.

A trading journal is not that different from any other strategic plan you can imagine. If you are starting to take your first steps in the world of trading and have no previous training or experience, your success could be temporary or, in the worst case, you could lose your investment. This is why a trading plan is important: to set your goals and how to achieve them. Every experienced trader has a thoroughly studied trading plan, which he follows closely and constantly updates. So, whether you are an experienced trader or a beginner, a trading journal can help you achieve the goals and successes you have set for yourself.

A Trading Journal is a general description of your planned trading activity according to the parameters you have chosen. For example, it could be the preparation of a list of trading activities, planned according to a certain style, a certain strategy and a certain temporality.

The main idea of the trading plan is to develop a set of rules to be respected. Once you have these rules in writing, it will be much easier to apply them, as you will have a clear action plan for your daily trading.

Furthermore, an effective trading plan can help you better

analyze the Forex market and apply your analysis to the trading strategy of your choice. A trading journal can avoid making spontaneous and irreversible decisions, which is especially useful when emotions start to kick in. The trading plan helps you avoid common mistakes allowing you to evaluate your profits and losses. The goal of the diary is precisely to think before acting and therefore be prepared to face the trading sessions.

For example, if a trader is in a winning position before a major economic release, the trading plan will let you know for sure whether it is better to let the position go or close it to avoid the sudden movement caused by the economic calendar.

Helps to manage emotions: having a framework that defines the rules to follow and eliminates any subjectivity in your trading activity allows you to better manage your emotions. Because the trading decisions you make are part of a trading plan and have a predetermined goal.

Another good reason to limit the number of trades is because without a trading journal, traders can make hasty decisions in the market, decisions that would most likely lead to losses that the trader will try to compensate with more trades, even with a larger volume. This is often done with a larger volume than used for previous positions, creating a higher level of risk to compensate. This is exactly what makes the vast majority of traders lose money on the Forex market.

To help you manage your risk. If you decide to take a position with a risk of more than 1% of your capital, including it in your trading plan will help you manage other open positions.

A good trading plan should:

- Include Trading Goals: These should be specific, measurable and time-consuming goals;

- Establish the method of technical analysis (graphs);

- Develop the trading strategy to follow with accurate entry and exit points in the market;

- Establish reviews to systematically manage open positions in order to have no doubts or remorse for a position closed earlier than expected or too late;

- To manage risk, a good trading plan should also include good risk management across the entire portfolio and also for individual positions.

How to develop a good trading plan

1. A reliable broker

Having a clear trading plan helps keep your mind fresh and focused on the most profitable decisions. As we have already said, trading is not 100% predictable. Even with a trading plan, decision making sometimes gets messed up in the heat of a trading battle. Mainly because Forex traders are human and therefore tend to make emotion-based decisions.

A trader who does not perform a previous analysis is equivalent to a driver who goes out on the road without checking the engine or the brakes. But before you even consider a trading plan, you need to choose the right trading software and a regulated broker.

For any experienced trader, having good tools to work with is just as important as having good skills to execute them. Likewise, no matter how good a trader is, without the right broker and the right trading platform, he will not be able to execute orders correctly.

Here are some points to help you choose the best broker and your trading platform:

- Does it give you access to the financial instruments you wish to trade?

- Is it competitive in terms of spreads and commissions?

- Which trading platform does it offer you?

- Does the platform it offers you have the functions you need?

- Is the customer service team fast and responsive?

- What kind of support can they offer you based on your current trading education?

2. Stay realistic

Do you think you can become a successful Trader? Many traders fail to trade in the markets. It is not so important to never lose, but to find out the reason for your mistakes.

Accept that trading success may take longer than expected. How does this affect your plans?

Are your goals realistic regarding your trading education?

3. Identify the market

Analyze the chosen market

Study the fundamental catalysts of this market

Is there enough volatility to meet profit targets?

Determine if there is liquidity to allow entry and exit. If not, consider other markets.

Is the time frame appropriate for your strategy? If not, consider choosing another market or period.

4. Work out your strategy

Try to develop a strategy that offers the versatility to leverage the market and generate profits when:

- The price is at the support or resistance level;

- There is a clear trend;

- Impulse changes occur;

- A gap occurs;

- An extreme reversal occurs;

- There is volatility in the markets.

5. Set limits

What capital is needed to operate in the chosen market?

What margin is required?

What is the minimum position size and the stop-loss percentage on the capital?

If the market is too volatile or margins are too expensive, continue studying how to save for more capital or consider a market that is more suitable for available capital.

Understand the advantages and disadvantages of the leverage available in this market.

6. Monitor the strategy

Where are the support and resistance levels?

Identify the supply and demand of the chosen market

What is your trading strategy: Intraday, Swing or Scalping?

Define daily and weekly price levels

Respect the rules you have set for yourself and plan:

- Financial leverage;

- Total risk;

- Daily risk;

- Order entry price;

- Order management;

- Order exit price.

After completing all of the above steps, one more thing is still required - patience. The market is like a shadow. If you run after it, you'll never catch it. You have to wait patiently for the market to come to you.

7. SMART

Specific

Measurable

Achievable

Relevant

Traceable

Having a SMART plan will help you monitor your trading performance.

Set your goals

Establish the goal development plan

This will help you decide how to achieve your goals at the right time. You can measure your success in terms of the benefits obtained from the operations carried out.

When setting goals, remember that they need to be SMART: specific, measurable, achievable, relevant and traceable.

8. Tools

To help you to better manage your risk, Admiral Markets has developed some of the most advanced risk management tools with Metatrader 4 Supreme Edition:

9. Psychology of the Trader

The trader must rely on his intraday trading plan or swing trading plan to suffer a series of losses without giving up, the time to find profits that replace the losses and generate capital gains.

Rules and routines. An effective trading journal has a set of rules and routines that allow traders to have a well-established framework of trust.

Historical data. Historical data provides the trader with confidence and experience to better enjoy his trading activity in the Forex market, stock market and commodity market.

Build a Trading Plan.

Determine the frequency with which you trade and the number of trades that open during that time interval.

To answer this question, you can check your account history and determine how many transactions you open on average per day or week and how long these transactions last. This is vital because your plan should clearly illustrate the time dimension you use in your trading.

Define your profile as a Trader.

Set specific goals and be consistent with the goals you want to achieve and the tools you need to use.

Establish a time horizon for achieving the main goal. Example: Become a profitable trader, you can set 2, 5 or 10 years to achieve this goal.

Choose the type of trading that's right for you.

Do you have a full time job? If so, swing trading is the type of trading for you. You can invest and trade in the Forex market, the stock market, the commodity market and only spend a few minutes a day analyzing the charts.

Do you have a part-time job? Day trading may be the best type of trading for you. You can trade during a full trading session and benefit from the most volatile hours of the day to try to generate profits day after day.

Are you inactive in terms of work? You may have enough time to refine your trading strategy and diversify your business between swing trading, day trading and scalping.

Evaluate your starting capital. This helps you better identify the type of trading that suits you best. Here you have to consider the investment you are willing to risk. For example, keep in mind that the greater the distance between your entry point and the Stop Loss, the greater the capital required to comply with the level of risk you have accepted.

Determine which market is best suited to your trading method. Here it is interesting to consider the expenses related to the operations, to know the amount of commissions and the size of the spread. Additionally, depending on the nature of the market, trading hours can vary and play an important role within a Forex strategy. For example, if you want to trade the stock market, take advantage of its volatility spikes during the early opening hours. The Forex market operates 24 hours a day, 5 days a week. Check out our Forex trading article to understand when it's best to trade.

Trading diary - find your style

How to design your trading plan:

Discretionary method

This type of method aims to make a decision based on the subjective analysis of the negotiations. Profitable discretionary traders in general are experienced traders who translate the price action of the foreign exchange or stock market very well. Therefore, this method is not based on systematic conditions for taking a trading position.

Mechanical method

Unlike the discretionary method, here every trading position is based on the systematic conditions necessary to take a position. If only one of these conditions is not present, the trade will not take place. Mechanical trading systems are very popular, because the part of doubt and subjectivity is non-existent.

Aggressive method

Aggressive management of a trading position means increasing the Stop Loss as fast as possible to ensure the gains of the position in the shortest possible time. The limit of this type of management is to see that the stop loss is reached with very little profit above the entry point, just before the movement actually progresses in the intended direction.

Conservative method

Conservative position management leads to a greater distance between the entry point and the stop loss. This allows the asset to breathe more, to give it more chance to see the movement moving in the intended direction. The limit of the conservative approach is to try to take the gains much farther, because the Stop Loss is just as far.

Risk management

The management of positions, as well as the respective risks, can be facilitated or automated thanks to the tools present in MetaTrader 4 Supreme Edition with the mini terminal that allows you to define a risk for a fixed position in euros regardless of the number of pips required by the stop loss of the position. Furthermore, it is possible to set a limit switch so that the management of the position is dealt with objectively and automatically.

Keeping a trading log allows you to measure the strategy used to better understand your trading behavior and report if any errors have occurred. Each position and session must be entered to really help the trader to analyze his trading system.

Test series in history

Historical background is very important in finding the profit and loss rates of your trading strategy. This step gives you confidence and experience in your strategy. And it will help you get through tough times (because there are always tough times, sadly). The most important thing is to be able to continue taking positions to find winning trades that will recoup your losses and increase your capital in the long run.

Trading Plan - Stop Loss and Take Profit

Another important point is that all trading positions in your trading plan must include a Stop Loss and a Take Profit. When setting the Stop Loss and Take Profit levels remember that stopping the loss is much more important than making a profit.

Trading signals

Input signals

Importantly, these signals should be as comprehensive as possible, to help you to eliminate subjectivity in your decisions. A good way to achieve this is to include indicators in your trading signals.

Exit signs

Much like input signals, traders should have a very clear idea of when to exit a trade.

When it comes to learning how to prepare an expert level Forex trading plan, opening a position at the right time and with the right tool is essential.

However, in some cases, it is possible to close a good position and continue at a loss because you didn't have enough patience. Or, conversely, you can close a winning position too early and lose the total profit that could have been made. This is due to the lack of exit signals from the Trading Journal.

Evaluate your Trading Journal

You need to know if your trading plan is adequate or in need of some improvement. To do this, start analyzing the input signals and the time period you are considering. Is the timing right for you? Remember that strategies with a success rate of less than 60% can be beneficial.

How? Here is an example:

the first ten positions in a row are lost. This represents a total loss of 10%, then you will win your next position with a profit of 6%.

The next two positions realize gains of 2% and 4% respectively.

This means you have made a 12% profit after losing the first 10 trades. This led to a 2% capital increase this month, with a success rate of only 40%. It is something you would get in a bank after two years of savings.

The problem is the following: most traders give up after 5 losses. We suggest you to:

Be patient

Reduce the risk between 0.5% and 1% per position

Try to keep your winning positions

Use a stop loss and a take profit

Set several goals to reduce risk and make a profit

Always practice on a risk-free demo account before switching to the real market

Trading Journal - Manage your investments

Once you've determined your trading system, start focusing on managing your capital. It should be clear whether your trading system allows you to trade multiple pairs and which ones. Improve capital management and include creating or revising the optimal exposure rule for trading.

To calculate this, it always takes potential double exposure on a currency pair. It doesn't matter if you trade to earn 1000 pips based on fundamentals or five pips based on scalping techniques with very small movements. Even if your fundamental analysis is correct, it could move 2 or 100 pips against you.

So what should you do?

In general, it is more advisable that the size of your position should be small, this will prevent you from losing a lot of money in case you make a mistake.

Control your emotions

Impulsive and emotional decisions begin in your mind.

Problems usually occur when a trader feels compelled to make a trading decision, i.e. to enter, exit or hold the same position. Keeping calm and patience while trading promotes positive results and success.

Answering these questions can help:

- What is the current state of your emotions?

- Does it work like you are at the casino?

- Are you optimistic or euphoric?

- Do you feel committed to staying disciplined?

We also recommend that you look into the latest innovations in the Forex market, as there are many tools designed to optimize your trading experience and make trading less stressful.

Here are some general trading tips:

- Don't try to become a full-time Trader right away;

- Keep your job full-time and work part-time as a first step;

- It is possible to trade as an experienced Trader, without leaving your job, after a lot of practice;

- Being a full time trader requires considerable capital, which usually has to be built up over time;

- Being a full time Trader is something you can aspire to, but it won't happen overnight;

- To achieve this, you need to be patient and focus on learning to operate;

- Only when you have followed these tips will you be ready to trade on a live trading account.

You put the icing on the cake

The main advantage of a trading journal is that it reduces the trader's attention request and the number of transactions. This helps the Trader to fully focus on the trades that are most likely to be successful.

Continuous analysis of charts and trades only leads to stress the trader. And this often leads to negative results.

Traders should use their trading plan as a rigid approach to the markets to stay focused on:

- find the best configuration;

- implement proper risk management;

- achieve long-term business goals.

On the other hand, trading is not limited to defining a trading plan. Traders must actively work to improve their trading technique and strategy.

Once the Trading Plan is established, traders should not go back and think this is the end of their learning or development curve.

CHAPTER TWELVE
METATRADER 4 OR 5

MetaTrader - The most used trading platform in the world

The MetaTrader or MT trading platform is a trading software offered by MetaQuotes Software Corp. There are several versions of this trading station: MetaTrader 4 and MetaTrader 5. Most Forex brokers offer MetaTrader 4 and there are also some online brokers who offer MetaTrader 5.

Private traders often wonder which broker to choose and especially which trading platform to choose: MT4 or MT5. In this article we will look at the differences between MT4 and MT5 and which trading site offers these platforms.

MetaTrader 4, more commonly known as MT4, was developed by MetaQuotes Software Corp and made available to the public in 2005. In 2013 and 2014 the MT4 platform underwent important updates, in particular with regard to the programming language made available to users.

MetaTrader 5 will be available to the public in 2010. The platform brings improvements to its predecessor, including the change of programming language from MT4 to MQL5. This change in the coding language allows for faster calculations and order execution for trading robots.

Although MT4 was initially adopted by brokers as an alternative to their trading platform, the MT4 platform quickly became the world reference for trading stations, being favored by both brokers and traders. Furthermore, the fact that both MetaTrader 4 and MetaTrader 5 are easily downloadable and that each of them has a version available in 39 different languages is a great advantage.

The success of the platform is linked to the full range of its functionalities and to the fact that it is not a simple trading terminal, but a complete tool that allows you to place orders, manage your positions, perform in-depth graphical analysis, develop indicators custom, create your own expert advisors (these famous trading robots also called "ea"), test strategies and indicators, access a large community...

How to get familiar with the MetaTrader platform

Any trader who wants to become familiar with the MT4 platform for the first time must dedicate some time to it. Indeed, the platform is a priori designed for more experienced traders, as it is not very intuitive.

It is important to understand that MT4 is designed for experienced traders, who spend time looking at their charts, doing analysis... Moreover, the buttons are relatively small and discreet in order to maximize the space for the charts, the trading terminal, strategy tester or interface for developing ea and indicators in MQL4.

For the MT5 platform, the idea was to make the platform more intuitive and more easily accessible for everyone, from experienced traders to beginners. Even if there isn't a radical change in terms of design, the buttons are larger and their icons easier to understand, although this slightly reduces the space available for graphics. A novice trader will find MT5 easier to learn than MT4.

A novice trader will be more comfortable on MT5 than MT4, the grip will be quicker and more instinctive. On the other hand, for an analyst, or a trader who needs to follow several markets at the same time, MT4 will be more suitable, especially if the trader has mastered the specific trading vocabulary, they will quickly orient themselves.

MetaTrader 4 vs 5 - Portfolio management

MT4 is a trading platform specifically designed for trading leveraged financial products, including Forex and CFDs. It allows the trader to access the Forex market, as well as commodities/indices/stocks via CFDs from a single platform, thus avoiding the need to switch from one platform to another depending on the asset he is working on and where he wants to position himself.

MT5 has taken this functionality and developed it so that a trader can access different portfolios of financial products, not just leveraged products. Consequently, a trader will be able to access financial instruments such as Forex, CFDs, futures, but also options, shares... It is therefore even easier for a trader to diversify financial instruments using the MT5. Investing in all markets with a wide variety of financial products has never been easier.

MetaTrader 5, while leveraging the strengths of MT4, offers greater flexibility in portfolio management, which is an undeniable asset. You can get more information on the MetaTrader 5 forum.

MT4 vs MT5 - Check chart analysis

By default, MT4 offers around thirty standard technical

indicators for volume, trend and oscillator monitoring. On the other hand, on the metrader 5 forum, thousands of indicators are made available to traders, and can be easily integrated into the platform. It is also possible to add indicators in addition to certain indicators, which can save space on the charts.

At the chart level, MT4 allows you to analyze prices from line, bar or Japanese candlestick charts. There is also the possibility to analyze renko charts via plugins downloadable from the forum. These features are also included in the MT5 platform.

The periodicities proposed on MT4 are the 9 classic time units (M1, M5, M15, M30, H1, H4, D1, W1, MN). The tick charts are accessible from the "new order" window or the "market observation" window. On the other hand, ticks have a rather short history that does not allow a real analysis.

MT5 has a slightly larger number of indicators and, thanks to its programming language, MT5 allows the use of custom and customizable indicators, more powerful than MT4. In fact, the language that is made to be read faster offers the possibility of developing more complex trading algorithms that will be read just as fast if not faster than on MT4.

The periodicities offered on MT5 are more numerous (21 periods offered in total). Even though the platform doesn't offer custom periods yet, it's very close to them. Furthermore, the ticks chart accessible from the "market observation" window has a much longer history than that of MT4, which gives rock climbers better visibility of the market in the very short term, so that their entry and exit positions can be refined as much as possible.

Overall, MT5 offers more flexibility and possibilities in terms of market analysis parameters. On the other hand, the MetaTraer 5 community provides traders with a large number of indicators and scripts of all kinds for both MT4 and MT5. Furthermore, both platforms allow the development of custom indicators directly from the MetaQuotes editor. However, due to its numerous time periods and its more advanced tick chart, MT5 is the one that stands out in terms of chart analysis.

Tips for the MT5 scalp

MT4 offers market depth, a similar tool to the order book used on futures. This tool gives access to prices and their evolution in the form of a table, and allows you to place orders very quickly with stop loss and take profit defined in points in advance. Market depth is particularly useful for opening and managing short positions, or for trading the economic calendar. Furthermore, in addition to market orders, this tool offers you the possibility to enter trigger orders such as stop orders or to limit orders with take profit and stop loss defined in points.

MT5 takes this tool and improves it adding a tick chart next to it. In this way, the scalper will be able to have visibility both on the depth of the market, but also on the ticks chart to more easily view the very short term supports and resistances and the trading volumes (volume that does not appear in the depth of the market on the MT4).

In addition to this easy-to-use position capture tool for

scalpers, MT4 and MT5 offer the ability to add a one-click position capture button at the top left of each asset chart. The trader simply needs to set the size of his position in advance based on his money management and trading strategy, and he will be able to open and close his positions in a single click.

MT5 Forex - Hedging

It is not uncommon for a trader to hedge the markets by deciding to simultaneously position an asset up and down. This hedging technique, known as hedging, is quite common and is not misused by day traders and rock climbers.

While it is possible to simultaneously enter up and down a market, in other words "hedger", on MT4, this possibility has been eliminated on MT5.

This is an important point for all climbers and traders used to hedging and hedging on the markets. In fact, while the MT5 platform offers greater comfort in analyzing scalping markets thanks to ticking charts and greater market depth, it does not allow you to hedge if the market moves in the opposite direction to your scenario.

Therefore, a scalper doing the hedging, or a day trader doing the hedging, will be better off using MT4 rather than MT5 as a platform, especially since it could be detrimental to a trader and his portfolio to change the strategy to which he is accustomed due to the impossibility of doing the hedging on MT5.

MetaTrader 4 opinions for the trading terminal

The trading terminal of the MT4 platform is a classic terminal, on which information about each position appears: order ticket number, date and time of position opening, opening price, direction of the order (buy/sell), volume, symbol, stop loss, take profit, current asset price, swap fees, commissions, comment...

It is possible for the trader to classify their positions: by symbol, by opening hours, based on current profits/losses.

It is also from this trading terminal that the trader can modify his order: add a trailing stop, modify the stop loss and take profit, make a partial closure of the position, etc.

In this tab the trader also has access to information on his balance, blocked margin, available margin, etc.

The MT5 terminal takes on all the functionalities offered by the MT4 platform terminal, except that it allows you to group positions. That is to say, if the trader has 5 open positions on the same asset, he will have a line that summarizes the total size of his accumulated positions, the total of his open P&L on this asset, the total of the swap commissions etc.

For all traders who use position building strategies, or strategies that lead them to open multiple positions on the same asset, such as pyramid trading or media strategies, the latter feature provided by the new trading terminal of the MT5 platform can be particularly useful for having a global view of your trading account by assets.

MQL4 vs MQL5 - Programming and development of algorithms

MT4 owes its success in part to the MetaQuotes Editor, its

programming software included in its trading platform.

In fact, integrating the MetaQuotes Editor into its trading platform, MT4 has made it possible to generalize the use of customized and tailored indicators, as well as the use of ea, the autonomous trading algorithms that were previously the prerogative of large investment banks.

To achieve this goal, MT4 has developed its own programming language: MQL4. It is a structured language that allows you to program trading algorithms or indicators. To do this, you just need to know the code, the main functions and test the algorithm conforming to it and then with the strategy tester before using the indicator or ea in real time.

The two main disadvantages of MQL4 are the difficulty of finding a coding error, the absence of a debugger is felt as soon as the code becomes consistent, and the delay in reading and executing.

MT5 wanted to take over MetaQuotes Editor, but chose to change the language from MQL4 to MQL5. It is a transition from a structured programming language to an object language. In fact, this modification allowed to optimize the execution speed of the algorithms.

This change in the speed of execution allows, among other things, the development of more advanced and powerful algorithms, which can come close to artificial intelligence. Coupled with the fact that MT5 was developed for STP Brokers, this enhancement allows for faster algorithm execution, an equally optimized stance and therefore more accurate account performance.

The MetaQuotes editor of the MT5 platform also includes a debugger, which will allow developers to spot errors faster, save time in correcting algorithms, and allow beginners to learn coding more easily to develop their own expert advisors that will make it easier to grasp of position, while having the advantage of being able to operate 24 hours a day, 5 days a week.

Money management and detailed reports

The MT4 trading platform not only allows the trader to analyze the markets, place orders, develop algorithms... but it also allows to analyze his closed positions retrospectively.

Indeed, the trader has the possibility to obtain a detailed report on his activity, a report based on the data of his closed positions. In this way, the trader will be able to analyze the evolution of his portfolio, based on reports that will allow him to improve his trading on an ongoing basis.

MT5 further enhances these trading activity reports adding standard risk control and performance analysis ratios. The analysis of a portfolio that you would like to present to an investor, the results of an expert advisor tested in real life or a simple monitoring of individual performance is now possible with professional precision.

MT4 avis - Platform for beginners

For novice traders, it is recommended to use the MetaTrader 5 platform, as this will allow the trader to familiarize themselves with the platform, to explore more basic indicators than MT4 and thus to test more combinations of indicators, and to be able to study in detail the evolution of its performance thanks to the detailed reports and different reports offered by the MT5.

Once the trader has become familiar with trading, has set up a rigorous strategy and begins to be interested in developing algorithms or ea, he will be able, depending on the constraints of his strategy to consider staying on MT5 or to switch to MT4.

MetaTrader 4 - Experienced traders

We recommend MT4 without hesitation. MT4 will provide you with significant visual comfort for continuous trading sessions, especially for traders accustomed to simultaneously observing an asset in different time scales, or used to study several assets at the same time.

You will also have the opportunity to buy and sell on an asset, which is quite common when you are positioning yourself in the short, medium and long term on the same asset, as well as when practicing pyramid or media strategies that include hedging (we specify that this type of strategy should be used by experienced traders, because if you don't master it, you will lose your capital).

Additionally, hedging is a significant activity in developing complex trading strategies involving hedging orders to protect your capital from volatility.

Expert advisors known as "MTFs".

For traders who use so-called "MTF" algorithms (Multi Time Frame: analysis of multiple time scales at the same time), as well as for traders who use algorithms that use hedging or who will likely open multiple positions simultaneously for both trading, it is imperative to use the MT4 platform and develop their own algorithms in MQL4.

In fact, on the MT5 platform, the inability to simultaneously open buy and sell positions can, at best, prevent the ea from opening positions, at worst, generate losses that can lead to a margin call due to ea's inability to properly adhere the strategy that is supposed to apply.

Traditional expert consultants

For the classics and those who monitor trends, who have only one position open at the same time, who open and close positions in the event of a trend change, MT5 is the most suitable platform, you will benefit from a faster execution than MT4 without running the risk that your algorithm prevents you from following his strategy on MT5.

MT5 and MQL5 language is also suitable for complex algorithms, which will benefit from faster position execution in speed compared to MT4. But this requires that the strategy is adapted taking into account the impossibility of hedging. To discover all the features of the MetaTrader 5 platform and to get to know it better, you can consult our Complete MT5 Guide!

CHAPTER THIRTEEN
MONEY MANAGEMENT

Trading requires a lot of patience, proper training, quick adaptation to market updates, and a host of other qualities. Success in trading also requires great rigor and organization.

Among the risk management tools that allow the trader to avoid mistakes and safeguard his capital, money management is the first and most important.

It goes without saying that Forex trading is a risky business and there are a large number of traders who are not winners. However, there are many tips that can improve your trading performance. A trader's financial health is measured by how well he can manage his trading capital. Money management trading helps you to determine your risks in advance, develop and improve discipline, and take your trading to the next level.

Incorporating these Forex trading money management tips into an overall strategy will help protect your portfolio. The most successful traders use these techniques. Unfortunately, most novice traders learn through experience. It is best to learn these risk management principles and avoid making these mistakes. Even if none of these Forex money management tricks are a guarantee against losses, they can always reduce them.

Now let's check out the money management tricks most practiced by professional traders. These Forex trading tips appear randomly and are also important. Take a look at these tips and try to implement them in your trading strategy.

We will tell you more about money management and how essential it is to make long-term gains. What many traders don't realize is that not only do they have to make short-term gains, but also know how to perpetuate them in the long-term. Long-term gains is possible thanks to Forex money management.

Definition Forex money management

What is money management?

Money management is a term used in the world of finance and especially in online investment to indicate the management of risks associated with investment. Money management is your ability to manage your earnings and investments so that you don't take risks outside of your trading strategy.

The reason why many traders lose money on investing is due to their lack of experience, which leads to neglect of money management principles in their trading plan.

Trading with money management is therefore a non-negotiable success factor for novice Forex traders and experienced traders. Below we will see more about money management in Forex trading for beginners, before moving on to the description of money management for advanced traders.

A good trader has a good investment strategy and a good money management tool. Your capital management is there to help you make more money without taking more risks. Here are some money management rules:

Stock exchange for money management

If you have just started trading online, you will need to train. Forex trading, like any other business, cannot be done without trader training. We recommend that you test your investment on a demo account first. Demo trading will allow you to set up a trading strategy, to avoid the mistakes of novice traders and above all to set up good money management.

When you feel that you have learned enough, you can start trading by investing amounts of money that you allow yourself to lose. Loss is inevitable in currency investments and you should get used to it. A fundamental principle of money management is not to put all your eggs in one basket. You need to diversify your investments.

The principles of Forex money management are quite easy to follow and risk management can make you earn a lot of money and most importantly avoid losing money.

Use of trading software for money management

The trading platforms of professional traders offer money management services.

Protect your capital

How to calculate the maximum loss of a trade.

Calculate the risk associated with each trading position. If the chances of profit are lower than the potential earnings, look for another trading opportunity.

To trade with earnings, you need to know in advance how much you can lose and gain on your position. Use our trading calculator to calculate the position size, lot, spread, swap and all other parameters of your position:

Forex excel money management

There is no need to look for expensive money management software, or Forex money management files. See your market exposure in real time.

Even if you want to make money as quickly as possible, the first and most essential thing you can do is to stay in trading without losing money. If you're broke, you obviously can't place winning orders. It is natural to lose a few trades from time to time, but the goal is not to spend all the trading capital.

A Forex trader should get into the habit of analyzing risks before betting money on a trade. One of the pitfalls of trading is trading around the clock. Beginner traders will try to rebuild their positions and take more. Several reports from the Autorité des Marchés Financiers (MFA) show that excessive trade generates losses more than anything else. You should therefore only trade when you have real trading opportunities.

The two rules of the Forex beginner are: make sure you have enough money to open 40 trading positions and don't risk more than 3% of your trading capital. This is one of the tricks of managing money on the stock market, even if it seems too simple.

Manage the stress in trading with money management

Trade only with money that you can afford to lose.

You never want to use the money you need to live. Forex trading is a risky investment and you should only use the money you can afford to lose on this type of investment.

This will help reduce stress and avoid the fear of doom, which will lead you to make mistakes.

Risk management

There are very few drawbacks when it comes to setting a stop loss. The stop loss allows you to better manage your feelings and puts some order at the exit points of your trading positions. Setting a stop loss allows you to lose no more than a predetermined amount. You should set a win/loss ratio and set the stop loss according to it. You probably can't trade without a stop loss. An interesting alternative is the use of trailing stop losses on the MT4 platform.

Since the foreign exchange market represents an exchange rate, many CFD brokers offer significant leverage to their clients. Leverage can amplify the gains and losses on the stock market. It is not recommended to use high leverage when you want to implement a trading risk management system.

The most important trick in trading is to cut your losses quickly and let your gains run their course. You add positions if you have winning positions and cut the losing positions before they are too big.

If you are a beginner, avoid prying on yourself. Leverage can only be used when you are used to losing money and know that not all trades can be successful. This way you won't suffer big losses in your portfolio - and you can avoid being on the wrong side of the market.

Leverage is one of the advantages of the currency market. It can help you to win more, but it can also work against you. Caution is advised.

Manage emotions and stick to your money management strategy

Forex trading can bring a variety of emotions, excitement and frustration. Clearing your mind of your emotional bias can help you make rational decisions. Making decisions based on your emotions is the surest way to lose money. Emotions can influence you to make many bad decisions, while trusting your reason can save you from losses.

When trading Forex online, the trader can face many obstacles with a lack of knowledge. These top five currency money management tips will provide you with the best insights and potential pitfalls you're likely to face.

Forex traders must accept that their orders can bring profits and losses. It is okay to think that there will be gains from trading, but to expect only profits is unreasonable. A winning trader is realistic and prepared for any result, giving the best of himself at all times.

Trading psychology is very important in manual trading, because it is a human who will make the decision to buy and sell. The best Forex money management strategies avoid stress and have an investment plan established in advance. Try to do the same.

Accepting a loss is very difficult and beginners will always want to recover after a loss. This is the most dangerous thing in trading. For example, $1,000 is lost by investing $5,000. The percentage loss is 20%. So, to cover the loss, you need to earn 25% to get back to the original amount. After a loss, the most important thing is not to try to recover, because very often you are not in a good psychological shape and this can make you lose even more.

Build a trading plan

You must have a trading plan and stick to your investment strategy. Your trading plan must include a Forex risk management system or a Forex money management system. A trading plan will help you keep your emotions and will also prevent you from trading when you don't need it.

With an investment plan, you need to know the entry and exit points in advance and know when to take the gains or reduce your losses without becoming fearful or greedy. This brings discipline to your investment, which is essential for successful Forex money management.

Understanding the risks of trading on the stock exchange

We must recognize that there is an element of risk in every stock market position and accept the fact that it is possible to lose money on any order.

We don't have to think in absolute terms. When investing, you should always think in terms of returns. If you can get a 10% return it's already huge, especially if you don't take a big risk. When entering a position, you have to weigh the pros and cons, the gain in relation to the potential risk. This is why we often talk about a gain/loss ratio of 1 to 4.

Traders who respect this trading rule are willing to earn 4 dollars for every 1 dollar lost. Your stop loss and profits should be set according to the rules of money management. Always evaluate the risk for each trade before thinking about the potential profit.

It is better to make small solid gains than large commercial gains. Entering the market with the mindset of a poker player is a surefire way to lose money.

Before you start trading, look at the size of your position. The size of the position will directly affect your investment risks and potential losses. The position size should match your equity. Quite often, traders take a maximum of 5-10% of their capital on one stock position, so they don't put all their eggs in one basket.

Forex trading is risky and you should never commit more than you are willing to lose. You should also deposit a reasonable amount into your trading account. The worst thing you can do in terms of risk management is to borrow to invest in the stock market. This will guarantee you some loss, you will be stressed and you will lack patience.

Trading money management - Stay informed

When trading Forex, it is a good idea to consult the Forex forums and keep in touch with other traders to keep abreast of market sentiment. A Forex trader should always follow the market news and techniques that other investors use to have a winning trading strategy.

Money management – Be optimistic but not greedy

Avoid being greedy in trade. Greed can lead you to make bad business decisions. Trading doesn't always mean being a winner and making big trades every time. It's about opening orders at the right time - and closing them at the right time. One mistake you shouldn't make is wanting to take your winnings too quickly for fear of losing. Good risk management is always associated with great discipline and the existence of a Forex strategy and trading plan.

To test your online investment skills and the MetaTrader platform, open a demo account.

How to apply Swing Trading Money Management

It is easy to access online trading training and learn money management with the intention of using it in your trading strategy. However, many traders fail to put all of these principles into practice. This is where the difference between winning and losing traders lies.

By conducting trader surveys, it is very easy to find the difference between winning and losing traders, beginners who have difficulty and professionals who excel - it is simply rigor.

Money management requires a solid organization. For example, you can write a series of money management rules on a post-it:

- I know why I open this trading position (technical and/or fundamental factors);

- I am going to make a stop loss;

- My maximum loss on this position does not exceed 5% of my trading capital;

- My risk/reward ratio is 1: 2 or higher (or 1: 1, 1: 3, 1: 4 depending on your trading style);

- The accumulated losses for the day (or week) do not exceed 20% of my capital. Otherwise I will stop trading for today.

This money management strategy can prevent you from trading too much and limit your risk exposure. It will tell you how much you risk and what the maximum loss is.

The limits of money management on the stock exchange

In the rules of money management, the concept of maximum loss in terms of the percentage of available capital is often present. This limits the risk of large losses, and makes it difficult to lose all your money on a series of losses (with a risk limited to 1% of the principal for each trade, it takes a series of 100 losses to consume all the money deposited).

It is easy to understand that with a capital of €1000, for example, this rule limits the loss to only €10 per position, which can cause positions to close early. The more capital available, the easier and more efficient the money management will be.

To counter this limit, the trader has no choice but to loosen the (mathematical but not behavioral) constraints of money management a little and take a bit more risk if he wants to make more attractive gains.

CHAPTER FOURTEEN
WHICH FOREX BROKER TO CHOOSE?

If you are wondering which broker to choose for your trading, this article is for you. You will learn how to select a good trading broker and you may find one thanks to our tips.

Definition of Broker: A Forex broker is a company that provides stock market investors with access to a Forex trading platform to buy and sell currencies. They can thus transact on the Forex market 24 hours a day. They are mostly offset by the difference between the bid and ask prices of a currency pair.

To start investing in the stock market and currency market, you must first find a reputable broker. Your first priority is to do your research so that you can make an informed decision on which broker to trade Forex trading. You should also make sure that it has a positive reputation and is able to meet your trading needs.

The vast majority of Forex brokers will allow potential clients to test their services with a demo or practice trading account, so that traders can have a good understanding of what Forex trading is.

How to find the best broker

We will now see how to choose the best broker based on the criteria to be taken into consideration.

Regulated Forex broker - It is important to open a trading account with a regulated Forex broker.

Spreads and brokerage commissions - Finding the broker with the lowest spreads is a good thing, but beware of different marketing techniques. A spread announced on the broker's website does not necessarily mean that you will always have it on your trading orders. As the article about the best spreads and brokerage fees shows, take swaps and commissions into consideration as well. Admiral Markets, for example, is one of the few brokers in France to offer a flat fee of 1 EUR per order on equity CFDs.

Order Execution Quality and Slippage - Having low spreads is a good start, but having orders filled at the asking price is even better.

Fund Security - Choose a Forex broker with bank accounts in Europe and especially with separate bank accounts.

Different Types of Trading Accounts: A good broker should offer you different types of accounts with different benefits for specific trading styles. See our section on account types.

Ability to choose leverage: Forex is a market that is often traded with leverage. To manage your positions well, being able to choose the leverage effect independently is very important.

The markets offered - It is always interesting to be able to invest in several markets at the same time. For this, a good choice is to work with a broker who offers different markets and trading instruments, such as stock indices, commodities, stocks, cryptocurrencies, bonds or ETFs (exchange traded funds).

What is the range of trading instruments of the broker

Although there are a large number of tools accessible for trading, only a few receive a lot of attention from traders, offering the best trading conditions.

The major currency pairs are EUR/USD, GBP/USD, USD/JPY and USD/CHF,

The main stock indices are the CAC40, the DAX30 and the Dow Jones,

The main commodities are gold and oil,

Bitcoin and Ethereum are at the top of the cryptocurrency family.

But the best trading brokers offer a wide choice of instruments and you can choose what to trade based on your trading strategy.

Trading fees - Choose a cheap broker

Each trading broker has a variety of account types that offer different spread and leverage offers.

Forex traders have access to a range of leverage depending on the type of account, up to 1:30 for retail clients and up to 1: 500 for professional clients. Leverage is a loan granted to margin account holders by their brokers. For example, applying a leverage of 1:50, a Forex trader with an account size of $1,000 can hold a position worth $50,000.

Leverage works in favor of the trader on winning positions as the profit potential is greatly amplified. However, leverage is capable of destroying a trader's capital quickly, as it also increases the potential for losses. Keep in mind that leverage should only be used with caution.

Secondly, the other important offers that affect your trading positions are spreads and commissions. A Forex broker makes money from his commissions and spreads. A broker who uses commissions can charge a percentage of the size of a position (that being said, this is more common with instruments like stocks and stock CFDs than with currency pairs). However, many currency brokers advertise that they do not charge commissions and instead make money with spreads, which are the difference between the bid and ask prices of a currency pair. The wider the spread, the higher the commissions (and the lower your potential profits).

A third parameter is the minimum initial deposit that an online Forex broker can request. Most Forex accounts can be funded with a very limited initial deposit.

And the last element is the ease of deposits and withdrawals. Each Forex broker has their own withdrawal methods as well as their own deposit policy. Brokers can allow account holders to fund their online trading accounts via PayPal, simply with a credit card or via wire transfers. Usually, withdrawals can be made via credit card or bank transfer. Brokers may or may not charge a commission for each service.

Trading with a No Swap broker

Among the costs that the trader has to bear is the swap, also called rollover. The swap consists of an interest paid or received by the trader for positions opened overnight.

The swap is applied on different types of instruments, including CFDs and Forex. Interestingly, Forex swap can make the trader earn money, depending on the currency pair and the position held. This is carry trading.

Traders can also trade swap-free by turning to futures contracts. This is because, unlike CFDs, futures do not carry evening swap fees, allowing traders to hold an open position overnight without paying any fees.

Which broker to choose for MT4 and MT5

The trading platform is the trader's portal to the financial markets and as such, traders should ensure that the platform, or any type of trading software, is simple to use and visually appealing. This is the case with MT4 and MT5, the most popular trading platforms for retail traders.

MetaTrader also has a range of technical analysis and fundamental analysis tools and it is easy to place Forex orders.

This is crucial when it comes to choosing a serious Forex broker: a well-designed Forex trading platform will have simple "buy" and "sell" buttons - and some even have an emergency button that closes all positions.

A poorly designed user interface could lead to costly order entry errors, such as accidentally adding a position instead of closing it, or running short when it was intended to be long. These mistakes can make your trading experience unprofitable and emotionally draining.

Make sure to choose a reputable stock broker that has a solid trading platform like MT4 or MT5 as it is the most popular choice among the best Forex brokers.

Other factors to consider are: customization possibilities, order types, automated trading options, backtesting, strategy developers and trading alerts. Most brokers offer free demo trading accounts so that traders can try the trading platform without any risk, before moving on to live market trading.

How to find a regulated broker

If you are looking for the best regulated brokers, a professional looking website does not guarantee that the broker is serious or trustworthy. You should check if your Forex broker is regulated and licensed by a serious regulatory authority, such as a Financial Conduct Authority (FCA).

Normally, brokers who comply with a regulation post the licensing information prominently on their website.

There are a lot of scams on trading sites today, and very often these sites have regulations that are not very strict, or not at all. For example, with the European passport, any financial company registered in one of the countries of the European Union has the right to offer brokerage services in other countries without the need for additional agreements.

Note that there are different regulatory bodies in different regions, so a good rule of thumb is to make sure that the Forex broker you are considering is licensed and regulated by the regulatory body in their region of business.

For example, in the UK, a good Forex broker will be an officially regulated and FCA licensed broker. In addition, EU brokers must act in accordance with the guidelines of ESMA (European Financial Markets Authority) and in France according to the rules of the AMF (Autorité des Marchés Financiers). In Australia, the main regulator is the Australian Securities and Investments Commission.

Due to concerns about deposit safety and broker integrity, trading accounts should only be opened with properly regulated brokers.

Beware of scams by looking for the best online broker

Unfortunately, many people mistakenly associate Forex trading with scams. The problem is that there are more and more unscrupulous companies selling false information. The number of Forex related trading scams has increased dramatically over the past few years, so it is important that you are able to identify a scam.

When traders register with an online broker, they should expect their personal data to be protected (i.e. not passed on to third parties).

When someone you don't know communicates with you via your personal phone number, for example, the entity that provided your information violated your privacy. Why? Because you did not allow your data to be accessible to the public.

Best Broker 2021 - Customer Service Test

Trading operations involve market movements within a short period of time, so customer service from a reputable broker needs to be available quickly. It should also be easy to talk to a real person, rather than just time-consuming and often frustrating self-help.

When determining which is the best Forex broker, a quick call can give you an idea of the type of customer service they provide, the waiting time and also the representative's ability to answer questions about spreads, regulations, leverage and business details in a concise manner.

Which broker to choose for Beginner Traders

If you are a novice trader, you probably won't need any extras, such as an advanced trading platform. But you may need some training and some support. This can be done through videos and tutorials or training articles written by experienced traders.

A good Forex broker should in fact always offer assistance to its traders, including good training on trading and markets. For Forex beginners it is very important to understand the jargon, so a broker with the right training tools is always better.

Choose your broker based on your investment style

The choice of broker should in particular be influenced by the investment style. Are you a short term trader or a long term investor?

Traders do not keep positions open for a long time. They are interested in quick wins above the market average due to short term price volatility and can trade a lot in a short period of time. If you consider yourself a trader, you will need to choose a broker with very low execution fees, otherwise the trading fees could drastically reduce your returns. Also remember that active trading requires experience, and the combination of an inexperienced trader and frequent trading often results in losses.

A long-term investor buys and holds his securities for a long time. It is content to let the value of its investments appreciate over longer periods.

Many investors will find that their investment style falls somewhere between that of the trader and the investor, in which case other factors will become important in choosing the most suitable broker, such as any custody and management fees.

Find a stock broker and ETF

Long-term investors, who are not interested in short-term trading, should choose a broker that offers a suitable offer.

Buying a long-term stock requires good fundamental analysis, but long-term investors will be happy to have a complete graphical platform to complete and refine their analysis.

Choose your broker based on your trading strategy

The choice of the best Forex broker can also depend on the trader's trading style. Although the general criteria remain the same, the trader may prefer one broker over another depending on his trading style.

Scalping: A scalper must choose a Forex broker that does not issue restrictions on trading. In fact, some brokers prohibit their traders from scalping or setting minimum distances for stock market orders, making scalping more difficult. Furthermore, scalping requires the lowest spreads and excellent quality of order execution. Indeed, the scalper needs speed and not to pay too many commissions per position, because he opens many positions per day.

Day trading: A day trader usually opens fewer positions than scalping, but it is also very short-term trading. You must therefore choose a Forex broker with low spreads, even if this is less crucial than scalping. Day trading is perhaps the most popular approach for retail traders, but it is still a risky business. This is why the broker you choose must offer serious support.

Swing Trading: A swing trader generally holds his positions open for several days. In addition to the above requirements, the swing trader will also need to pay attention to the swap fees.

The trader can choose to trade with an NDD (No Dealing Desk) Forex broker or Market Maker.

An NDD broker uses external liquidity providers and acts as an intermediary between the trader and the financial markets.

A Broker Market Maker is a market maker, which means that it is directly the counterpart of the trader.

Retail traders generally prefer to avoid Market Maker brokers due to the risk of price manipulation, as the broker himself sets the prices.

Start with a broker who offers a demo account

Choosing a Forex broker to start trading is sometimes a

difficult task. However, an essential element not to be overlooked is the availability of a demo trading account.

In fact, before starting trading in real with a broker, even for an experienced trader, it is essential to test it through a demo account.

A demo account is a virtual money trading account. It allows you to practice trading without risking your funds when you start, but also to take the tools offered by the broker of your choice. It is also an opportunity to test the availability and competence of customer service before eventually choosing this broker permanently.

Demo trading therefore offers several advantages to novice traders, in addition to being completely free, it would be a shame to do without it due to the impossibility of the broker.

Tips for choosing and getting started with the best broker

As we have just seen, there are a number of factors that should be taken into consideration when choosing a good online broker. With the elements mentioned above, you now have the keys to making informed, efficient and smart decisions and to choose the best online broker for you.

Your first broker will not necessarily be your broker for life. Your trading style may change and your investor needs may change at the same time. But you have a much better chance of being successful as an investor if you take the time to choose the right broker to get started.

It can be tempting to simply sign up with the broker you've seen advertised, but to be successful in trading you need to

Forex Trading for Beginners

pay attention to detail and make informed decisions, even when choosing a broker.

Following this guide on which Forex broker to choose, you may have already found the broker that will best suit your needs, whatever they may be.

Once you've chosen your Forex broker, it's time to get started. Don't just open an account and start trading, use all the educational and analytical resources at your disposal, start defining your trading strategy and practice as a demo account. You have spent valuable time finding your broker, now is the time to take advantage of their services.

CONCLUSION

If you are reading the conclusion, it means that you have reached the end of the book.

I hope it was a pleasant reading and the content was interesting.

Hope all of this has helped to improve your way of trading Forex.

I also hope that with this book you will discover the method to make your trading more profitable, but above all, that you will learn the tools to try to safeguard your capital.

As I always say, trading doesn't mean playing at the casino.

Trading has become their job for many, and for some, the possibility that has allowed them to significantly increase their standard of living.

But behind all this there is study, preparation, discipline, organization and above all, never improvisation.

I wish you every success in trading and in other types of business, have a good life!

CRYPTOCURRENCY INVESTING

Blockchain Revolution

How To Become a Crypto Millionaire Investing and
Trading Bitcoin, Ethereum and Other
Cryptocurrencies with the Best
Strategies in the Market

INTRODUCTION

There are people who, thanks to trading, have changed their lives and the lives of many people who have believed in them. It is enough to mention the name of Warren Buffet or George Soros because dreams and visions begin to appearin the heads of many traders.

Trading success is achieved staying grounded.

Starting from this belief, I wrote this manual in a simple way with the aim of helping newbies to find the right way to be successful, but above all to find the right methods to avoid losing money, very often, saved with many sacrifices.

Trading is not synonymous with gambling. Cryptocurrencytradingis neither a game nor a hobby. Your approach must be extremely serious and disciplined, especially your attention must be paid to safeguarding the capital you decide to invest. Knowing your character, your fears, your goals, knowing how to use all this to your advantage, is certainly an added weapon.

CHAPTER ONE
BLOCKCHAIN

In recent years, you have surely noticed the term "blockchain" being pronounced with increasing frequency. It is understandable when you consider the fact that many individuals are comparing the importance of blockchain technology tothat of the World Wide Web in the 1990s.

But what is blockchain? How does it work? Above all, how can you position yourself to capitalize on this innovation that could offer a huge growth opportunity?

Blockchain

Put simply, we could define blockchain as a shared database, a digital ledger, an archive of financial transactions that are saved on multiple computers in different places.

The database grows steadily as new transactions are added, also called "blocks". This forms a continuous chain of data in which the records are public and verifiable. As there is no head office, it is more difficult to hack information as it exists in millions of different places.

There are three main technologies that combine together to create a blockchain. These include private key cryptography, a distribution network with a shared ledger, and an incentive to maintain network transactions, record keeping and security. These combine to make blockchain technology a decentralized, transparent and immutable system.

Decentralization

Most traditional forms of payment are centralized. For example, your bank stores your money and to pay someone else you will have to go through the bank. This has several weaknesses:

- all data is stored in one place, making it an easy target for hackers;

- if the centralized entity shuts down or becomes corrupted, no one has access to the information it holds.

In a decentralized system, such as that created with blockchain technology, information is not stored by a single entity. Everyone in the network owns the information and can access the history of transactions, but cannot modify it. This immutability is another fundamental pillar of blockchain technology.

Immutability

Once something has been placed on the blockchain it cannot be tampered with. There is no possible way to "tinker" with the registers. This is because the underlying technology uses cryptographic hashes. In the context of payments, this means that transactions are taken as inputs and passed through a hashing algorithm that gives them an output of fixed length and size. This means that each hash can identify a very large set of calculations or a string of data.

Transparency

Perhaps the most interesting aspect of how blockchain works is the fact that it offers a high level of transparency and privacy at the same time. A user's identity is hidden behind complex encryption and can only be identified by their public address.

At the same time, while the user's identity is secure, one can still see all the transactions that have been made on his public address. This level of transparency does not exist in the current financial system and that is why blockchain technology is changing the world of finance, as we will see later in this article.

How does it work

Let's supposethatDavid wants to send Paul some money. Using blockchain technology this transaction would be represented online as a block. This block would be distributed across the blockchain network which is a special type of peer-to-peer network where the workload is partitioned among the participants rather than a central server.

Once the network verifies that the transaction is valid, the block is added to the chain and reconciled across the network, creating a permanent record. David's record of ownership of money then passes to Paul. In essence, the technology helps to cut the middleman out, but with full transparency and privacy.

How it works in the real world

One of the first real-world uses of this technology was in cryptographies like Bitcoin and Ethereum. This is due to the fact that technology allows digital information to be distributed and not copied, which means that each data can have only one owner which is essential when it comes to payments; in fact, a digital master book.

How Blockchain Works for Bitcoin

In 2008, someone using the pseudonym Satoshi Nakamoto created Bitcoin. Since the Bitcoin blockchain is decentralized, it is not controlled by a single central authority, unlike traditional currencies which are issued by a central bank. Instead, the Bitcoin blockchain is maintained by a network of miners (sometimes called "nodes"). These nodes are custom built computers that solve complex mathematical problems to get the transaction through.

Let'simagine that Davidmakes a Bitcoin transaction. This transaction would originate from David's digital currency wallet which will be protected by a private key. This key is nothing more than a digital signature from David, which provides mathematical proof that the transaction comes from that wallet.

If more people make more transactions, they will all be grouped into a block that will be organized by strict cryptographic rules. This block will then be sent to the Bitcoin network and once validated it will be added to the previous blocks, thus creating a chain of blocks.

Although this mightseem like a very long and convoluted way to make a transaction, keep in mind that all of these transactions are transparent and listed on the Bitcoin ledger (which you can search using a Bitcoin explorer). Furthermore, multiple parties need to authenticate the transaction and even if one part of the network were to collapse, the whole network would not collapse.

How Blockchain Works for Ethereum

Following the hype and the success of Bitcoin, a number of other companies have begun building platforms with blockchains that have been easier to use in the real world and by businesses. The second largest digital currency in the world by value- after Bitcoin - is Ethereum. It is essentially a blockchain platform that specializes in smart contracts and is linked to a digital currency called "Ether".

Ethereum's blockchain is public, just like Bitcoin's, and it allows people to build decentralized applications on its platform, which specializes in smart contracts. These are contracts that are automatically executed when certain conditions are met by all interested parties. This level of automation helps speed up the process.

How the wallet works

A blockchain wallet is nothing more than a software program that allows users to buy, sell and monitor their balance sheets with digital currencies such as Bitcoin and Ethereum. It is important to note that a blockchain wallet does not store cryptocurrencies. It simply keeps a record of all currency related transactions (your public and private keys) and stores them on the blockchain.

There are several types of block chain wallets available.

Hardware wallets are hardware devices such as USB sticks that store private keys for a user. There are also software wallets, such as desktop, online and mobile applications, which store private keys for transactions made.

Blockchain technology itself, its uses and the services surrounding it are big business. It is the reason why many large companies are investing billions of dollars in its development. However, there are some blockchain stocks that stand out from others.

Before delving into this topic, you need to learn more or improve your knowledge of blockchain technology andbetter understand how to use blockchain.

How to invest in blockchain

To demonstrate how many investors are interested in blockchain stocks, just take a look at Riot Blockchain. It was a penny stock that went from just $8 per share to $40 per share in 2017 when they changed their name from Bioptix Inc to Riot Blockchain.

The company was a manufacturer of diagnostic machinery for the biotech industry. After changing its name and changing its brand to have a focus on buying cryptocurrency and blockchain assets, the shares have skyrocketed on investor hype. Over time, the company was investigated by the Securities and Exchange Commission.

This is an example of why investors need to do their research before buying the potential of blockchain technology. However, there are some well-known large companies that are investing billions in technology that all traders should be aware of.

The 3 Best Sharesfor 2020

According to a report by the World Economic Forum, about 10% of the world's gross domestic product (GDP) will likely be stored in blocks by 2027. Companies at the forefront of providing blockchain-powered services will be at the top of investor lists for 2020 and well beyond. Below you can find a list of just 3 stocks that can get you started and understand how to invest in blockchain, and that most investors may find interesting for 2020 and afterward.

IBM

IBM is one of the leaders in the development of blockchain technology. The company is supported by more than 1,500 industry experts, participating in more than 500 blockchain projects. One such project is the IBM Food Trust platform which was launched with Walmart in 2018. The goal was to improve food safety processes through an integrated supply-side blockchain.

According to Forbes, IBM " may be the largest and most successful of the blockchain companies". One reason is that the company helped create Hyperledger Fabric, after donating 44,000 lines of code to the project that formed the core of a new blockchain with faster speeds and greater privacy. Hyperledger Fabric is the gold standard for enterprise blockchain projects.

Over the past seven years, the IBM stock price has suffered

from the lack of innovation of their counterparts like Microsoft and Apple. However, it is firmly at the heart of blockchain development, and investors will be on the lookout for signals that help achieve the company's bottom line and mark a turn in the fortune of its share price.

In the long-term monthly chart of the IBM stock price, the downward trend from mid-2013 to the end of 2018 is evident. The coronavirus pandemic has made its effects felt, but IBM appears to be recovering and investors will now be interested to see if the IBM share price will manage to increase its momentum during 2020. Blockchain technology is new, but it helps to be at the heart of its development.

Alibaba

Alibaba is China's largest e-commerce and technology company. In November, Ant Financial, the fintech arm of the Alibaba Group, launched the test phase for its blockchain network aimed at supporting small and medium-sized businesses.

The group has also started a partnership with the Chinese government for the use of blockchains in the healthcare sector. The Chinese government has already announcedthatit wants to be a world leader in blockchain technology, and Alibaba looks set to take advantage of this, as it has not only built a large blockchain patent library, but is already using the technology in its subsidiary and e-commerce Lynx and T-Mall, winning a practical and real advantage.

On the long-term weekly chart of the Alibaba stock price, it is clear that the company has done well - even before excelling in adopting blockchain technology. The success of its e-commerce platform offers great support to investors who still distrust the potential of blockchain. The coronavirus pandemic, on the other hand, appears to have favored Alibaba thanks to the increase in online orders as a result; combined with the success in both areas it could be a powerful driver of Alibaba's share price throughout 2020 and afterward.

MasterCard

Mastercard ranks third in the world among the best blockchain innovators with over 100 blockchain patents filed. The company's advancement in blockchain technology is interesting as the technology itself is designed to make centralized intermediaries obsolete.

However, the company is using the technology to reduce transaction costs and increase fraud protection. With over $21 billion in fraud losses suffered by banks in 2015, there is a huge advantage in using technology that allows transparency and privacy at the same time, in addition to its immutability.

The way Mastercard has approached blockchain technology is evident of an innovative and forward-thinking company that shareholders and investors will be pleased with.

The long-term monthly chart of the Mastercard stock price shows a very impressive upward trend. The share price is trading at a high level, and has been doing so since 2006. How the company has adapted to this new technology that threatens parts of its business could mean that the upward trend is here to stay.

CHAPTER TWO
ICO

Anyone who has the slightest familiarity with the world of cryptocurrencies, has at least once heard of ICOs (Initial Coin Offering).

This is a fundraiser aimed at collecting economic resources for those start-ups that develop projects in the blockchain field. ICOs exploded in 2017 only to have a big drop in 2018.

At the moment, they almost seem to have been replaced by IEOs.

Currently, it is no longer possible to invest directly in ICOs.

To better understand what ICOs are, just think that it is the acronym of Initial Coin Offering.

How they worked was not too different from IPOs that take place on the stock market and have the same purpose.

A start-up that operates on the blockchain, in fact, decides to take the big step going public, or opening up to investors.

The ICOs made it possible to obtain the necessary funds to continue their projects. Unlike a regular crowdfunding campaign, however, ICOs offered investors a real advantage.

Investors, in fact, were rewarded in tokens. As we will see, these are cryptocurrency units issued by the start up and given as a reward to investors during the ICO.

In this way the start-up receives funds and the investors,

instead, receive tokens which, if the project of the financed company goes through, will be worth much more than what was paid.

Obviously the advantage of ICOs lay in the fact that, if you could evaluate a start-up well, the profits that could be obtained were enormous.

Differences Between IPO and ICO

Let's go into more detail, recalling other important differences between IPO and ICO.

The main one concerns the fact that, in ICOs, unlike what happens with IPOs, the company that initiates the fundraising is not required to meet particular criteria.

Virtually anyone can open a fundraiser for a blockchain-related project.

Warning: this does not mean that all ICOs are destined for success. Many of them, in fact, start and fail after a short time.

The lack of proper regulation of ICOs has caused their decline. To date, in fact, it is no longer possible to participate in these collections.

Alternatives to ICOs

Normally, when an ICO was launched, participants were rewarded in tokens or cryptocurrencies.

Conceptually, the ICO is very similar to the IPO of the equity world. Everything, however, takes place on the blockchain in a decentralized manner.

Most of the people who wanted to make money from ICOs understood today that the best way remains to speculate on virtual currencies.

Today, when this tool is no longer available, many investors have nonetheless grasped the basic principle and found an alternative way to earn from emerging cryptocurrencies.

How to invest in ICOs: White Papers

Everything about investing in ICOs was extremely complex.

When approaching emerging cryptocurrencies in general, in fact, it is necessary, as already mentioned, to remember that not all projects are valid.

In any case, it is good to specify that protections existed and still exist.

In fact, every single ICO had to present a specific prospectus, technically known as a WhitePaper.

For the sake of completeness, it must be remembered that the White Papers are not subject to the control of external bodies.

In light of this aspect, it is not uncommon for them to highlight above all the positive and advantageous aspects of the project. This is why the sector has been closed to the public of retail traders.

Crucially, in spite of everything, it was vital that you read it carefully before joining any ICO.

There were some aspects to pay particular attention to when

reading the WhitePaper of an ICO and that can help you, today, to understand how to evaluate a young cryptocurrency.

In this category, it is possible to include information about the people behind the project (previous experiences in other similar projects in the first place), but also everything related to competitors.

ICO rewards the tokens

In the previous lines we mentioned that, when participating in an ICO, it was possible to be rewarded in different ways. One of these is token distribution.

These are "tokens" which, in the case of ICOs in the crypto world, correspond to a certain amount of the future cryptocurrency.

Going deeper, we also find different types of tokens.

Here's what they are:

Equity tokens

These tokens are similar to the shares of companies listed on regulated markets. Whoever owns them can claim a right towards the start-up that issued them. Right now, this type of token cannot be issued for reasons of legality. The current legislation, in fact, assimilates equity tokens to shares.

Utility tokens: in this case, we are dealing with tokens that have nothing to do with the world of stocks. This means that they can be traded on the markets and used within the various platforms.

Do you want to make money with cryptocurrencies, but you don't know where to start or are you confused with all the information you find on the net?

A very important parenthesis when talking about what ICOs are concerns the analysis of regulations.

Token class 2 a

Class 2 a tokens are representative of assets and entitle you to a specific payment both at sight and in the future.

Depending on its configuration, the token can be classified in the context of securities, but also in that of similar or financial instruments.

Furthermore, the class 2 a token can be included in the category of equity instruments

Token class 2 b

First of all, remember that, in this case, we are dealing with tokens aimed at providing services or receiving intangible assets.

It happens that the discipline of the ICO loses all the connotations of the offer of financial instruments. In practice, in the initial phase of the ICO, various advantages are highlighted, dedicated to users who acquire the tokens first.

Token class 3

We are dealing with tokens that confer co-ownership rights. The aforementioned rights are managed by the platforms themselves.

In these situations, the owner is given an economic compensation following the use of the platforms by a third party.

Stop ICOs with online trading

The halt to ICO investments came from September 2017. The Popular Bank of China's decision to shut down the ICO market in China has led to a chain reaction.

Leading financial authorities around the world have gone to great lengths to issue stringent industry regulations. Among these also the ESMA (European Security and Markets Authority), with two press releases of November 2017.

Don't get us wrong, ICOs haven't been made completely illegal. However, there have been many in the following years, but the policy on risk prevention in online trading has led to making them inaccessible to retail traders like you.

Investing in ICOs today is no longer safe as it is a possibility that is no longer offered to you by the main online trading platforms.

Successful ICO

To fully understand the peculiarities of ICOs, it is appropriate to call into question some successful examples.

Let's start with thatof Ethereum. To do this, we have to take a step back to 2013. In that year, the very young VitalikButerin launched a 42-day ICO, with the aim of financing the

Ethereum project.

What were the results? A gain of 31,591 Bitcoins, corresponding to approximately 18 million US dollars.

In 2018, other successful ones were also launched. Among these, it is possible to remember the Cypherium project, promoted and carried out by professionals with experience in Amazon, Google and Microsoft.

In this case, we are dealing with a project that has a completely new blockchain as its goal. Specifically, we are dealing with a multi-level governance that, according to some, could lead to a new decentralization in the world of cryptocurrencies.

To mention, when talking about the successful ICOs of recent times, is also the LociCoin project.

What is it about? An ICO launched with thegoalof creating a cryptocurrencyfor the purchase of intellectual rights.

The project in question aims to streamline the process of acquiring patents, which are now subject to both national and international rules that are often excessively rigid.

Most successful ICOs: how much did they raise?

To make you understand how much money has been invested in ICOs, take a look at some of them:

Telegram Open Network - $1.7 billion;

Dragon Coin - $320 million;

Huobi - $300 million;

HDac - $258 million;

Filecoin - $257 million;

Tezos - $232 million;

Sirin Labs - $157.9 million;

Bancor - $152 million.

The list could go on and on!

We will limit ourselves to mention the example of CoinLancer, a project that aims to improve the freelance world lowering transaction fees.

We conclude talking about Omega One, a project that intendsto solve the defects of ICOs, intervening on problems such as lack of liquidity and attacks by computer hackers.

CHAPTER THREE
IEO

What is an IEO

An Initial Exchange Offering (IEO) is a token sale supervised by a cryptocurrency exchange. IEOs are available exclusively to exchange users, although some IEOs may occur on some exchanges. Just like ICOs, IEOs allow investors to obtain new cryptocurrencies (or tokens) while raising funds for promising crypto projects.

Many people in the crypto world call Initial Exchange Offerings the next step in the evolution of ICOs. Since ICOs are unregulated and most of them turned out to be scams, STOs should have solved the problem. However, most STOs remain constrained by slow and expensive processes and suffocating regulations. IEOs are the middle ground that tackles problems on both sides.

Although exchange-assisted ICOs have been something worthwhile for some time, IEOs started gaining ground after the launch of the Binance Launchpad in late 2018. There have already been more than 50 IEOs in 2019, which have garnered over $159 million, according to ICObench.

IEOs try to promote only legitimate projects because they challenge the credibility of

the exchange itself. Therefore, the control process goes deeper. However, not all ideas manage to get support from an exchange. Additionally, exchange offerings are more accessible than STOs, as they allow almost anyone to participate and invest (except for countries with regulatory restrictions, see below), and the token sales team is less likely to be impacted by lawmakers due to the mandatory KYC/AML control of investors, as this service is performed by the exchange.

Essentially, the IEO is another way to crowdfund for various cryptocurrency startups through a crypto exchange that acts as a broker. With the help of the crypto exchange, projects are able to gain significantly more exposure, interest and credibility.

After an initial phase with a successful IEO, the token issuer pays a commission due to the established amount of tokens for making use of the services offered by the IEO platform. Quickly the tokens are listed on the exchange where investors can access instant liquidity.

Characteristics of Initial Exchange Offerings (IEO)

As with ICOs, IEOs have a limited amount of coins offered at a fixed price, limits on the minimum and maximum number of tokens that the individual user can purchase, soft caps and hard caps and the specific cryptocurrencies that are accepted.

However, unlike ICO tokens, IEO coins are already mined before the crowdsale. Furthermore, they enter exchanges several days or weeks after its IEO, which makes it more convenient for investors (immediate liquidity). Furthermore, the IEO process naturally involves an intermediary (the IEO platform) who is trusted to manage the funds. This also serves to increase investor confidence, which is lacking in most ICOs.

Pros and Cons of IEOs

IEOs are essentially advantageous thanks to:

- greater investor confidence.

- In fact the investors are not dealing with the IEO project team directly, but with the exchange. This makes the whole process more credible and safer in case things go wrong;

- security for both token issuers and investors.

- Token issuers also gain as IEO platforms handle all regulatory aspects, such as the mandatory KYC/AML checks for each participant;

- frictionless process.

- IEO platforms ensure that almost anyone, regardless of their experience in the crypto world, can easily contribute;

- guaranteed exchange listing. IEO tokens are listed on the IEO exchange right after the IEO;

- scam removal.

- IEO project teams are neither anonymous nor fake, so they won't disappear after raising the funds;

- benefits for projects, such as greater marketing effort

by the exchange, more credibility, more exposure and interest in the project;

- benefits for exchnage, including new users who sign up with them only to buy and trade IEO tokens;

- benefits for holders of native exchangetokens.

- Most exchanges use IEOs to add another use case to their native token (if it has one) which is then likely to increase in value.

However, IEOs are also subject to the following risks and concerns:

- unclear regulations and restrictions.

- Many countries have issued restrictions or completely banned ICOs, which could reflect negatively on IEOs as well. Although it is slightly different, the fundamental principles of an IEO remain the same;

- all investors must comply with AML/KYC.

- The crypto community is known to be full of privacy obsessed people, so going through the AML/KYCprocess might be a big no-no for some of them;

- market manipulation and coin concentration.

- Most IEO tokens are mined early, so you should always

double-check your token distribution and allocation details before investing. Both the project team and the IEO exchange could keep an unreasonably large portion of the tokens for themselves, which could lead to pricing meddling later on. Furthermore, it is now known that the majority of exchanges participate in "wash trading";

- limited number of investors.

- There have been a lot of complaints from investors that not everyone is able to buy tokens during IEO sessions.

The first large-scale IEO was famously thatof BitTorrent launched by TRON through the Binance Launchpad in January 2019. About 60 billion BTT tokens were sold in a few minutes for a total of about 7.2 million USD.

After observing the success of Binance's IEOs, major exchanges have started copying the model. Another notable IEO was launched on Bittrex International. Veriblock (VBK) and raised $7 million in 10.4 seconds. Later, this record was surpassed by the IEO Blockcloud operated on OKEx's Jumpstart, which sold all $2.5 million in BLOC tokens in just one second.

CHAPTER FOUR
DIGITAL TOKEN

A token is a set of digital information within a blockchain that confers a right on a particular subject, tokenization is the conversion of the rights of an asset into a digital token registered on a blockchain.

One of the words that recur most frequently when talking about the new economy and blockchain is certainly that of token. However, not everyone knows that two distinct meanings and aswell asmany peculiarities can be attributed to the term token, depending on the context in which this term is used.

The Token in Cryptocurrencies

Obviously, the sector to which reference is made to attribute a first meaning of token is that of cryptocurrencies, in fact starting from the assumption that a cryptocurrency is an "electronic money" (even if here the meaning of currency should certainly be deepened, but only for simplification it is defined as such) based on blockchain or other distributed ledger, we can certainly say that each of these cryptocurrencies (Bitcoin, Ethereum etc.) has its own transaction register on which exchanges are stored. Tokensare in fact fractions of an issued cryptocurrency, which are exchanged between users through exchanges that are stored on the aforementioned register. To simplify, this type of "token" should be defined as "coin",a term that although it indicates the same concept (when we refer to cryptovalue or a fraction of it), in reality, is less confusing.

There is in fact another type of "token" also called token, which unlike those mentioned above, does not have its own register, but uses the register of another coin. For example, through Ethereum's smart contracts, anyone can issue their own tokens, evenwith an ICO (Initial Coin Offer) and record the transactions relating to that token on the Ethereum blockchain instead of necessarily building their own. These "tokens" acquire the unique token appellation.

The token therefore has the same characteristics as the cryptocurrency (security and non-censurable transferability) but is not "native" and above all "internal" to the blockchain on which the transactions concerning it are stored but represents the digital twin of a real asset, a right "real", but which exists outside the blockchain system.

A further difference is expressed in the fact that the issuance of tokens (tokens that do not have their own blockchain) is not particularly complicated:essentially it is enough to write a smart contract on the mainnet of another coin, for example the Ethereum network. The creation of a new coin, on the other hand, is a much more complex process, as it is necessary to develop a new protocol, create the mainnet, make sure you have a sufficiently powerful hardware to make it "run" and above all hopingthat someone will use it.

Hoping to have clarified this first difference and focused attention on the term token intended as a token created using a blockchain of an existing coin, we can certainly say that a token is a set of digital information within a blockchain that confers a right to a particular subject. Consequently, tokenization is the conversion of the rights of an asset into a digital token registered on a blockchain, where the real asset and the token are connected by a smart contract. Therefore tokenizing means generating a token in the virtual world and connecting it to an existing asset in the real world through the use of smart contracts.

What is "tokenizable"

Theoretically, anything can be tokenizable, so much that in the not too distant future we hope and expect a real revolution comparable to what was the advent of the internet in our society: in fact, the blockchain promises to revolutionize not only all aspects directly linked to finance, but also public and civil services. It is likely that we will soon live in a fully tokenized economy, where every form of value storage and public recording will be represented by a token.

Currently, several sectors are experimenting with tokenization, which has already been implemented not only in the real estate sector (with luxury condominiums enabled for tokenization on Ethereum) but also in sectors such as works of art and sports. The strength of the tokenization of an asset lies in the fact that it is possible to make liquid assets otherwise indivisible, to manage assets plastered by excessive bureaucracy through the concrete implementation of the concept of "democratization" of the shareholding. Not only that, it is possible to digitize anything exploiting the flexibility and security of the token to implement a series of previously unthinkable commercial initiatives. In the real estate sector, for example, the purchase of a small fraction of a property also allows small investors to enter a market that is usually closed to them, without resorting to mortgages and intermediaries from credit institutions. For manufacturers, the advantage of this type of financing is to offer greater flexibility and capital inflows in the short term.

Same concept for the tokenization of some works of art, where participants in special auctions received digital shares of the work. Also in the world of sport, some companies have decided to manage business decisions through decentralized platforms that allow the sale of shares and rights to fans around the world quickly and safely, giving fans the advantage of being able to access exclusive content and services.

In other sectors, its products are being tokenized creating special rewards consisting of tokens to encourage purchases and retain customers.

Token, stock exchange and circular economy

The use of computer tokens is also very useful in the stock market sector. There are already projects for the tokenization of "stock exchanges" with the development of decentralized platforms, or infrastructures for the exchange of shares, thus protecting them from manipulations other than the "natural" ones of the market. To encourage projects of this type, the tokenization of company shares has begun to be evaluated.

Another fundamental aspect of tokenization is the absolute predisposition of this revolution to the creation of a circular economy. It is now known that the linear economic model "production-consumption-waste" which is based on the use of large quantities of resources and energy with relative waste of materials that can easily be put back into circulation, is less and less in line with today's reality,and will necessarily have to transform itself into an economy capable of being able to self-regenerate, and the use of tokens and the tokenization process represents the perfect case use.

CHAPTER FIVE
START INVESTING IN CRYPTOCURRENCIES

For several years, virtual currencies such as Bitcoin have been recognized as an essential and very attractive investment vehicle for investors.

The volatility of cryptocurrencies offers traders numerous trading opportunities. Therefore, digital currencies have become increasingly popular in trading strategies in orderto diversify their investment portfolio.

Today, in 2020, there are two ways to invest in cryptocurrencies:

- buying cryptocurrencies on an exchange platform to hold them in an online or offline cryptocurrency wallet;

- trading these financial assets via CFDs directly on a trading platform

Cryptocurrency Trading and Cryptocurrency Trading Strategies.

But what exactly sets a successful cryptocurrency trader apart from other investors?

And more importantly, how do you need to prepare to take on these financial markets and become a successful cryptocurrency trader?

Investing in Cryptocurrencies

What is a cryptocurrency

Despite being a global phenomenon, cryptocurrencies are sometimes difficult to understand, however their definition is relatively simple.

A cryptocurrency is a 100%, fully decentralized digital currency that is only traded in pairs. All validated cryptocurrency transactions are recorded on what is called the blockchain.

The principle of a cryptocurrency is to provide a monetary alternative for people looking to regain control of their money becoming their own bank. Some properties of cryptocurrencies are revolutionary.

Among the features of these 2.0 currencies, decentralization and peer-to-peer exchanges allow their users to not trust their money towards banks and to carry out transactions without intermediaries.

Therefore, central bodies no longer have control of the change in the money supply (inflation vs. deflation). Furthermore, they cannot refuse or cancel a transaction or block funds, as they have no power over cryptocurrencies.

Investingin Cryptocurrencies With CFDs

Unlike cryptocurrency exchange platforms that allow you to trade your dollars for cryptocurrencies and then keep them as long as you want in your virtual wallet, the benefits of investing in cryptocurrencies with CFDs are greater, especially for those who want to take advantage of rapid price changes.

> *CFD stands for"Contract For Difference" and is a type of derivative product. Therefore, it is a financial instrument whose valuation depends on another instrument called an "underlying".*

> *Using a CFD, you never own the underlying instrument, asyou are only investing in the price change between the opening and closing of the contract.*

Advantages of trading cryptocurrencies via CFDs

- Bullish and bearish investments: you can make money as cryptocurrency prices rise and fall

- Leverage:take advantage of margin and leverage which increase market exposure

- High volatility: maximizes the volatility of the cryptocurrency market

- Better liquidity: get better prices and shorter execution times that allow you to increase performance through better liquidity

- Reduction of the risk of loss, theft and cyber attacks related to storing your cryptocurrencies in a wallet, since you don't have tokens that use CFDs

- Flexible trading hours: trade on a 24-hour market

- Regulated and safe environment: benefit from a safe and regulated business environment with protections as a private operator, such as negative balance protection

- Low starting capital required: start trading cryptocurrency CFDs with relatively low capital

Disadvantages of trading cryptocurrency with CFDs

- You do not actually own cryptocurrencies: you do not have cryptocurrencies since you use CFDs on cryptocurrencies

- Leverage: you need to master leverage. Traders risk losing their deposit faster when using leverage, so use it with caution

- High volatility: the volatility of cryptocurrency prices is high. It is for this reason that we need to understand the concept of volatility and integrate it into a rigorous trading plan

Characteristics of Virtual Cryptocurrencies

There are no coins or bills. Everything is on the Internet and on computers

Like any other currency, a cryptocurrency can be used to make purchases when accepted by merchants, to send money to someone, to receive money, etc.

Decentralized

There is no government or country that controls cryptocurrencies unlike traditional currencies.

The total money supply of a cryptocurrency is often limited. In this case, it is determined at the time of creation of the cryptocurrency and indicated in its technical document. The bitcoin money supply, for example, is not expected to exceed 21 million BTC tokens.

Without intermediaries

To execute a transaction with a cryptocurrency, it is not necessary to use a trusted third party such as a bank or other intermediary to validate it. Transactions are carried out on a peer-to-peer basis via electronic wallets that are carried out in applications to buy cryptocurrencies, websites or even exchange platforms.

Based on blockchain

Traditional currencies under the control of central banks such as the Fed (Federal Reserve) for the US dollar (USD) or the ECB (European Central Bank) for the euro (EUR).

In the case of cryptocurrencies, all transactions are performed on the blockchain, which acts as a large, transparent and tamper-proof accounting book open to all.

Encrypted

The term "cryptocurrency" comes from the principle that it is an encrypted currency. It can only be used by the person with the decryption code that allows, for example, the use of cryptocurrencies in a wallet.

Safe

Since the funds use an advanced cryptographic system with a combination of public/private keys, your funds are safe. Furthermore, the blocks that belong to the blockchain (those that group all validated transactions) are linked together by complex computer formulas that avoid any data manipulation.

Fast

Validating the blockchain transaction is much faster than most traditional operators such as Visa or SWIFT. Some transactions are validated almost instantly.

Irreversible

Once a transaction involving cryptocurrencies is confirmed, it is no longer possible to withdraw. Therefore, it is impossible to cancel a transaction if a cryptocurrency transfer has failed or your tokens have been stolen.

(Pseudo) Anonymous

Depending on the cryptocurrency you use, you can enjoy a greater or lesser degree of anonymity.

Even if you receive cryptocurrencies at encrypted addresses that don't directly reflect your identity in the real world, once you share this address with someone to receive funds, that person can see all the movements taking place in that direction.

CHAPTER SIX
INVESTING IN CRYPTOCURRENCIES SUCCESSFULLY

Success in trading can take on different meanings for every trader who has decided to invest in cryptocurrencies.

For some, being successful could mean making a profit on a real trading account or demo trading from the 30 minute chart. For others, it could mean making a profit from a short position in cryptocurrency CFDs. Ultimately, however, success most likely comes down to a profitable return on the capital that everyone has invested and therefore exposed to risk.

Of course, as with any other business, the tools we use will have an impact on our overall success. After all, no one wants to spend a great deal of time researching and analyzing a trading opportunity with a high probability of success, only to end up with a platform that is either unresponsive or suffering from the technical issues that prevent them from completing the strategy.

Here are some of the fundamental tools for increasing the odds of long-term success as a cryptocurrency trader.

Choose a trusted broker

Those who decide to physically purchase a cryptocurrency will have to do so through a cryptocurrency exchange system. These are often unregulated entities that are prone to attacks. For example:

In 2018, Japan's Coincheck was hacked and more than $500

million worth of digital currency was stolen.

In 2017, Youbit - a South Korean stock exchange - had to close and declare bankruptcy after being hacked twice.

In 2014, MtGox - a Japanese exchange that handled nearly 80% of all global Bitcoin transactions - closed after 850,000 Bitcoins disappeared from its virtual vaults (worth around half a billion dollars at the time).

Even when it comes to CFDs, the broker with whom you decide to invest in cryptocurrencies holds the capital with which you will then have to trade. Therefore, it is important to choose an entity that offers the highest possible regulatory oversight, safety and assurance.

The trading platform

Your trading platform and charts help you visualize the historical price movements of the financial instrument you are trading, as well as provide you with the orders you need to place and manage your trades. Some people may have a separate charting platform from their brokerage platform. With the new and advanced trading technology, however, it is now possible to have the trading platform and brokerage platform in one software with the MetaTrader product suite.

The trading strategy

Trading is all about making decisions about how to buy, sell, or sit idle on a particular market. If a trader has been successful over a substantial period of time there will be a greater chance that they are using a trading strategy or methodology to help in their decision making. Trading strategies are used to help simplify the information process which can include when to trade and when not to trade, what times to focus on, which technical indicators to use, how to enter and exit, and so on.

Of course, the tools used will depend on the trading styleof each one. This is the first thing to establish when starting to invest in cryptocurrencies. After all, if your goal is to trade cryptocurrency CFDs from the hourly chart, which involves multiple buying and selling throughout the day for short-term profits and closing positions at the end of the day, using a weekly long termchart for price analysis can only prove to be of little use.

Trading styles generally incorporate one or both types of analysis:

- Technical analysis. This type of analysis involves analyzing the price movement of financial products, in this case of cryptocurrencies, to identify repeatable patterns of behavior. Many traders use technical indicators applied to cryptocurrencies to find clues and price levels in which the market may move.

- Fundamental analysis. It involves analyzing news announcements related to financial products, and in this caseto cryptocurrencies, such as the new developments and uses of the technology behind crypto, namely the blockchain.

There are also types of events that are uniquely related to cryptocurrencies, an example is the "halving", which we will explore further on.

Here are some trading styles that you can apply to invest in cryptocurrencies:

- day trading

  This style involves buying and selling in various trading positions several times a day, often closing all trades by the end of the day. Traders using this style mainly rely on technical analysis tools such as trading indicators and chart patterns in their trading decisions. Investing in cryptocurrencies is worthwhile when using this type of trading style, as intraday traders need to trade the right tools to profit from different types of market conditions, such as rising and falling markets;

- swing trading

  This style involves buying and selling financial assets with the purpose of holding trades for several days and, in some cases, several weeks. Traders using this style of trading often use a mix of technical analysis and fundamental analysis, such as analyzing new developments in "blockchain"cryptocurrency technology, to aid in their trading decisions.

CHAPTER SEVEN
HOW TO TRADE CRYPTOCURRENCIES

A Few Steps to Facilitate the Process

Work on your trading plan

First of all, it is important to know what kind of trader you are to confirm that cryptocurrency CFDs are the products you need. Think about your personality, your financial goals, seed capital, risk tolerance and the time you are willing to devote to trading.

If trading cryptocurrencies through leveraged derivatives such as CFDs seems like a good option for short-term trading, it is essential to work on your trading plan, test and follow it at all times.

A trading plan is simply a detailed description of how you will conduct your business: style, strategy to follow, risk management, objectives, etc.

Therefore, the idea is to develop a number of rules to follow in order to better manage operations. Therefore, you will avoid operating spontaneously without any strategy.

A trading plan is not a quick fix. Sometimes it takes time to develop a profitable trading strategy.

Don't forget also that some strategies only work in certain market situations, such as side consolidation or, conversely, in a market with a strong trend.

To tailor your trading plan, it may be worth keeping a trading journal and taking advantage of the option to trade virtual funds to practice.

Choose a broker with advantageous trading conditions and a trading account tailored to your needs

After designing your trading plan, you will have a more appropriate idea of your needs.

This will allow you to choose the correct platform and account type to start trading with a regulated broker that offers you the best trading conditions.

Without the right broker and trading platform, you will not be able to analyze or execute your trades quickly and correctly, which will affect your overall performance.

Start trading knowing how the market works

You can now start trading with cryptocurrencies! Here is an example of cryptocurrency trading that shows how much you can win or lose in one position.

Hypothesis:

Let's assume BTC/USD is the pair you want to trade with. Believe that Bitcoin has reached significant support and will recover soon. Therefore, open a position in the Bitcoin vs USD pair through a CFD to take advantage of the price increase.

For example: Bitcoin's bid/ask price, or "Bitcoin price", is 7000/7034. As a reminder, the selling price is always lower than the buying price. The difference between the two prices corresponds to the spread.

Therefore, you make a 1 contract buy/sell contract on the BTC/USD pair at $7000. Since the leverage is 1:2, this means that you need to set aside $3,500 (the margin) to open a buy position on a contract from 1 BTC/USD.

Winning position

Your ideal scenario is realized and the pair rises to reach the $7200 level. The new Bitcoin price is 7166/7200. Therefore, you decide to close the position (and thus sell) with a sell price of 7166.

Since the Bitcoin price at the time of purchase was 7000 and the price at the time of the sale was 7166, you took advantage of a $166 price shift. Therefore, your gross profit is $166 since you only opened one contract.

Losing position

Bitcoin's value does not appear to recover from the expected level and is accelerating downwards. You decide to close your position with a new price at the price of $6834/$6868.

Since the price of Bitcoin at the time of purchase was $7000 and the price at the time of the sale was $6834, you have lost $166. Therefore, the gross loss is $166 since you only opened one contract.

Check your money management

You are probably wondering why many traders lose money investing in cryptocurrencies. The answer is actually quite simple. They don't have a trading plan and don't use risk and money management tools to control their risk and protect their capital!

Therefore, risk and money management is essential if you want to be successful in long-term cryptocurrency trading while preserving your capital.

That is why it is important to always make sure that you manage risk as outlined in the trading plan. To be sure, it's important to always stick to your business plan. Also think about the following questions:

Do you use a risk/reward ratio to place stop-loss and take-profit orders that fit your strategy?

Do you risk more than 1% of your capital in one position?

Have you recently increased the size of your position just because you made some winning trades?

Do you have a well diversified portfolio?

Do you often deviate from your trading plan?

Follow cryptocurrency prices and market news

The most important thing in cryptocurrency trading is to always monitor your investments. Follow the cryptocurrency price in real time and market news. In fact, many movements in cryptocurrency quotes started with the "most popular" cryptocurrency news of the moment.

Discover the events that have the greatest influence on the price of cryptocurrencies

The cryptocurrency market is a new market whose fundamentals are still quite vague. This is why the greatest influence on prices continues to be the evolution of the relationship between supply and demand. Among the most influential factors for cryptocurrency prices are:

- market sentiment;

- news on cryptocurrency trading platforms;

- the evolution of the level of acceptance of cryptos;

- speed of execution and scalability of tokens and blockchains;

- the number of cryptocurrencies issued relative to the total money supply;

- the process of reducing miners' premiums (halving);

- cryptocurrency reputation.

Best time to trade cryptocurrencies

There really are no better times to trade in the cryptocurrency market. In fact, it never stops working. Therefore, every part of the world manages Bitcoin and the rest of the cryptocurrencies, which means that there will always be movements.

It can be interesting to trade when multiple exchanges are active, such as when European and American sessions are active. You can also trade at night and on weekends.

Mistakes to avoid whenstarting to invest in

cryptocurrencies

- Don't define the trader's personality, risk profile and trading plan before starting to trade with real money

- Set unrealistic goals

- Don'tinvest in yourself (always try to improve knowledge through free cryptocurrency training)

- Trade an asset without knowing the details of the CFD

- Don't diversify your portfolio enough

- Don't accept you lose

- Lose patience

- Don't manage emotions

- Don't let your profits run and don't limit your losses

Which cryptocurrency to invest in 2020

Now that you know exactly what a cryptocurrency is and how it works, you are probably wondering which cryptocurrencies will be exploited in 2020 and in the coming years.

You must first understand that every cryptocurrency is different. Each of themhas its own advantages and challenges. Therefore, the best cryptocurrency to invest primarily depends on your goals in trading and your interest in cryptocurrency and what it contributes. Currencies that are already very popular often benefit from greater confidence and higher price movements than you can.

Future of Cryptocurrencies

The fall in cryptocurrencies after the peak in late 2017 led many people to believe it was the end of cryptocurrencies. But after several years, there are still many virtual currencies that currently offer attractive valuations.

The cryptocurrencies that will be exploited in 2020 should be small tokens that are not very popular (and often not available for trading) or major cryptocurrencies such as Bitcoin or Ethereum.

In any case, the most promising cryptocurrencies in 2020 are those that continue to evolve and offer more and more innovative features for their users.

The cryptocurrencies of the future must provide a real solution to the problems of legal currencies and an alternative to the challenges of our economy. It is also important that your adoption continues to support your development.

CHAPTER EIGHT
BITCOIN

Bitcoin is a digital currency, or "cryptocurrency", as it uses cryptography to secure transactions within its infrastructure, which represents a distributed online database, or "blockchain".

The abbreviation for Bitcoin is BTC. The same principle applies to USD (US dollar) and EUR (Euro).

Bitcoin can also be paired with other currencies. In that case, the name of the bitcoin CFD contract could be, for example, Bitcoin CFD against US dollar, or BTC/USD.

Bitcoin offers the opportunity to make fast, secure, low-cost peer-to-peer (P2P) payments without the need for a bank or central processor.

System transactions are performed directly between users' digital folders and are verified in the blockchain. Transactions are digitally signed with unique private keys, proving they come from the wallet owner.

History of Bitcoin

When a new block is created in the chain, it is rewarded with 12.5 Bitcoins. This happens approximately every 10 minutes.

This is a reward for the so-called "mining" process, which wastes electrical energy and computer power in maintaining the network.

Mining involves many people and specialized companies around the world and creates the core value of Bitcoin.

The system automatically generates new Bitcoins and self-regulates the speed of this process so that there is no way to circumvent global rules and earn Bitcoins faster than with investments in mining hardware and with higher spending on electricity bills.

The block reward will be halved in 2020 and will continue to be halved every 4 years until 21 million Bitcoins are generated. This means that Bitcoin has fundamental potential for value growth.

The image shows that there are more than 16 million (76% of the total) of Bitcoin on the market in 2018. The image also indicates rapid growth in its supply between the beginning of 2009 and 2013. We have seen that during 2018 the value of cryptocurrencies plummeted, so we need to be aware of the effect this can have on their demand.

Who invented Bitcoin

Bitcoin is believed to have been created by Satoshi Nakamoto, who announced its invention on October 31, 2008 on an encrypted mailing list in a research paper called Bitcoin: A Peer to Peer Electronic Box System. What's more interesting is that its name is likely a pseudonym used by the unknown, or by the people who originally designed Bitcoin. In 2016, Craig Wright, an Australian businessman, declared himself "Mr. Bitcoin", a statementthat has been widely accepted by prominent members of the Bitcoin community.

Bitcoin's financial history dates back to 2010, May 22, 2010, when someone bought a pizza. If you haven't heard of this groundbreaking event, don't worry, you're not the only one.

The pizza wasn't the most important part of the transaction - but what was used to pay for it. The meal cost 10,000 Bitcoins: it was the first time this virtual currency was used to buy something in the real world.

The day is now celebrated by Bitcoin enthusiasts every year as Bitcoin Pizza Day.

Things have changed since then. Bitcoin's use and value have skyrocketed. If that pizzeria had taken over those 10,000 Bitcoins, it might not have made history, but today it would have around $20 million in its pocket.

There are a lot of things you can buy using Bitcoin - besides pizza. There are even more places that accept it. According to www.coindesk.com, the number of merchants accepting Bitcoin has exploded. Many of them are online e-commerce sites, but a growing number of offline stores also accept BTC. The list is constantly expanding, and you will be able to spend bitcoins literally anywhere.

Common household items:

- video games;

- gift cards;

- travels;

- food;

- car;

- tips and charity;

- online and offline stores.

Most Bitcoin payment processors will also provide a QR code on the box, which represents the address and amount of the Bitcoin payment.

QR codes are very convenient, so it's easy to pay through the Bitcoin wallet application from your smartphone. Just scan the QR code and enter the recipient's Bitcoin address and the requested payment amount. Once the transaction is submitted, the payment is complete.

Traceabletransactions

Bitcoin is completely transparent. All Bitcoin transactions are public, traceable and permanently stored on the Bitcoin network. Bitcoin addresses are the only information used to define where Bitcoins are allocated and where they are sent.

These addresses are created privately from each user's folders. Since users normally have to reveal their identity to receive services or goods, Bitcoin addresses cannot remain anonymous. The Bitcoin network is a peer-to-peer network, and it is possible to record the user's IP addresses.

Countries that accept Bitcoin

The legal situation varies from country to country, but the list of countries that accept BTC is constantly expanding.

Bitcoin operates independently of any central bank, unlike other currencies such as US dollar and Euro.

The Bitcoin network has no other central point or administrator, which makes it a decentralized digital currency.

The fundamental value of Bitcoin is generated through "mining" and is closely linked to the costs of electricity and hardware, while the rest of its value is driven by its limited quantity, slow generation process and increasing demand.

Bitcoin is spreading around the world as a valid payment method for which various goods and services can be purchased; which is driving demand further.

Legality

Regulations vary from country to country. At the moment, only Japan officially recognizes Bitcoin as money, while in other countries there is still no specific legislation.

But domestic financial regulators can be expected to be increasingly interested in Bitcoin and other cryptocurrencies as blocking technologies are spreading rapidly and the size of this economy is growing.

Bitcoin Trading

Bitcoin is a volatile asset, with daily price changes of over 10%, making it highly risky for investing and trading.

Of course, there is no high reward without high risk and it is vital that you do not invest or use funds that you cannot afford to lose.

The causes of the collapse of Bitcoin in 2018

Over the course of 2017, the cryptocurrency market increased by 2000%. However, in 2018 the trend reversed and collapsed.

This led toa capitalization loss of approximately $700 billion. One of the advantages of CFD bitcoin trading is that the trader can trade going short and thus take advantage of the bearish trend.

The causes of the collapse were:

- ICO offers;

- money laundry;

- tax evasion;

- computer theft;

- market evolution;

- low or non-existent regulation in some cases;

- excessive speculation;

- investing in Bitcoins without buying them – CFDs.

Trading Bitcoin CFDs is probably not that different from trading any other currency pair, product or CFD that shows a strong trend.

The beauty of trading lies in its diversity, and through studies of price shares, traders should be able to make profits that make them financially independent and stable. So let's see how to trade with Bitcoin.

Bitcoin CFD traders should focus on:

- follow the trend (bullish trend until proven otherwise);

- proper money management;

- the main sessions London, New York and Tokyo;

- buying on BTC/USD price drops is important because it gives traders the opportunity to enter most of the market and follow the momentum. Of course, the trend will change, but BTC/USD is showing an exceptionally strong trend right now.

Proper money management is the holy grail of bitcoin trading, and if applied correctly in a strong trending environment, it should theoretically generate huge ROI.

CHAPTER NINE
RIPPLE

Most of the world's population has already heard of Bitcoin since its explosion in 2017, but the cryptocurrency family extends far beyond that. Those who have explored the topic a little more may have also heard of Litecoin and Ethereum.

Another cryptocurrency that has caused ripple effects across the digital currency market is Ripple. Even though Ripple has its own currency, its value is perhaps more considerable thanks to the ultra-fast payment system that supports it.

Ripple is a company born in San Francisco from the design of a payment system similar to the blockchain system. It is a protocol that works similar to a payment system, a remittance network, and currency exchange. It works with cryptocurrencies, fiat coins and commodities.

Ripple allows customers to integrate the protocol into their systems. National Bank of Abu Dhabi has recently started using blockchain technology for some of its transactions, such as international transactions. This allows its clients to transfer funds of various amounts virtually in real time.

Ripple uses a Bitcoin-like blockchain, but Ripple's cryptography is called "Ripples".

In terms of market capitalization, Ripple is the third largest cryptocurrency - after Bitcoin and Ethereum.

The abbreviation for Ripple is simply XRP. It can also be paired with other currencies, as well as USD (US dollar) and

EUR (Euro).

The name of the currency pair Ripples vs. US dollar is therefore XRP/USD.

Ripple VS Bitcoin

Ripple is considered a competitor to Bitcoin and has some advantages over its more famous "cousin". Ripple does not depend on a single company to secure and manage their transaction database. Therefore, there is no waiting for block confirmations. According to Market Mogul, there is a difference between the time of liquidation of Bitcoin and Ripple. Bitcoin's settling time increased, reaching 168 minutes on March 27, 2018, while Ripple took an average of 3.7 seconds. Money transfers between Spain and Mexico made by BBVA revealed that Ripple takes only seconds, while a standard wire transfer would have taken four days.

Both currencies share many similar characteristics, and Ripple is similar to Bitcoin crypto with a few differences:

- Ripple offers faster settlement time,as explained above;

- Ripple uses an iterative consensus process,Bitcoin uses so-called mining;

- Currency vs. Network Transactions: Bitcoin is a decentralized digital currency, while Ripple is basically a transaction network that also includes a digital currency.

You cannot mine with Ripple. The Ripple cryptocurrency was born with a fixed number of Ripples (XRP) and has no expansion built into it, according to the rules of the Ripple protocol. Therefore, there is no need to mine new coins.

The total number of XRPs created is 100 billion, but the flow of XRP is controlled by Ripple. This has been criticized by Bitcoin sympathizers who praise Bitcoin for not being centralized on its creation or distribution.

Ripple responded announcing its intention to freeze 88% of its XRP assets and sell one billion XRP each month. Both freezing and constant flow will allow ripple traders and investors to have some level of predictability with respect to supply.

Ripple emphasizes its role in the "global settlement network", which simply allows financial parties, such as banks, to reduce transaction costs. At the same time, it also offers an advanced service with direct and instant transactions. The image below shows how Ripple allows payments to cross the world in the blink of an eye.

Payments are cryptographically secure and designed to fit into a bank's existing infrastructure. Ripple highlights the following four main features:

- distribution: banks can deal directly with each other without intermediaries;

- security: confidentiality of transactions;

- scalability: high levels of processing;

- interoperability: ability to connect multiple networks together.

The network for investing in Ripple allows you to complete payments faster (almost instantaneously) and cheaper, safer and with direct access. It's no surprise, then, that Ripple is increasingly being used by the banking sector, which hasn't capitalized as much on new technologies as some other sectors of the industry.

Blockchain

Ripple uses a structure that processes payments in a similar way to the concept of blockchain. It is a "storage ledger" for processing transactions that allows you to work across borders and with any payment size.

Ripple cryptocurrency helps facilitate transactions between two parties if direct exchange is not possible and has no counterparty risk as it is not dependent on third parties.

Investingin Ripple

Ripple is believed to have been founded by Ryan Fugger, but has seen a great deal of development since its initial creation.

Ripple's growth began in 2004 when the creation of RipplePay was founded by Ryan Fugger. In 2011, the system was redesigned, making it faster and much more efficient than Bitcoin. In 2012, OpenCoin, Inc. was formed.

Soon after, the Ripple Transaction Protocol (RTXP) was developed based on Fugger's concepts. The protocol is able to process the commissions and waiting times of the corresponding traditional banking system.

Since 2012, Ripple has also focused on expanding the banking market.

In short, the future for this financial product looks bright. Ripple's network is much faster at processing payments than its competitors and is aligning multiple partnerships with global companies:

- 60 institutions from around the world, including famous companies such as UBS, RBC, UniCredit and Santander;

- 40% of Japanese banks will be linked to Ripple;

- RBS and BAML will use Ripple for both retail and commercial payment services from 2018;

- Abu Dhabi National Bank uses Ripple for international transactions.

Of course, Ripple isn't as popular as Bitcoin. However, with the growing interest in cryptocurrencies in general, in addition toRipple's amazing fast network and ability to offer payment solutions, it looks like it will be a big contender for the market leader in the coming years. The volume division for XRP is shown below.

Ripple operates independently of any central bank in a similar way to other cryptocurrencies, such as Bitcoin, Ethereum and Litecoin. This is a major difference

from well-known currencies such as US dollar and Euro.

These coins are distributed and printed in the US and EU by their respective central banks.

Ripple decides the flow of XRP, which is set at one billion XRP every month. However, unlike "fiduciary currencies" like USD and EUR, Ripple has a maximum supply of 100 billion XRP, which is available under the protocol.

Risks of Investing in Ripple

As with any financial asset, there is a risk that the price will go up and down. Ripple is subject to market fluctuations, such as supply and demand. However, price fluctuation is what allows traders to trade Ripple.

Considering the great acceptance of Ripple as a financial network by both major banks and many financial companies, it is unlikely that major disruptions will occur in the future.

Last but not least, each Ripple account must have a minimum reserve of 20 XRP and a transaction fee of 0.00001 XRP for each trade. These actions are designed to limit hackers who intentionally want to overload the network. In general, these ground rules are not heavy.

It is legal to invest in Ripple. Regulations vary in detail from one country to another, but the general expectation is that national financial regulators are interested in investing in Ripple and other cryptocurrencies.

For example, a law has already been passed in Japan to normalize and regulate digital currencies such as Bitcoin and XRP.

Investing in Ripple is as safe as using Bitcoin, Litecoin,Ethereum, or any other product. We suggest trading the XRP vs USD pair.

Most traders prefer trading on the Forex and CFD market, but cryptocurrencies offer a wide mix of tradable instruments.

Invest in Ripple Successfully

Operating in a shorter period of time always requires more practice and experience than operating in longer periods of time. Yes, there are more trading opportunities when investing in the 15 minute chart, but there is also more confusion and traders need to be more critical with the settings they choose.

In trading based on technical analysis you should always check if there is a possible news event or data release that could lead to spontaneous and rapid price increases. We are fundamentally cautious at these times andwe prefer to trade with normal trends rather than sudden price spikes. In particular, technical traders want to trade technically andto avoid price movements based on specific events.

The next step when trading shorter time slots and daily trades with XRP/USD is to consider the direction of the broader trend. This is one of the main reasons why we have added the 144 EMA near the chart.

The price must be above the EMA before trading any of the intraday setups.

If the price is below the EMA, we will omit any intraday

settings.

After that we will look for long trades that are based on break or bounce settings when using trend lines and MT4 Pivot Points.

The trendline is a dynamic tool that traders need to draw on the chart.

Pivot Points are automatically added to static support and resistance levels.

Both Pivot Point (PP) indicators and trend lines can be used for pause and bounce settings:a pulse above the trendline or PP is an interruption pattern, a return on the trend line or PP is a rebound configuration.

Of course, this is just a rough idea of how to approach intraday trading. There are many different types of trading methods that could be used to enter the markets. You can find other articles that delve into various trading strategies in our educational section.

It is possible to make a profit in trading Ripple but it is always important to realize that trading involves risk, which means that you can lose money. There are a couple of key elements that you must always keep in mind when trying to make money trading in the markets.

It is important to keep in mind that trading requires patience and discipline. This is the "trading psychology" part and it is an important aspect to remember before entering the markets. If you don't, you may be tempted to trade forthe"payback", negotiateand analyze more than you should, and/or suffer other traps that lead traders to lose habits and false prejudices and turn this into a casino.

The other key aspect is risk management. When traders take a lot of risks, it becomes a gamble and the possibility of losing all trading capital increases. It is possible that this situation will degenerate over time. To avoid losing all trading capital, each trade should be divided into small amounts of capital, such as 0.5%, 1% or 2%. A period of losses will generally not lead to a significant decrease in the account and will allow traders to continue investing for another day.

Last but not least, traders must approach the markets with a solid trading plan that indicates how to analyze the charts, how to trade, manage settings and exit the market. Each trader has their own strategy and prefers different types of tools and indicators. This is why it is important to practice your trading plan first on a demo account or a real account with little risk.

Excitement for Ripple grew when a new high against the US dollar was reached on May 17, 2017. The price action took a steep rise, but that moment was an unsustainable energy explosion in the long run. The price has corrected as the markets do.

CHAPTER TEN
DASH

The cryptocurrency Dash was first released in 2014. This open source cryptocurrency offers simple and scalable solutions. Open source means that technology and software are created, tested and improved with the collaboration of users.

The Dash is the first fully decentralized digital money system and is increasingly accepted by companies on the Internet. Dash allows you to make instant and private payments online, as well as in physical stores. Being a "Blue Chip", you can get the Dash (cryptocurrency) in most exchanges.

Dash cryptocurrency is another alternative to decentralized digital currency.

It is a type of open source Peer-to-Peer cryptocurrency that offers features similar to Bitcoin but with some more advanced features, such as InstantSend instant transactions and PrivateSend transactions which we will explain later.

It should be noted that Dash is the first decentralized autonomous organization and that it uses two layers in its architecture to lead the network.

On the one hand we have the first level with the miners who are responsible for the security of the network and where the transactions are recorded in the blockchain, and on the other hand we have the second level consisting of "Masternodes" which make it possible for the crypto dashboard from Dash to enjoy advanced features.

Dash first appeared in January 2014, it started being called XCoin using the XCO code, a month later it was called Daskcoin but it wasn't quite convincing. In the third month, in March, it was in fact changed to Dash, which is the name we know it by today.

Dash is a play on words that stands for "Digital Cash", that is digital money.

In the first two days of the launch, 1.9 million coins were minted, which represents about a quarter of Dash's current issue.

According to CoinmarketCap, in June 2017 the daily volume of Dash was about $100 million per day and market capitalization exceeded $1.4 billion.

Dash shares many features with Bitcoin and other major cryptocurrencies. The main point in common is the ability to send cash digitally over the Internet.

However, there are also some differences between Dash and Bitcoin including speed, cost, and governance. In all these aspects, the Dash is better positioned than the rest of the cryptocurrencies.

But without a doubt, the main advantage and difference between the cryptocurrency Dash and the Bitcoin is privacy. Both currencies operate through blockchains that allow financial transactions to be carried out without intermediaries.

Like Bitcoin, the cryptocurrency Dash guarantees anonymity as it is not obliged to reveal personal information (name, address). However, the big difference is that the solid coding of the Dash blockchain prevents the tracking of your transactions and thus ensures anonymity.

A Valid Alternative to Bitcoin

The Dash managed to improve the original idea of Bitcoin in terms of speed, cost and governance. Let's review these three crucial points one at a time.

Speed

The transaction speed between Dash and Bitcoin is not comparable. Confirming Bitcoin transactions can take more than 10 minutes. The Dash (cryptocurrency) completes a similar transaction in just 4 seconds. The speed difference is amazing.

Costs

Bitcoin transaction fees are around $6. The Dash reduced this rate to less than half a US dollar. However, Dash cryptocurrency fees are expected to increase in line with revenue.

Governance

The Dash demonstrates how changes in currency development can be incorporated without the need for hard forks or bifurcations. The concept of hard fork refers to the implementation of two different solutions. Bitcoin has incorporated several hard forks in its development. Bitcoin

Cash is an example of a currency separating from its main currency, Bitcoin. The Dash manages this type of process through a voting system, which accelerates the implementation of changes.

How the Dash is issued

The issuance of new Dash cryptocurrency coins occurs through a process of mining. This process is the most common way of crypto coins to reward users who record transactions in the blockchain. The time it takes for the Dash to "pull" a block is less than two and a half minutes.

The newly issued Dash cryptocurrency coins are divided into three groups: miners: about 45% of new coins are given to miners to encourage high electronic participation in the blockchain process;

- masternodes: they also receive about 45% of the new number;

- development team: the remaining 10% is used to finance and support the marketing, customer service and development team.

You may not know the terms miners and masternodes, so let's see what they mean!

What are masternodes

Masternodes are based on the Proof-of-Stake (PoS) algorithm, a concept that allows the user to mine or validate transactions in bulk based on the amount of coins in their possession.

Bitcoin, for example, is based on the concept of Proof of Work (PoW). This implies that its blockchain must be validated by all nodes on the network.

The difference between masternodes and standard nodes is that the former reduce the number of nodes required to validate to carry out a transaction. This makes the total number of nodes manageable and solves transaction scalability problems.

As an economic incentive for their work, masternodes receive 45% of the new cryptocurrencies issued. Governance also has an impact on the future direction and course of the currency.

Unlike minors, masternodes don't need to protect the network via PoW, but they use secondary functions like PrivateSend, InstantSend and the governance functions we talked about above.

PrivateSend and InstantSend functions

PrivateSend and InstantSend are two additional functions of the Dash, which are based on the management masternodes. These functions have the following advantages;InstantSend allows you to sendtransfers in less than a second, while PrivateSend hides the details of the transfer and information about the sender and recipient. This is made possible by the fact that this feature mixes all transactions, making traceability difficult.

How the price moves

Between 2014 and 2016, the change in the price of cryptocurrencies was reduced. Since 2017, the price has taken off and volatility has risen tremendously, thenthe price fell sharply.

The Dash crossed the magical $100 line in March 2017. This first bullish move was just the beginning, reaching $200 in May to reach $400 in August. Over the next three months, the price remained at a range of $250 to $400, until the wide range of cryptocurrencies caused a spike.

In November 2017, the price continued to rise until it stopped at around $1600. This was its highest peak since then, the value of the cryptocurrency from Dash maintained a downtrend to reach $175 in June 2019.

Opinions

The advantages of Dash in terms of speed, cost, privacy and governance have given this cryptocurrency a solid niche in this new world of financial products. However, we think we have to wait a little longer to see if it can be extended.

Zcash

Zcash is a cryptocurrency that was born at the end of October 2016, and was listed at 33 Bitcoins in the first minutes of the negotiations.

The Zcash cryptocurrency automatically hides the identity of senders and recipients, as well as the amount of all transactions we carry out in its blockchain. Only those with a view key will be able to see the content of the operations.

Zcash is based on peer-reviewed cryptographic research. It has been programmed by a team of IT security engineers on an open-source platform. The whole programming has been based on the proven code of Bitcoin. Zcash uses advanced digital-cryptographic techniques, as "zero knowledge tests". The goal of this technique is to ensure the validity of transactions without showing additional information about them.

This algorithm is called zero-knowledge proofs and allows the creator of the transaction to include a validity test in it, without the need to transmit any information other than the fact that the transaction is true. In other words, no information is transmitted that anyone can read.

You can receive, store and spend money while showing transactions to only chosen parties, instead of showing transactions to everyone on the Internet. This is a big difference with Bitcoin and Ethereum, which cannot function without exposing all of their transactions to anyone on the Internet.

After debuting on the currency trading platforms in October 2016, the Zcash reached $1,000 per unit, rising to the level of the pioneer Bitcoin, currently around $100. Zcash is attracting the interest of Russian, Chinese, Venezuelan and Brazilian consumers. In Brazil, the currency is also used to pay taxes and utility bills. A maximum production of 21 million units is expected.

User privacy protection is precisely what sets it apart. But this opacity is, as expected, in the spotlight: it does not offer the transparency required by the authorities seeking to prevent it from being used for money laundering, terrorist financing, tax evasion or fraud. Zooko Wilcox, CEO of Zerocoin Electric Coin Company, which operates Zcash, hopes this feature will help companies overcome reluctance to use their currency as a reliable alternative to traditional state-controlled ones.

CHAPTER ELEVEN
ETHEREUM

Ethereum (ETH) is an open-source software platform based on blockchain technology, which allows developers to build and release decentralized applications. It is actually much more than a cryptocurrency, which is only a part of Ethereum's offering.

Bitcoin and Ethereumareboth built using distributed public network technology - known as blockchain. All their other features are different.

Bitcoin offers a single application - a peer-to-peer digital currency system that allows online payments. It is basically a coin in its essential form.

While Bitcoin uses blockchain technology to track who owns Bitcoins, Ethereum uses blockchain as a platform for running almost any decentralized application. Bloomberg once described it as "shared software that can be used by everyone but is tamper-proof". So the possibilities are truly endless!

Where does ethereum come from and who is its founder

Ethereum was originally created by VitalikButerin, a cryptocurrency researcher and programmer who previously worked on Bitcoin in 2013. An online crowdfunding done in 2014 was the key part of the platform's funding. The system went into operation on July 30, 2015, and was populated by 11.5 million "coins" ready for pre-sale.

How Ethereum works

In the Ethereum blockchain, instead of "mining" as with Bitcoin, users work to earn "Ether", a type of cryptocurrency that powers the wider network. In addition to being a tradable cryptocurrency, Ether is also used by developers to pay for services on the Ethereum network.

Investing in Ethereum CFDs and other cryptocurrencies without risk

The best way to practice cryptocurrency CFD trading is to open a free demo trading account. Both beginner and advanced traders can start from a demo account. This provides the entire live trading experience, including all the real-time information and analysis from the live markets, even without using your capital.

History of Ethereum

Since Ethereum's inception in 2015, its cryptocurrency, Ether has shown slow progress in its first year. But 2017 was a completely different story. The cryptocurrency started the year with a meager pricing of $7.76, and by the end of the year it was over $700, an increase of over 9000%! Unlike Bitcoin, that set its record at the end of 2017, Ethereumwas at his top in January 2018, reaching a peak of over $ 1300 in mid-January.

As with other cryptocurrencies, however, 2018 proved to be a test year for Ether, and its price has progressively declined since then, settling around $130 towards the end of the year. 2019 saw a first upward phase, peaking on June 26 at 361.61, and then returning to decline, closing the year at 127.55. The first month of 2020 the price resumed an uptrend.

As the public has become more and more informed about how to trade Ethereum and Bitcoin, more interest has been generated. The case of the Aether is even more interesting. It had a steep price hike almost exclusively because it is very much like Bitcoin, and investors wanted to jump on the boat early when prices were moderately low.

Of course, as with all markets, what goes up can go down. As well as 2017's fantastic gains were driven by some sort of multiplier effect of rising prices that pushed investor demand, which in turn pushed prices higher, thus triggering higher demand once the market started selling out in 2018, we saw a reverse reaction. A correction in investor demand frightened by prices, which has led to an increase in sales, driving prices down and thus further holding back demand.

Investingin Ethereum

The first half of 2019 got off to a good start for Ether investors, with prices exceeding USD 350 at one point. But in the second half of the year, the cryptocurrency returned most of these gains but still holds more than 15% above its annual opening price in November 2019.

While trading is currently in neutral mode, a break below USD 150 could clearly be considered a bearish signal and lead to a decline towards and even significantly below the psychological important level at USD 100 in 2020.

In any case, given the current situation of uncertainty due to the coronavirus pandemic, we recommend that you always keep yourself updated on the latest economic and financial news before making any investment.

Recommended strategies to invest in Ethereum

Technical trading and proven tools should be applied to the chart when trading Ethereum, which in turn could be a good basis for successful trading Ether CFD against the US Dollar. Considering its volatility, scalping strategies should be applied in intraday trading.

Those looking to trade ETH/USD need to prepare for some price instability, where steady profits could turn into losses in a split second.

A "flash crash" occurred on June 21, 2017, when the price dropped from around $320 to 10 cents. He recovered later, but investors and traders certainly took a hit during that time. Mr. Adam White, Vice President of GDAX, explained that an investor placed a multimillion-dollar short selling Ether order at 12:30 pm on Wednesday. The size of the order caused a drop in the price of the currency (which was already volatile).

As is well known, when the price reaches the stop loss, it creates additional momentum and potentially strong movement in a very short amount of time.Each closing of a buy position is an automatic sell on the market and vice versa.

Trading with ETHEREUM/USD

Proper money management is the foundation of any trader's success or failure. When used correctly in high trend cases, it can produce a great return on investment (ROI).Due to the high volatility, losses may also occur, so it is extremely important to use proper money management. Market stability could be achieved when power shifts from investors looking to profit from price fluctuations, to consumers actually using cryptocurrencies.

When that happens, volatility should stabilize. Traders should treat crypto trading the same way they would treat any investment in the initial start-up phase. Furthermore, intraday traders should definitely focus on the most important trading sessions, as the major trading centers provide the highest volatility in ETH/USD. Fortunately, the MetaTrader 4 (MT4) platform offers the tool during the main market sessions - 24/5.

Bitcoin VS Ethereum

In 2017, the Ether was very hot. The sentiment towards Etherum was very positive at that time.

Of course, some of this sentiment has cooled along with the decline in the value of the ETH/USD CFD pair from its 2017 highs. It is a general truth, however, that sentiment will decline for any market that has undergone a severe value correction.

There are investors who believe that cryptocurrency prices will recover. One factor in Ethereum's favor is the potential of its platform, and in 2019 we started to see signs of institutional adoption of the technology.

Banking giant JP Morgan made headlines in early 2019 when it launched its JPM coin, which was touted as the first cryptocurrency backed by a US bank. While many news outlets have acknowledged that this new digital token uses blockchain technology, what many have not mentioned is that JPM's proprietary Quromblackchain is actually an enterprise-grade version of Ethereum. Where all this will actually lead is far from clear, of course, but this kind of concrete example of real use of Ethereum technology could serve to rekindle confidence.

That said, we must point out that the vast majority of Ethereum trading and cryptocurrency trading in general is pure speculation, and the current utility value for users is close to zero. Not many people use blockchain protocols, unlike many people who trade crypto. We may also see regulations coming in terms of trading, issuing and holding new currencies in the near future.

In 2018, the bubble burst and both currencies saw their price plummet, but never reached historical lows. 2019 saw an interesting new increase for Bitcoin, which was also reflected in the chart of those who had decided to invest in Ethereum, but with much less intensity.

In early 2020, Bitcoin nearly skyrocketed against the US dollar driven by uncertainty in traditional markets as many investors view it as a safe haven asset. Despite this, BTC collapsed coinciding with the stock market crash in mid-March when several European governments decreed the confinement of their citizens and the closure of economic activity following the Covid-19 pandemic.

Bitcoin was close to $5,000 as investors preferred to turn to traditional safe haven markets such as gold. At the end of June 2020, the most valuable cryptocurrency on the market recouped what was lost at the beginning of the year exceeding $9,000, according to the Coinmarketcap website.

Ethereum took a similar path in its price movement against the USD. ETH/USD was worth $7.65 on January 1, 2017 and a year later it was above $1,300. Between 2018 and 2019, like Bitcoin, its price plummeted and sometimes even dropped to $100. In 2020, Ethereum's chart was similar to Bitcoin, bouncing to around 250USD in February, falling in mid-March to 106 USDand recovering what was lost in the following months, to USD 244 at the end of June.

Who will have the best results in the future? This is very difficult to say, but Bitcoin's leadership role could give Bitcoin a bullish continuation, and reach new highs. It is likely that the highest Bitcoin price has not yet been quoted.

From this point of view, the Bitcoin chart seems to have the advantage, as it is considered the market favorite. The difference is clearly seen when compared to Ethereum, which although it has had its rallies, it does not move the same volumes.

However, both instruments have risen and decreased a lot over the past three years, so keep in mind that there is always a risk that prices will move sharply in the face of unexpected news.

Each cryptocurrency has a different method and set of rules that go hand in hand with its creation, distribution and protection or security. It is useful to know the details of each cryptocurrency, whether it is Bitcoin or Ethereum trading, the important thing is to be comfortable with its parameters.

There are several fundamental differences between the two cryptocurrencies, below hereare a couple of examples to understand if bitcoin or ethereum is better.

The Bitcoin supply is limited to a maximum of 21 million, while the Ethereum supply has limited growth every year.

Bitcoin was created in 2009 and has a block time of 10 minutes, while in Ether it is around 14 seconds.

It's not mandatory to trade an instrument you like, but having faith in its long-term potential and design could make it easier to invest in Ethereum or Bitcoin and aim for bigger goals. This particular factor is very personal and depends on each trader.

Bitcoin remains the best known cryptocurrency and seems to be no threat that it could lose that position. Therefore, the possibility that Bitcoin will be able to maintain this status over the next few years is entirely acceptable.

The advantage of Bitcoin's leadership role is that it could attract more investors. Cryptocurrencies in general, but Bitcoin specifically, may be increasingly attractive to large investors, perhaps even institutional investors. Bitcoin is well positioned to receive even more attention than in the past, Ethereum may receive a lower volume of investment, but this remains to be seen.

Bystaying abreast of certain developments within each cryptocurrency, you also gain key insights into possible price reactions. For example, the Bitcoin Cash hard fork, far from the original Bitcoin, had a temporary impact on prices, so tracking trends like this can be important.

From this point of view, Ethereum is slightly more stable than Bitcoin, taking into account the most recent split. Either way, it doesn't hurt to monitor each cryptocurrency's latest trends and see if either of them offers less risk and more stability. This too can change from month to month, as the trends and news updates in this space continue to be dense and fast.

Trading is not only based on long-term potential or fundamentals, but also on the volatility and price actionof a cryptocurrency. This is especially important when trading Ethereum or Bitcoin in shorter time periods for example.

Slow moving instruments do not offer attractive trading setups because it is difficult to make a profit by entering and exiting if the price goes up or down. Volatility is the key, as it offers more opportunities for traders.

Price action is alsofundamental- it is important to review Ethereum or Bitcoin trading charts and familiarize yourself with the tool. This is even more true for short-term charts, where price action can sometimes be quick and unexpected. Some tools also fit your trading style more naturally. You should always make sure you know how to trade Bitcoin CFDs before trading with real money.

CHAPTER TWELVE
HALVING BITCOIN

2020 was a historic year for financial markets, with all types of assets experiencing great market volatility and extraordinary price changes. However, it will be this May 2020 that will shake up the cryptocurrency market.

The "Halving Bitcoin" event predicts that production of this digital currency will be reduced by 50%. This event is written in the rules of the underlying Bitcoin code with no one in control of the process, creating unique trading opportunities to know this tool and its properties well.

Halving Bitcoin

Bitcoin's unique digital design predicts that every four years there is a seismic shift in the cryptocurrency. For the third time in 11 years of history, in May 2020 it will undergo another major change.

To understand the halving of Bitcoin it is important to understand the basic principles of Bitcoin itself.

The code predicts that only 21 million Bitcoins can be produced. About 18 million Bitcoins have already been produced through the so-called "crypto-mining". Bitcoin mining is abig business where miners use high specification computers to help process Bitcoin transactions. These transactions are added as "blocks" to the blockchain ledger, which is the technology behind cryptomination.

The miners doing this work need considerable computing power, which comes at a cost. That is why when a block is added to the blockchain, the miner who worked it is compensated with Bitcoins, also known as a "miner's grant" or "block grant".

This is also how new Bitcoins are added to the supply chain, as a fixed amount of new Bitcoins are released in each bulk transaction. Miners can sell their earned bitcoins through an exchange.

The Bitcoin halving refers to the 50% reduction in compensation to the miners who maintain the Bitcoin network. What excites traders and investors the most is what could happen to the Bitcoin price during this period.

When and how it will happen

The Bitcoin halving is performed, as we anticipated, about once every four years or whenever 210,000 blocks are mined. The halving in May 2020 will take place in block 630,000. Although blocks are added to the blockchain approximately every 10 minutes, the exact date and time can be difficult to pinpoint, as the compound effect of small variations can make a big difference.

Many analysts predicted that Bitcoin's halving would likely take place between May 10-12. It looks like it will be like this.

According to the most accurate estimates, the 2020 bitcoin having will be on May 12th.

This halving will drop the miner's rewards from 12.5 bitcoins per block to 6.25 bitcoins.

When Bitcoin was first released, the reward for the miner was 50 bitcoins.On November 28, 2012, the amount dropped to 25 bitcoins.On July 9, 2016, it dropped to 12.5 bitcoin.

However, what excites most cryptocurrency traders, investors and enthusiasts is the fact that the amount of bitcoins entering the supply chain will be reduced while demand will remain at the same level. This shift in supply versus demand could help raise the price of the cryptocurrency.

Since Bitcoin halving has already happened twice in the past, let's take a look at the change in the price of bitcoin at that time.

While it is impossible to say for sure how prices will react to the 2020 Bitcoin halving, we can see how the Bitcoin price has reacted to previous bitcoins.

In both previous Bitcoin halvings, the price of bitcoin saw its value rise a year earlier and a year later. Both cases were in a general context of cryptocurrency market growth and global economic stability, which makes 2020 a very different year due to the impact of Covid-19.

Another important factor to remember is that this event is highly anticipated and therefore part of the potential increase in the value of bitcoin may already be included in the quoted price before the Bitcoin halving. However, to capitalize on any potential Bitcoin halvingmovement, it is essential to have the right tools in place.

A great way to get started is to open a free demo trading

account to practice your trading ideas and strategies in a virtual environment until you feel ready to invest with real money. It is a great way to develop your skills until you are ready for a real trading account. Moreover, you'll have access to a variety of benefits, including free market analysis, access to advanced Trading Central indicators and tools, and much, much more.

CHAPTER THIRTEEN
HOW TO TRADE

Anyone who is minimally interested in learning about cryptography has taken part in some form of trading. As more and more attention is being paid, new participants want to enter the market and get their slice of crypto cake.

<u>how to trade cryptocurrency</u>

So, you have some money you want to invest. How do you intend to proceed? The portals that connect our world to the crypto worlds are called "exchanges". There are a lot of exchanges out there, but before you choose to invest in any of them, there are a few things you need to watch out for. Let's call it the "Exchange Checklist".

<u>Validity</u>

Before doing anything, first make sure that the exchange is available in your area. For example, Coinbase, one of the largest exchanges, is not available in India and Indonesia. So before you do anything, check this out.

<u>Reputation</u>

The next thing you need to check is the reputation of the exchange. Are people happy with their services? Has it been hacked recently? How safe is it? Have people complained? Twitter and Reddit are great sources to check this out.

<u>Exchange rates</u>

The next step is exchange rates. Different exchanges have their own exchange rates which can vary. Do your homework here and look for 3 or 4 exchanges and their rates.

Security

Always choose exchanges that need an identity verification from you. While they may take some time, they are easily 100 times safer and more secure than anonymous exchanges. Ultimately, it's your hard earned money. You have to take an extra step to keep them safe.

How to start trading

To protect your cryptocurrency, you need to have a wallet. The wallet saves your private key and public address which helps you to store, send and receive cryptocurrencies. While this should be very clear to you, let's take a quick overview of the meaning of the private key and the public address:

- private key: the private key gives you the right to log in and send your money;

- public address: this is the address where everyone will send you money.

One thing to remember before continuing, the public address is what you will give others to send your money.

DO NOT and we repeat DO NOT give your private key. The private key is for you and you only. If you give your private key to strangers, they will have access to your money.

All crypto wallets fall into the following two categories:

- warm preservation;

- cold room.

Hot storage vs. cold storage

Before we go deeper, let's use an analogy to understand the difference between the two. The warm wallet is like the wallet you carry in your pocket. It gives you easy access to your money, but is quite vulnerable.

The cold room, on the other hand, is like your savings account. Highly impractical for everyday use, but extremely safe when comparing the two.

Warm preservation

An internet-connected wallet is called "hot storage". Below are some examples of hot wallets,but before we get to the heart of each of these wallets, let's look at the pros and cons of hot wallets.

Hot Wallets pros:

- it gives you quick, easy and immediate access to your funds;

- getting easy support in different devices;

- very easy to use and ideal for beginners.

Hot Walletscons:

- vulnerable to hackers and cybercrime;

- unless the keys have been carefully saved, if the device is damaged, the wallet will also be damaged;

- the device where the warm wallet is stored, such as the laptop, phone, etc. is also susceptible to physical theft.

So now that you have a general idea of what a Hot Wallet is, let's look at some of the more popular types.

Hot Wallet: exchange wallets

This is the simplest wallet you can ever create. In fact, if you followed our instructions and created your Coinbase account, guess what? You have already created your exchange wallet!

The benefits are obvious. It is already linked to your account and gives you quick and easy access for trading. In any case, this also means that you are vulnerable to attack. Remember that exchanges are a constant target for hackers. We recommend that you do not keep an important part of your cryptos in exchange portfolios, but only keep what you need for trading.

Hot Wallet: desktop wallets and mobile wallets

Desk wallets and mobile wallets have become increasingly popular. Desk wallets offer more security than exchange wallets. Their setup is also very simple. All you have to do is downloadingthe client to your laptop/desktop and you're done! MultiBit provides an excellent desktop wallet to store Bitcoins.

However, there is a problem with desk wallets. They are not the most flexible options. After all, wallets cannot be accessed from any other desktop, apart from the one where it was downloaded.

That's why, for more users who want flexibility, mobile wallets are a pretty affordable option. Setup is as simple as downloading an application to your phone. MyCelium is a pretty popular mobile wallet for both Android and iOS.

The problem with both of these wallets is that, being stored on an internet-connected device, they are vulnerable to viruses and hackers.

Hot Wallet: multi-brand wallet

Have you ever seen one of those old school lockers that require multiple keys to open? Or those treasure chests that need 3 or 4 people to be opened at the same time?

This will give you an idea of how multi-signature wallets or multi-sig wallets work. Most ICOs use multisig wallets to raise and hold their funds. So why would you want to use multisig wallets?

To protect against corruption: we have all heard stories of ICOs making millions of dollars in their sale to the crowd. What's stopping all these developers from taking the money and running away? Human greed is powerful, after all. In situations like these, it is much more prudent to accept funds in a multi-digit wallet, where all the money and power does not depend on a single human being.

More security and insurance: since the funds are in a multisig wallet, they will automatically be safer because they no longer depend on the whims of a single person. Moreover, if I send my money to an address with multisig wallets, I will also feel reassured that my funds are not being mishandled.

Cold room

While hot wallets offer great accessibility, the fact remains that they are extremely insecure. That is why it is more prudent to save most of the funds in a ColdWallet. A Cold Wallet is completely cut off from the internet, which automatically keeps it safe from hackers and viruses.

Examples of cold storage wallets include:

- hardware wallet;

- paper wallet.

Before learning how to set up each of these aspects, let's try to understand the pros and cons of refrigerated wallets.

Pros:

- 100% safe from hackers and viruses;

- a great place to store and safeguardyour coins for a long period of time.

Cons:

- extremely impractical for day to day transactions;

- it is not suitable for beginners;

- it is still vulnerable to human inattention.

Well, now that we've covered that, let's figure out how to set up Cold Wallets.

Cold room - Hardware Wallets

Hardware Wallets are physical devices where you can store your own encrypted currency.

The most common form of Hardware Wallet is the USB style which was advocated by the French company Ledger. The reasons that have brought so much popularity to Hardware Wallets are the security and storage capacity of a Cold Wallet. This makes transactions very simple. Basically, it works and nullifies the biggest drawback of Cold Wallets.

Pros of Hardware Wallets

As this is a cold wallet, your private key will be safe. Keys are stored in the secure area of a microcontroller and cannot be transferred outside the device

They are designed to be elegant and can be carried easily.

Transactions are extremely easy. All you have to do is enter your wallet and then follow the instructions provided to make your transactions. The wallets UI interface is very simple to use.

Extremely safe and secure. As for the writing, there have been no cases of hardware wallet hacking.

It has the ability to store multiple addresses for sending your funds.

The wallet is protected by a pincode, so even if it falls into the wrong hands, they will not be able to access your funds. By entering the wrong pin code 3 times, the wallet will be closed. In case of closure, it is still possible to recover the funds by following the details of the restoration.

Cons of Hardware Wallets

Like all products, these wallets can also have design flaws. Recently, a design flaw was discovered in Ledger which made it potentially vulnerable. Ledger has faced the problem ever since.

It is a real physical item, which means it can be stolen or damaged.

They are not the most versatile when it comes to storing cryptocurrencies. Trezor stores 10 types of coins, while Ledger stores about 23.

Finally, you will need to trust that the company that is creating your Hardware Wallet is ethical and will not try to interfere with the design of it. It calls for trust in an environment that should be trustless.

So, now that the pros and cons have been addressed, let's see how you can create it! Without doubt the two most popular Hardware Wallets in the world are Trezor and Ledger Nano S.

Trezor

Trezor is a Prague-based company that has made one of the

simplest and easiest to use Hardware Wallets ever. It's really stupidly simple to use and the design is so sleek and light that you can take it anywhere. It is compatible with Windows, Mac and Linux and its use is simple, just plug it into your laptop and connect it with one of the following interfaces:

- My Trezor;

- Multibit;

- Electrum.

Ledger Nano S

Ledger, is a Paris-based company that has given the crypto community one of the most user-friendly, stylish and popular Hardware Wallets. They store all your data in a smartcard that keeps them safe from hackers. To use it, simply connect it to your laptop and connect it to one of the following interfaces:

- Mycelium;

- Electric;

- Green address;

- Greenbits;

- CoinKite;

- Copay;

- MyEtherWallet.

Cold room - Paper Wallets

Paper Wallets are often considered the safest way to store your cryptocurrency. The idea behind a Paper Wallet is very simple. You set up an offline wallet by following a few simple instructions and then simply print the private and public keys on a piece of paper. The keys will also be printed in the form of a QR code which you can scan to gain access to your funds.

So, the questions you need to ask yourself now are: do you need a Paper Wallet?

The answeris:it depends.

Are you going to use your funds fairly regularly? Then no. Paper Wallets will be a nuisance when used this way. Then you better get yourself a hardware portfolio.

However, if you are planning to hold your funds for an extended period of time, then, without a shadow of a doubt, the Paper Wallet is the way to go.

CHAPTER FOURTEEN
TOP 10 CRYPTOCURRENCY INVESTORS

The popularity and values of cryptocurrencies today are undeniable.

Far from the initial skepticism of 2009, when Satoshi Nakamoto published the historic "White Paper" with which he presented Bitcoin, this and other cryptocurrencies have gained an important place in the contemporary financial world, and more and more products and services can be paid for with cryptocurrencies.

Although cryptocurrencies have had strong price fluctuations that may have raised some doubts among potential investors, the truth is that most of those who have opted to invest their money in cryptocurrencies have achieved good economic results.

This list ranges from those who have built great fortunes by investing and trading with cryptocurrencies, to others who have created some of the cryptocurrencies that are among the most popular today.

1. The first is Chris Larsen, co-founder of Ripple, American, a graduate of Stanford. He owns 17% of the company that controls 61 billion of the 100 billion XRP tokens that will be issued in total. His fortune in cryptocurrency is estimated at $7.5 billion.

2. Then, we have Joseph Lubin, a Canadian creator of ConsenSys, and co-founder of Ethereum, another cryptocurrency of the most used today. Lubin studied at

Princeton and his fortune is estimated to be between 2 and 3 billion.

3. There are Winklevoss brothers (Tyler and Cameron) co-founders of Winklevoss Capital. They started investing in Bitcoin starting in 2012 and created the Gemini Exchange, which is widely recognized in the cryptocurrency world. His fortune is around $1 billion.

4. On this list, there is also Matthew Mellon, who passed away just as we are writing this article, who was a Bitcoin investor when the majority of the public still did not know about cryptocurrencies and who, after selling his Bitcoin had invested $2 million in Ripple, also obtaining a large capital gain from this investment. Now, after his death, the question iswho will take care of the Ripple package that was his property and that he had declared to keep stored in various Hardware Wallets in the name of different people and in various places in the United States.

5. In the world of cryptocurrencies, everyone knows about the CoinBase Exchange, whose mobile application is among the most downloaded in the United States. Its CEO is the American Brian Armstrong, who studied at Rice University and who,thanks largely to CoinBase, has brought his fortune to almost $1000 million.

6.Matthew Roszak is an American entrepreneur who initially made his fortune with several software companies before delving into the world of cryptocurrencies. His investments in cryptocurrency as well as his Tally Capital and Bloq projects have allowed him to build a fortune of about $900 million.

7. Another Canadian in the ranking is Anthony Di Iorio, who

studied at Ryerson University and has invested in several cryptocurrencies, including Qtum, Verchain and ZCash. He is among the co-founders of Ethereum. His fortune exceeds $750 million.

8. An American Brock Pierce, administrator of the Bitcoin Foundation, was one of the first to bet on cryptocurrencies. During the first decade of the 21st century, he founded Internet Gaming Entertainment, a highly successful internet gaming platform. His fortune exceeds $700 million.

9. Another important name to list is Michael Novogratz, an American CEO of Galaxy Digital, one of the largest cryptocurrency trading houses on Wall Street, who firmly believed in the cryptocurrencies in which he has invested millions of dollarsand this has allowed to increase his fortune now estimated at around $700 million.

10. The list ends with the Chinese Changpeng Zhao, a graduate of McGill University, is also one of the brightest minds in cryptocurrencies. He has been involved in several cryptocurrency projects, including his most recent and already legendary, Binance, which appears out of nowhere in 2017 to become the world's largest exchange in less than a year. His fortune ranges from $1 to $2 billion.

CHAPTER FIFTEEN
CRYPTOCURRENCY IN THE FUTURE

Web giants and central banks find them particularly interesting,but the Financial Action Task Force (the intergovernmental organisation founded at the initiative of the G7 to develop policies to combat money laundering) - fears that they may also be used in illegal contexts to promote money laundering and finance international terrorism. Cryptocurrency, which has been in use for more than ten years now, has various potentials but also numerous risks, about which we have not yet been able to shed any definitive light.

Blockchain and Cryptography: the ingredients of cryptocurrencies

Cryptocurrencies are valuable digital representations that use peer-to-peer technologies (i.e. between two devices directly, without the need for intermediaries) to purchase goods and services. The nodes of the networks are made up of computers that can potentially be distributed all over the world, on them are run special programs that perform coin purse functions. Transactions and release take place collectively on the network, so there is neither centralised management nor control authority.

The decentralised control of each cryptocurrency works through a blockchain, which acts as a database of public financial transactions. The blockchain consists of a constantly growing list of records, called blocks, which are linked and protected by encryption.

Bitcoin: the cryptocurrency of the mysterious nakamoto

There are over 6,000 cryptocurrencies in the world. The first to be known on a large scale, and perhaps the most famous, is Bitcoin. It was created in 2009 by a mysterious computer scientist whose only known alias, Satoshi Nakamoto. To date, a Bitcoin is worth just under 9 thousand euros, a value that it has maintained with some fluctuations over the past year. A limited number of Bitcoins are expected to be issued over the next few decades: 21 million units by 2140. Despite their popularity, the security of Bitcoins is not certain: the writing at the base of the blockchain could hide some imperfections easily exploitable by cyber criminals.

Ethereum and Altcoins

Over the years, other cryptocurrencies have emerged, Altcoins, which claim to offer users more advanced privacy and security requirements than their big sister. One of the best known is the Ethereum, born in 2015. It is able to securely digitize the conclusion of a wide variety of contracts: financial transactions, electoral systems, domain name registration, crowdfunding platforms, intellectual property and insurance. The main difference to Bitcoin is that the Ethereum is not only a network for the exchange of monetary value but a network that supports a multitude of transactions. Ethereum contracts pay for the use of its computing power through a cryptocurrency, Ether, which also has the function of supporting the platform. To date, an Ether is worth just under 300 euros, since its inception it has only exceeded 1000 euros in 2018.

Potentials and risks

After the financial crisis of 2008, cryptocurrencies have enjoyed considerable success, presenting themselves in the world of markets as the new way of giving and receiving guarantees in financial transactions. Buying them, however, is not for everyone; on the contrary, due to their volatility, cryptocurrencies are considered a high risk investment. As of today, cryptocurrencies cannot be considered currencies, but financial investments. They are not comparable to money for two reasons: first they are not a widespread and efficient payment instrument, the second reason is the instability of their value. As financial investments they have a high volatility, they can therefore please risk lovers and those who appreciate their presumed anonymity.

Anonymity: reality or utopia?

The standard blockchain we started to know with Nakamoto is not a totally anonymized system but a pseudo-anonymized one, it is in fact possible to trace Bitcoin flows very effectively and, consequently, to trace the transactions made to specific identities present in the system. As far as the legality of the transactions is concerned, everything depends on the type of platform on which it is traded. If someone wants to commit an offence, they can easily go to the Bitcoin: all they need to do is keeping away from regulated markets (platforms that group anonymous codes) that respect the rules of the countries where they operate and instead choose platforms that do not care about legality. In regulated markets, in fact, not only does the blockchain make it possible to trace transactions and discover offences, but market operators have the right to intervene and possibly notify the competent authorities of the country in question.

The Zuckerberg Libra and stablecoins

For some years now there has also been talk of Stablecoins, a new type of cryptocurrency. The most famous example is the Libra, launched in 2019 by Facebook creator Mark Zuckerberg. But the project is still frozen, while another Stablecoin, Gram, designed by Pavel Durov, died before it even saw the light, invalidated by the American Sec.

But how does this new generation of cryptocurrencies differ from the Bitcoin? In order to overcome the instability of the value of cryptocurrencies, some issuers promise to anchor the trend in a basket of existing coins or public financial assets. But how credible is this promise, given that we are not talking about sovereign states, but about private operators? Even Stablecoins remain bets. What is certain is that the Financial Action Task Force has sent a report on these new cryptocurrencies to the G20 finance ministers and national bank governors, which it is monitoring from 2014, in which it reiterates the risk that they will be used for money laundering.

Digital public coin

This year, however, following the digital opening imposed by the Covid emergency, central banks have become interested in the world of cryptocurrencies and are preparing to mint coins made of bits. According to the Bri (Banque des RèglementsInternationaux), 80% of the central banks are working on it, 40% have started experiments, 10% have set up pilot projects. The Fed is also carrying out research with the MIT on the subject and China launched a programme at the beginning of the year, in open challenge to the dominance of the dollar.

It is only a matter of time before the central banks will sooner or later have to produce digital public money. However, the issuance of this currency is a Pandora's box, because it opens up technical and political questions both in monetary policy and in banking and financial supervision. So we just have to wait.

CHAPTER SIXTEEN
LIBRA FACEBOOK

Libra is the cryptocurrency announced by Facebook in June 2019 and promises to revolutionize the universe of payments and financial transactions. His announcement aroused praise and consensus, but also doubts and criticisms. In the months following the launch, financial authorities around the world moved to verify the controversial aspects, some of the world's top economic and financial leaders expressed opposing positions and some of the organizations that initially supported Libra pulled back.

The latest in order of time is Vodafone: the company, initially among the supporters of the project, has made it known that the resources previously allocated to Libra will be redirected to its consolidated digital payment service M-Pesa, currently active in 6 African nations. To this day, many people fear that cryptocurrency will never see the light, despite Facebook, until recently, seemed willing to continue on its way. On the other hand, at the end of January Mark Zuckerberg announced the international launch of WhatsApp Pay, a payment system via chat. It is not yet clear how the new solution will fit into the "Facebook ecosystem" of payments. But let's see what Libra is and how it works, what has happened so far and what to expect from the future.

The Launch of Libra

"We want to make it easy for everyone to send and receive

money just like our apps to share messages and photos" wrote founder and CEO Mark Zuckerberg on June 18, 2019 in a post on the social network with which he broke the news and provided additional details. The project, which should take off in 2020, is not limited to creating a new cryptocurrency but involves the development of an entire ecosystem: a global financial infrastructure accessible to billions of people. The initiative is governed by the Libra Association, a non-profit association based in Geneva, which currently includes about 20 members including companies, non-profit organizations and international academic institutions, but the goal is to reach 100 members by year. In the meantime, however, after the official announcement, Libra has come under pressure from many quarters, particularly over the issue of its regulation. In the first week of July, the US Federal Reserve declared that Facebook's plans to create a digital currency "cannot go on" until all controversial issues are clarified. The company initially responded that it relied on constructive dialogue. Then, at the beginning of August, Mark Zuckerberg, in a post, took a kind of backtrack, warning that Libra and its subsidiary Calibra could experience significant delays or even never be launched. A tactic to counter the pressure and criticism that rained down on him from many sides since he announced the Facebook cryptocurrency?

In the first week of July, the US Federal Reserve stated that Facebook's plans to create a digital currency "cannot go on" until all controversial issues are clarified. The company initially responded that it relied on constructive dialogue. Then, at the beginning of August, Mark Zuckerberg, in a post, took a sort of backtrack, warning that Libra and the subsidiary Calibra could experience significant delays or even never be launched. A tactic to counter the pressure and criticism that rained down on him from many sides since he announced the Facebook cryptocurrency? Or an authentic back-of-front?

One thing is certain: all the banks want to see this clearly. On September 16, representatives of the US Federal Reserve, the Bank of England and 24 other central banks met with representatives of the Libra project in the Swiss city of Basel to discuss how the blockchain will operate and the objectives pursued.

Libra's path seems increasingly uphill: at the end of September 2019 some relevant financial partners such as Visa and Mastercard began to review their involvement in Facebook's cryptocurrency, worried about the decisions that regulators will make. After that, in October 2019, Paypal, eBay, Visa, Mastercard and Booking definitively announced their defection. But in the meantime let's see what led to its birth and why.

On June 18, 2019, with a post on Facebook, the founder and CEO of the social network, Mark Zuckerberg, launched the new currency called Libra and at the same time the non-profit association of the same name together with other 28 international organizations around the world. The news had been anticipated the previous week, but for some time, at least for a couple of years, the Internet giant had been working on the operation. For the past year and a half, Facebook has had a fluctuating relationship with cryptocurrencies. On the one hand, it has shown interest, also leaking news on possible acquisitions in this area (for example, Coinbase, a well-known cryptocurrency exchange company). On the other hand, digital currency ads have often been blocked and banned on its platforms for long periods.

The turning point was a gesture by Zuckerberg that was passed over in silence by the media: in January 2018, it acquired a license in Ireland to offer personal loans to its 2.07 billion users. Then over the past six months the interest has gradually become more concrete with various rumors about the issue of a possible cryptocurrency by Facebook, until the official announcement.

Facebook has therefore officially entered the world of payments, more precisely in that of cryptocurrencies. The declared objective is to provide access to the financial system to the approximately 1.7 billion unbanked adults present in the world today, that is, all those who do not have a bank account or similar services.

The founding members

There are three key elements of the Libra project: the association of actors that governs it, the blockchain on which it is based and the cryptocurrency with which it is used. In short, Libra is a non-monolithic ecosystem, which brings together companies, associations and investors from different sectors for the first time. As for the association that governs the project, it is called Libra Association and it is a non-profit based in Geneva, which initially included 28 members including companies, non-profit and multilateral organizations, academic institutions from all over the world.

These organizations join the association by actively participating in the Libra network, running a validation node on the network, and serving in governance in exchange for rewards generated by transaction fees, conversion fees, and deposit interest.

The founding members who in June 2019 pledged to work for the development, dissemination and acceptance of the new cryptocurrency were:

- payments sector: Mastercard, PayPal, PayU (Naspers' fintech arm), Stripe, Visa;

- technology and marketplaces sector: Booking Holdings, eBay, Facebook/Calibra, Farfetch, Lyft, MercadoPago, Spotify AB, Uber Technologies, Inc. ;

- telecommunications sector: Iliad, Vodafone Group;

- blockchain sector: Anchorage, Bison Trails, Coinbase, Inc., Xapo Holdings Limited;

- venture capital sector: Andreessen Horowitz, Breakthrough Initiatives, Ribbit Capital, Thrive Capital, Union Square Ventures;

- non profit and multilateral organizations, and academic institutions: Creative Destruction Lab, Kiva, Mercy Corps, Women's World Banking.

The conditions required to become a member must be at least two out of three of the following:

- value: more than $1 billion in market value or more than $500 million in customer account balances;

- scale: reaching more than 20 million people per year, in multiple countries;

- sustainability: to be recognized as Top-100 by third-party or media associations in the area of sustainability (e.g. by Interbrand Global 100, Fortune 500, the S&P Global 1200, the FTSE Eurotop 300).

Funding Members will be remunerated for their work. They will in fact be entitled to the Libra Investment Token, a second token of the platform, linked to the returns from the securities held by the Libra Reserve. Facebook apparently worked for over a year on a project which it then shared both governance and potential revenues with other players. The White Paper also talks about the future objective of further opening the network, even making it totally permessionless, consequently modifying the remuneration mechanism envisaged today. However, neither Apple, nor Google, nor Amazon, nor Microsoft are among the partners and there is no bank either. All technical information can be found on the website www.libra.org.

Founding members: the defections

The presence of the giants of the payment world, from Mastercard to Visa, from PayPal to Stripe, should have worked as a guarantee for the reliability of the project. Instead, between September and October 2019 these actors all abandoned. EBay and Booking, part of those hi-tech groups that should have adopted Libra as a payment tool, have also decided not to participate.

On October 14, The Libra Association formalized its board of directors and executive team, with CEO David Marcus (former blockchain Leader at Facebook). Of the initial 28 members who showed interest, 21 formally signed the statute of the Libra Association, the entity in charge of managing and governing the cryptocurrency blockchain architecture. The Association has seen the defections of Mastercard, VISA, Paypal, Mercado Pago, eBay, Stripe, Booking Holdings, leaving PayU as the only payment company at the moment.

In addition to the aforementioned David Marcus (Calibra), who was in charge of the project from the beginning, Matthew Davie (Kiva), Patrick Ellis (PayU), Katie Haun (Andreessen Horowitz) and WencesCasares (Xapo) were appointed to the board. The board then voted on the association's executive team consisting of Bertrand Perez, chief operating officer and president, Dante Disparte, head of policy and communications and vice president, and Kurt Hemecker, head of business development.

At the same time, again on October 14, the association confirmed that it had received indications of interest from more than 1,500 counterparties, with 180 counterparties that meet the criteria required to become founding members. Objective: reaching100 members.

Vodafone also left the game on 22 January 2020. It was the eighth defection from the Libra Association: practically a third of the initial members left. Vodafone has declared its intention to concentrate its resources on the M-Pesa project, a system for the transfer of money and microcredit launched in 2007 by the subsidiary Safaricom, currently only available in some countries: Kenya, Tanzania, Afghanistan, South Africa, India,

Romania and Albania. Now Vodafone would aim to expand M-Pesa to other countries.

How the Calibra Wallet Will Work

Libra is not the only entity that was revealed to the world on June 18. In fact, Calibra, a company directly controlled by Facebook, was also officially presented. Calibra is the first wallet available to manage the new cryptocurrency and transact through this digital currency. Its prerogative is to simplify the user experience with respect to the complex management of private keys and public keys which is instead normally provided in all blockchain platforms, including Libra.

Wallets are widely used by all cryptocurrency holders and it will be interesting to see if other wallets integrate the possibility of making transactions through Libra. However, Calibra will certainly be the only tool to be perfectly integrated with Whatsapp and Messenger, the main messaging platforms managed by Facebook, thus making the exchange of money as simple as sending a photo.

Calibra will also have the role of ensuring compliance with AML (Anti Money Laundering, Anti-Money Laundering) regulations and carrying out the KYC of users ("Know Your Customer", the recognition process used by companies to verify the identity of their customers) in compliance of the regulations in force. It will also open up new scenarios for digital identity management, potentially enabling an evolved "sign in with Facebook" button that can be used not only for registration on sites, but also for access to services that require KYC such as financial or insuranceones.

Similarities and Differences With Other Cryptocurrencies

Facebook's Libra is a cryptocurrency. But there are currently at least 2,238 cryptocurrencies in the world. What are the peculiarities of the digital currency that will be issued starting from 2020 by the social network of Mark Zuckerberg? Fabio Pezzotti, Founder, CEO and President of Iconium Blockchain Ventures explains: "If we consider the degree of decentralization, in the case of the Libra project this is limited when compared to permissionless and open-source infrastructures such as Bitcoin and Ethereum with miners or nodes of the order of thousands, and in fact the minimum requirements imposed by the association are very restrictive (for example a minimum of $10 million investment) and can only be met by a few organizations in the world. In other words, unlike Bitcoin, Libra will be a permissioned platform. Each of the Libra Association members will own a validator node. In permissionless platforms such as Bitcoin and Ethereum, anyone can participate in the validation process, while in Libra the validators will be dozens of large international companies".

As for the blockchain used, Facebook first acquired the entire team of the ChainSpacestartup, to develop a blockchain capable of supporting 1000 transactions per second and create a new programming language known as "Move" to develop on it. Security is one of the key principles on which this language is developed, with which it will be possible to create new assets, logic and decentralized finance applications on Libra.

Libra cryptocurrency is guaranteed by a basket of fiat currencies (for now Euro, USD, GBP, Yen) which will allow it to have a stable value over time and allow consumers and merchants to overcome the volatility risks that today disadvantage cryptocurrencies as a means of payment. There will be no monetary policy, it is possible to generate new Libra by depositing fiat money and vice versa it is possible to burn Libra by withdrawing fiat money.

The arrival of Libra could definitively unmark the difference created between cryptocurrencies and private digital forms of value transfer Facebook's entry into the market has certainly attracted attention of many professionals and not. Finally, each of these assets is finding its position within the market: Bitcoin an attractive safe haven asset from a speculative point of view, Libra a currency to make payments and maybeother projects in an ever-expanding market.

Facebook Updates Its Digital Currency Project

Of the changes made to the original project listed in the White Paper, the main one aims to dispel the concerns of financial regulators that Libra may interfere with the national currencies and monetary policies of individual countries, thanks also to the fact that it can immediately reach apoolof 2.5 billion potential users, the number of Facebook subscribers to date. To achieve this, the system will now also offer single currency Stablecoins, in addition to the original Libra backed by a basket of currencies and debt securities, such as Librausd (USD), Libraeur (EUR), Libragbp (GBP) and Librasgd (SGD). This will allow people and businesses in regions whose local currencies have single-currency Stablecoins on the Libra network to directly access a Stablecoin in their own currency.

Single currency linked Stablecoins will be usable anywhere in the world. A key objective of the economic project of the Libra network is the trust in an efficient payment method. Each Stablecoin on the Libra network will be fully backed by a pool of high quality liquid assets and backed by a competitive network of exchanges that buy and sell each coin. This means that Libra owners should have a high degree of certainty that they can convert Libra into local currency, the White Paper states. Libra, therefore, now appears almost like a digital version of currencies.

Furthermore, the association, aware of the fact that several central banks are now moving to create their own digital currency, hopes that its system can be perfectly integrated with central bank digital currencies (CBDC) as soon as they are available.

Facebook asks Finma for approval

The Libra "2.0" project was presented for approval to Finma, the federal supervisory authority on financial markets in Switzerland, the country where the Libra Association is based.

CONCLUSION

If you are reading the conclusion, it means that you have reached the end of the book.

I hope it was a pleasant reading and the content was interesting.

I hope all of this hashelped to improve your way of trading in cryptocurrency, but not only that!

I have also tried to help you understand how important it is to have a trading plan, or understand what your goals are or how best to manage risk.

I also hope with this book you will discover the method to make your trading more profitable, but above all, thatyou will learn the tools to try to safeguard your capital.

As I always say, trading doesn't mean playingatthe casino.

Trading has become their job for many, and for some, the possibility that has allowed them to significantly increase their standard of living.

But behind all this there is study, preparation, discipline, organization and above all, never improvisation.

I wish you every success in trading and in other types of business, have a good life!

DAY TRADING

Your Millionaire Guide

A Beginner's Guide To Day Trading, You'll Learn
How To Make a Living and Use the Best Trading
Tools, Money Management and Advanced
Techniques to Make Money

INTRODUCTION

There are people who, thanks to trading, have changed their lives and that of many people who have believed in them. It is enough to mention the name of Warren Buffet or George Soros because dreams and visions begin to start in the minds of many traders.

Trading success is achieved by staying very down to earth.

Starting from this belief, I have written this manual in a simple way with the aim of helping newbies to find the right way to be successful, but, above all, to find the right methods to avoid losing money, which are usually saved with sacrifice.

Trading is not synonymous with gambling. Trading on the financial markets is neither a game nor a hobby. Your approach must be extremely serious and disciplined, you have to pay particular attention to safeguarding the capital you decide to invest. Being aware of your personality, your fears, your goals you can use this to your advantage, making it your secret weapon.

CHAPTER ONE

WHAT IS DAY TRADING

What is day trading?

When we talk about day trading we mean a way of trading in the markets with trades that open and close on the same day. Those who do this type of trading tend not to have positions held overnight, but they try to close them every night and reopen them the next day. Day trading is a short term strategy that aims to profit from small intraday price fluctuations rather than longer term market movements.

When we talk about day trading we refer to a way of trading in the markets with trades that open and close on the same day.

The meaning of day trading is in direct contrast to traditional investment techniques that involve buying at a low cost, holding and then selling at a high cost. Day traders must therefore think differently from investors, focusing on the price action of an asset rather than its long-term potential. This is why day trading strategies tend to use a lot of different technical analysis solutions and require the trader to stay up to date with the latest news.

Pros of day trading

There are many markets on which day traders can operate: futures, stocks, forex and commodities. Stocks are very popular because they allow you to eliminate the risk of gapping overnight markets by being able to close them at the end of each day. The rise of technology in recent years has definitely made this way of trading more and more popular.

Cons of day trading

Day trading is not for the part-time trader. It requires concentration and dedication, as it involves quick decisions and the execution of a large number of operations in a single day. Day traders don't necessarily have to trade all day, but they need to stay alert and stay ahead of the markets. Day traders can be limited by the resulting costs. For example, if you buy and sell stocks you will pay a commission. As with all types of trading, day trading carries a market risk which can be substantial when using leveraged instruments.

CHAPTER TWO
PSYCHOLOGY AND MINDSET

Trading errors

In Gann's theory the psychological aspect is of great importance. The volatility and unpredictability of the financial markets require traders to have steady nerves and continuous critical analysis of their actions. Among the mistakes that are most frequently committed by operators, emotion is the most recurrent; dominating fear, hope and greed is the first task that every good trader should set himself.

Basing one's speculative actions on the evidence of the facts is only possible by creating a trading plan before operating, since hope or expectations manifest themselves with such fascination as to mislead even the best trader; acting in accordance with rumors or on the basis of false hopes is unfortunately a recurring behavior, which often leads to even bearing large losses before closing the position. According to Gann, a healthy fear of the market is the first sign that reveals the potential of the successful trader. Speculating is a business where losses are inevitable and physiological to a certain extent. The trader who monetizes a loss after a speculation and doesn't get too excited is mature enough to do his job. The feeling of fear, which must be avoided, greed, or the desire to improve one's position, is another personal aspect that must be mastered. Greed stimulates emotion and this can lead the operator to hope that the market will still see his expectations and may also be induced to make investments for an amount not justified by good money management rules. Therefore, to have a logical rather than an emotional approach, it is necessary to prepare in advance an operational plan or trading plan , that allows us to fix exactly the operations we want to do. According to Gann, the most important thing to do, when drawing up an operational plan, is to set stop-loss signals or to set price levels, beyond which a "coherent" buy or sell order is given.

Equally important is that the trader does not try to tell others what he is speculating on. This behavior, in fact, can only lead him to increase self-esteem and convince him, even more, that he is on the right side of the market, thus feeding his hopes on the price list rather than on predictive analysis on quotes. Gann advised buying when bad news arrived and selling when good news came in, which could prove to be unfounded.

The trader should behave independently, this means that he should develop his beliefs only after carefully studying the markets, without following the advice of others. In drawing up an operational plan, an accretive type process should always be followed, increasing positions on a financial asset only after it has already provided earnings.

If the speculations are made by two people, Gann recommends dividing the tasks as follows: the one should set the buying and selling times while the other should identify the levels around which to set the stop-loss. The operational plan is essential in order not to suffer a type of emotional behavior when operating in the financial markets. Obviously, once the trading plan has been drawn up, it is essential to follow it without being misled by emotional factors, as we have already said.

Speculating is a profession where losses are inevitable and to some extent functional.

Therefore, drawing up a trading plan is necessary to have a logical approach, rather than an emotional one ; being able to eliminate the intrinsic emotionality of trading is almost impossible, but it is certainly the right way to follow.

Beware about your decisions

Discipline is one of the most important elements that experienced traders have in common. Keep an eye on your bad habits and try to solve them as soon as possible. Trade in a disciplined manner if you decide to establish a carefully thought-out set of rules to govern your trading decisions, and then stick to them. Find ways to avoid breaking your rules and try to solve every problem before it becomes one!

Also, as a day trader, it is a good idea to reevaluate your rules at the end of each month, due to the shorter lead times of this style of trading.

But there are sources of inspiration that you should follow in order to arrive at the expected results more effectively.

Money management

Money management is essential in day trading although, ultimately, it is one of the essential elements of trading in any investment time frame. Of course, if you intend to trade for many years to come, you will need to apply successful money management strategies. There are entire books devoted to this subject, which contain many different approaches, and you need to take the time to find a method that you are comfortable with.

The risk / reward ratio is important. Remember: it doesn't matter to make a profit 90% of the time if your losses are much larger than your wins. What is important is that your wins are greater than your losses.

Stop loss

Never forget to use stop losses to manage risk when placing your orders to enter the market. This is your main "insurance": you must be aware that these should be the most important elements when opening a new position, as they will protect you from operations that evolve in a different way than expected. Standard stop losses may be subject to slippage when price gapping occurs, however, guaranteed stop losses will always close positions at your chosen level.

Determine your best strategy

No strategy always works, but even a simple day trading strategy can help a trader try to spot low-risk, high-yielding trades at important points in the day. Some traders would also use the failure of a trade as an opportunity to set up another. Should the level be "broken", it can signal the start of a new trend, presenting another opportunity to try to make money.

Controlling emotions in online trading

Mindfulness means "conscious attention" and is "a way of focusing attention on the present moment, paying attention to your thoughts, your emotions and the signals that your body sends you the moment they occur, observing them without prejudice ".

Mindfulness

In fact, Mindfulness is not a kind of religion or spiritual practice, it is simply a form of "Training the Mind". Even the Marines use it: they call it "Mind Fitness".

Equanimity and Impermanence are the two fundamental principles underlying Mindfulness. Don't be fooled by big words, they are much simpler and more intuitive than you imagine.

Equanimity is about accepting your every thought, emotion, every impulse or feeling, without trying to suppress them or resist them. Mind you: Equanimity does not mean resignation. Equanimity does not push you to give up in the face of reality, rather it helps you to observe it for what it really is, allowing you to act accordingly._The principle of Impermanence teaches that everything around you is in a perpetual state of change.

Financial markets, for example, are uncertain and always changing. You can't do anything about it, that's their nature.

By accepting the markets for what they are, you will be able to ease your "performance anxiety": to be clear, that anxiety that pushes you to remain with an open position even when the market is clearly communicating that the time has come to close it.

How to manage information

In addition to performance anxiety, another great challenge that every trader often faces during his trading day is undoubtedly having to manage a huge load of information from all over the world.

Charts, indicators, latest news, economic calendar, etc., in short, you know what I'm talking about. In these situations of enormous pressure and confusion, Mindfulness will help you choose the most important information to focus on with extreme clarity , greatly reducing stress and improving your performance.

Self-awareness is the ability to step outside oneself and begin observing oneself from the point of view of an external and impartial spectator. By becoming aware of yourself, you will be able to get out of the flow of automatic actions you take without even thinking about it, and you will begin to direct your attention and energies according to your will.

While you are trading, where do you put your attention? On the results you are getting (Profits & Losses) or on your Trading System? In trading, the best decisions are made when focusing on the Trading System rather than the results obtained, as by focusing solely on the results, your future expectations and how much you think you will gain / lose from your positions, you will fall back into that performance anxiety. I was telling you about earlier.

If, on the other hand, you turn all your attention and all your energies on the development and improvement of your Trading System, you will avoid sleepless nights and anxieties of all kinds, and the results (profits) you will get will amaze you! Van Tharp, a legendary trader, used to say that: "You don't trade according to the market, you trade according to your beliefs about the market." It is extremely important, therefore, to recognize what your beliefs and convictions are. regarding financial markets and trading in general, because only in this way will you be able to understand the reason for your behavior and your reactions in front of the monitors.

The first step to trading more effectively is to become aware of your thoughts and everything that goes through your head when trading the markets._The key concept to understand here is that you are not your thoughts. Thoughts are only the fruit of the incessant work of our mind, they are not reality.

That said, none of us are able to choose the thoughts that go through their heads, but we can choose:

- how much attention to devote to each thought;

- what meaning to attribute to each thought.

Mistakes to avoid in online trading

One of the mistakes that can cost us dearly in the markets is to emotionally attach ourselves to any thought, for example: "I am holding the long position on EUR / USD open because I am sure the Euro will appreciate". In fact, this strong attachment risks hindering us from observing reality for what it is, and does not allow us to realize that perhaps the time has come to close.

Most traders, including professionals, have a secret dream: trading without the interference of emotions. In fact, we often perceive the emotional impact on our decisions as negative and detrimental to our performance. In reality, emotion is not only a key element of our decision-making process, but it is also the first element of every decision, because we first feel and then think.

Emotions provide us with messages about what we are experiencing, and as such, they are valuable data on which we can rely to direct our actions. Therefore, our goal should not be to be able to trade without emotions, precisely because we will only get better performance when we start trading taking into account our emotions. Instead of suppressing or ignoring the messages transmitted by our emotions, it is essential to learn how to manage them.

The first step in learning how to manage your emotions is simply to start feeling them.

How to manage the impulses

A sudden urge or desire to act. "The impulses we feel during our trading days can be of various types:

the urge to close the position too early to pocket the profit;

the urge to risk more than usual;

the urge to stay in front of the screen all day for fear of missing the right opportunity.

Being irrational reactions of the mind, impulses and sudden stimuli to act are very dangerous for our trading and the only way to follow to manage them is to "ride the wave". In fact, the impulses to act are like the waves of the sea: they come and go, they don't last forever.

Riding the wave therefore means observing the arrival of the impulse, accepting the impulse for what it is. By continuing to observe the impulse without following it, you will notice that its "impact force" will decrease until it disappears. And the more you train yourself to ride the waves of your irrational impulses, the less vehement will be the future waves that will hit you. By practicing Mindfulness, you will also gain greater control over your behaviors and you will be able to resist impulses, inhibiting them without too much effort.

Manage insights

Intuition is not something mystical or magical, it is simply a process that our mind uses to make future decisions using the information it has gathered in the past. An event experienced in the past, very often re-emerges in the form of a body signal: George Soros, for example, when he experiences severe back pain, interprets it as a signal that something is about to go wrong in his portfolio of securities. Therefore, when making trading decisions, logical reasoning alone is not enough: before deciding if something is good you should also listen to what your body communicates to you.

It is also true that making any decision involves a considerable expenditure of mental energy, and this "decision fatigue" has an extremely negative impact on the decisions you make every day.

To make intelligent decisions in line with your long-term goals, it will be useful to keep an eye on these 4 aspects:

- The sleep. Scientific studies show that sleeping a few hours a night leads to less feeling the weight of losses, and at the same time pushes to over-emphasize the positive results (in trading: profits).

- Exercise. Exercise increases the oxygenation of the brain, and this helps our mind to think more clearly.

- Food. Scientists recommend starting each day with a large breakfast, then continuing to eat at regular intervals to better manage your insulin and glucose supplies.

- Rest and Recovery. Alternate 90 minutes of trading with 20 minutes of recovery (i.e. leisure).

Manage your habits

Most of the actions that we repeat constantly and prolonged over time soon become a habit, that is an automatic behavior that we adopt unconsciously, and that we can only modify through a conscious effort. A habit, therefore, is "cemented" through the repetition of the same action over time, a repetition that develops new neural pathways in the brain that help you perform that specific action almost effortlessly.

However, it is very likely that over time we have automated behavior that is no longer useful or even harmful to our performance in the markets.

It usually works like this: in the past you have developed one or more habits in your way of trading for the sole reason that in that market moment those habits have made you a lot of money. As you know, however, financial markets are constantly evolving, and what was useful and profitable in the past may no longer be, today or in the near future.

I advise you to start observing your trading habits carefully, so as to identify and stop any counterproductive behavior. Use Mindfulness! As you practice the Mindfulness exercises I illustrated above, you will develop a greater awareness of your behaviors and your "automatic responses" to external events, and you will therefore also notice a series of habits that hinder your decisions and your performance on markets. After you become aware of your "bad habits", be very careful to replace them with new habits that are more effective for your trading.

Manage stress

Imagine this scene: you are in front of your PC and wait for the data on the American GDP to betray the news. The news comes out and the market begins to react: your heartbeats increase, your stomach contracts and your muscles tighten. The amygdala has just activated your stress response. You must know that each of us responds to stress in a different way, each of us experiences stress in different situations. This is because stress is not an external factor: stress is a perception and, as such, it is different for each individual. The external event can also be the same, but if this event will be perceived as a risk, it will determine in us a certain type of reaction, if instead the same event will be perceived as an opportunity, it will determine a totally different reaction.

Our performance will be poor both if we perceive too little stress and if we perceive too much of it. The optimal stress level for our performance is in fact a middle ground between little stress and too much stress, and we reach this optimal state every time the energies and efforts required by the market coincide with our ability to deal with it.

To feel the level of stress you are experiencing in the present moment, listen to your body: put your attention on the area between the chest and the abdomen: usually the stress is felt there. As soon as you have identified the area of your body that is most sensitive to stress, let this become your "Stress Barometer". By constantly placing your attention on this area, you will soon become more aware of your stress level and learn to manage it better.

Stress is an indispensable factor for our growth: by constantly pushing ourselves beyond our limits, it allows us to fully develop our potential. In order to avoid turning this precious ally into our worst enemy, however, we must always keep in mind the so-called "oscillation process". The "swing process" consists of alternating each period of stress with a period of rest and recovery. In fact, the problem for many of us is not too much stress, but the absence of recovery periods.

Physical resistance of the trader

Closely related to the concept of stress, is the concept of resilience. Resilience is defined as "the ability to recover quickly from times of difficulty", and can increase or decrease in the same way that the muscles in our body grow and shrink : with training.

The more we expose ourselves to difficult situations, the more our resilience muscle grows and strengthens. Furthermore, Jon Kabat-Zinn, the father of Mindfulness, has promoted several scientific researches aimed at measuring the impact of Mindfulness on resilience. From the studies carried out, it clearly emerges that Mindfulness significantly increases the level of resilience in individuals who practice it.

331

The importance of being patient

Trading is a way to make money. For some, it will be a business, for some a game. What you cannot forget is that emotions play an important role in life and also in business. And a very important skill that every trader should master is to have patience.

Some are more patient than others. Some people tend to speed things up. They want to know everything at once, they rush to trade different goods, use new indicators and open transactions. Others prefer to have a solid foundation, read and learn, try the features one by one, and be prepared when they finally enter the business.

If you are part of the first group, you don't have to worry. Patience is a skill. It is something you can learn through practice.

To put it plainly, patience is the ability to wait. Sit back and see what is happening on the chart. Analyze and wait. Wait for the right signals, wait for the right time to enter a position and then wait a little longer to see how the market is developing.

Patience is something you can learn

You already know that patience is something that can be learned. You are probably wondering now how to do this if it is not in your nature. You can do something as simple but effective as writing a short note for yourself. It could be "Be patient" or "Patience" or just "Wait". Put it in a visible place. You can even paste it directly into the trading image so that it is there every time you trade on your platform.

Waiting for trade can be tedious

Familiarize yourself with different trading strategies. Invest your time in learning how they work. You may be interested, for example, in how to combine RSI with support/resistance to create a powerful strategy. When choosing a strategy, stick to it. Don't be discouraged even if the signs to enter haven't appeared for a long time. Eventually they will.

Long wait for a good entry point

You wake up, sit down at your computer and log into your account. Choose the EUR/USD currency pair, set the Japanese candlestick table and 5 minute time candles. After this you need to add the indicators. However, it is important to remember that too many indicators could increase the chaos on your chart. The levels of support/resistance in combination with the RSI indicator would be sufficient.

Grab your coffee and wait. You are looking for the places where the price touches the support/resistance level and there is a divergence showing the RSI Indicator.

Waiting for the right opportunity pays off

After about 3 hours of waiting there is a signal for a good input point. It is at this point that the price reaches the resistance level and the RSI goes to create a divergence. A short position opens for about 30 minutes.

About 3 hours waiting for a good trade signal

After completing your order, forget about it. You did what was in your hands. Now take a breath, relax, take a walk or read a newspaper. Take a break from the markets for about half an hour so you can return with a clear head.

Always remember that patience is the key to success. You can learn it. And don't forget that there are free demo accounts where you can practice trading various assets, strategies and indicators without the risk of losing your money. You can also train your patience.

CHAPTER THREE
THE BEST TOOLS AND
SOFTWARE FOR DAY TRADING

Many new traders make the beginner's mistake of using the wrong tools. Important to your success will be finding and using the right day trading software and the right day trading tools. While an experienced trader can settle for instruments that are not exactly ideal, novice traders need every possible advantage.

This means making sure you are equipped with the best trading software, scanning software and charting software.

I often talk about trying to ride a road bike on sand. It doesn't matter if you have a $ 2,000 road bike, you can't ride a road bike on sand.

If you ride a used $ 200 beach bike on fat tires, you're having a blast! The guy on the road bike will wonder why you're making it so easy.

It is because you are using the right equipment for the environment. It's not about how much money you spend, it's about using the right tools. Simplify your life using the best tools below.

Day trading software

There are a few different items you will need for day trading, including:

- Online broker

- Scanning software

- Charting software

- Breaking News Software

Now we are going to analyze which are my favorite day trading software, why to use them and why they are crucial for traders!

Online Broker: Lightspeed Financial Broker

There are hundreds of brokers to choose from and all of them offer traders a different experience.

I generally group brokers into various categories depending on the services they provide or the financial instruments they specialize in. There are options, forex, stocks, long-term investments, and scalping brokers.

There are some things that are important for day traders, such as hotkeys, direct access routing and quick executions.

Because of the above I use Lightspeed and I consider them the best broker and one of the best tools for any trader.

If you trade with a $ 500 trading account, CMEG (Capital Market Elite Group) is your best bet! They allow unlimited daily trading with a balance of $ 500 min (no restrictions of day trader patterns)

Inventory Scanning Software: Trade-Ideas

Now that you have your own funded broker you are ready to start trading! It is useful to have a way to find the actions to trade. Based on my Gap and Go and Momentum trading strategies, there are only a few stocks that are worth trading on any given day.

Knowing how to identify those stocks before they take the plunge is what separates the most profitable traders from everyone else.

Trade-Ideas is great for all my stock scanning software. You can use their predefined searches to see HOD movements, volume peaks, Biggest Gainers/Losers, Turbo Breaks, etc.

Or you can do what I did and build custom scanners using their set of hundreds of filters to tell scanners exactly what you want to see.

Do you like to trade with the Flags of the Bull? No problem. Flat Top Breakouts? Simple. It is the best software in the world able to scan the market and find winning stock settings better than Trade-Ideas.

Graphics Software: eSignal Charting

At this point you have your broker, you are all equipped with Trade-Ideas, and you are ready to get charts of the highest quality. You can safely use the charts that are provided by default by your broker.

These will work for some time, but eventually you may want to level up and use graphs that allow you to draw and write custom formulas.

This is where eSignal comes in. ESignal allows me to easily

run graphs on 8 monitors without any delay.

This is pretty impressive. It is important because it allows you to keep an eye on several titles at the same time. Besides being fast and reliable, eSignal allows you to install custom scripts. They are used as custom indicators for reversals and automatically draw support/resistance lines.

Breaking News Provider: Benzinga

Every morning it's good to start the day with a review of the actions gapping up on our Trade-Ideas scans. From there we need to look for the news catalyst, why these headlines move higher. Sometimes they move in sympathy with the market or a strong industry, but other times they have a unique catalyst such as earnings.

It is important to understand why a title moves because some catalysts are stronger than others! We could use Benzinga Pro to search for the latest titles. Then during the day listen to Radio Benzinga Pro.

They read the headlines and inform us when the stocks are up, inform us about the news, etc.

TAS market profile

TAS Market Profile is one of the best day trading software programs out there. There are a couple of different packages that you can choose from depending on what you are looking for.

It also has a suite of TAS indicators that offers 7 of their proprietary indicators including: TAS Market Map, TAS Boxes, TAS Vega, TAS Navigator, TAS Ratio and TAS Compression

Levels.

Worth taking into consideration is the TAS Market Map, TAS Vega and TAS Boxes for active and valuable trading decisions.

They also offer TAS Scanner. This unique tool allows you to see actions moving in different periods of time with different levels of buying or selling confidence at key levels. It is a powerful addition to your charting software and is something I use every day.

Indicators and scanners work on many different graphics platforms, including eSignal, Tradestation and Bloomberg.

CHAPTER FOUR
RIGHT STOCKS TO TRADE

Choosing the right stocks to trade

Intraday investment

As can be seen from the name itself, intraday trading (or day trading) presupposes the opening and closing of an operation on the same day, but also a very rapid operation. With this type of trading, the trader never leaves his positions open overnight, because he opens and closes them during the course of the day. To be successful with this strategy, it is therefore important to know how to choose the shares to buy, especially if we consider that the time to think is reduced. Often people are unable to generate profits from intraday trading because they fail to select the proper stocks.

1. Buy only the most liquid shares

Stock liquidity is the most important factor to consider in intraday trading. The more "liquid" shares have huge trading volumes and therefore can be bought and sold in large quantities without significantly affecting the price. Conversely, less liquid ones do not allow traders to buy and sell in large quantities due to the lack of too many buyers. However, some may argue that "illiquid" stocks offer great earning opportunities due to rapid price changes. However, statistics show that volatile stocks show more movement in a short period of time. Thus, most of the possible gains dissipate while the downside risk still remains! In any case, the liquidity of the securities depends on the quality of the trades put in place.

2. Stay away from volatile stocks

It is commonly known that a low daily volume of stocks traded or those for which big news are expected always move unpredictably. At times, the stock can show volatility even after the announcement of big news regarding the company in question. This means that day traders should stay away from these types of stocks. Usually, the greatest volatility occurs on small-cap stocks, while mid-cap stocks have a much more linear trend. But in addition to being volatile, these stocks also have low daily trading volumes, which also makes them less liquid.

3. Buy stocks with good correlation

Another way to make intraday trading more profitable is to opt for those stocks that have a higher correlation with major sectors and indices. This means that when the index or sector sees an upward movement, the stock price will rise accordingly. Stocks that move according to the "group sentiment" are always the most reliable and often follow the expected movement of the sector. The strengthening of the Indian rupee against the dollar, for example, will generally affect all information technology companies that depend on the US markets.

4. Follow the trend

One of the most important "tricks" of intraday trading is that following the trend will almost always bring benefits. During a bull market, traders should try to identify those stocks that are potentially bullish. On the other hand, during a bear market, it is advisable to find those stocks that are bound to decline instead.

5. Buy after doing research

Looking for quality companies is one of the pillars of intraday trading. Unfortunately, most day traders today don't do any research before buying. First, you need to identify the benchmark index and then find the sectors that are of interest to you. The next step is to create a list of various stocks belonging to these sectors. Traders don't necessarily need to understand which are the leading companies in the industry, but rather identify the stocks that are more liquid. It is therefore necessary to rely on technical analysis and determine the support and resistance levels together with the study of the fundamentals of these actions, so as to find the most profitable ones for intraday trading.

Medium-long term investment

Actions

Before investing, we need to start from the basics and be aware of what stocks are.

Shares are a financial instrument that allows you to purchase a portion of a company: in fact, they represent a share owned by the company that issues the share.

Ownership of the shares gives the right to participate in the operating and financial results of the company, as well as control of a portion of the company assets.

How the stock market works

The stock market is divided into "Primary Stock Market" and "Secondary Stock Market":

Primary stock market

Newly issued securities are placed in the "Primary Stock Market", here we will find:

New bond issues (such as BOTs or BTPs)

New issues of shares

IPO (initial public offering), i.e. the first public offering of shares belonging to companies that have just been listed on the market

Secondary stock market

The Secondary Stock Market is what interests us most because it is where the trading of shares takes place.

Within the Secondary Market, anyone can buy shares of any company listed on various international markets.

To understand how the stock market works, let's take a trivial example:

I decide to sell 100 Apple shares for $ 200 each.

You think Apple stock is worth more, so you sniff out the deal and buy my 100 shares at $ 200 a share.

The sell and buy orders (which are anonymous) coming from all investors are thus compared, and, since ours are compatible, the trade is made.

What stocks to buy

Now I will give you my personal opinion on which stocks to buy and how to choose the best ones when making an investment with a medium-long time horizon.

First of all I want to give you some positive news: the fundamental characteristic for a successful investment in the stock market is common sense.

In fact, I can assure you that all those mathematical formulas are not necessary for small investors.

Obviously, there are some notions that you need to know, even when deciding on what to bet based mainly on common sense, and below I will explain them one by one.

Behind the shares are the companies

First, remember what you are buying when you buy shares: you are buying shares in a company that you believe is valid.

You will become a full shareholder of the company, albeit at a low percentage of the company's total outstanding shares in the market.

So, if you invest in Amazon stock, you won't be able to sit on Bezos' right on the board of directors, but you will share the fate of his company.

Invest in what you know

If you don't know a business, what's the point of focusing on a company operating in this business?

It pays to invest in sectors and companies that you fully

understand.

If you don't know anything about biotechnology, how can you tell if the patents of a company like Bayer are valid compared to those of the competition?

On the other hand, if you are interested in video games, movies or technology and are about to release a new Netflix series or a latest generation Nvidia video card, you could consider buying their shares.

Think about what your skills or passions are and specialize in those fields.

The market looks to the future

The market is forward-looking, i.e. it always looks to the future.

In fact, all official or verified announcements regarding future events will be taken into consideration immediately by the market.

Sometimes this also applies to rumors.

For example, if Apple presents a new innovative iPhone model, the price movements will be immediate and will not wait for the actual release of the smartphone.

Then, when this new product is actually available to the public, the listing will not move in view of the launch of the new device.

In the period of release of the iPhone X (09-2017) the price of Apple shares did not react in a particular way. The significant change occurred in the previous months, - at the beginning of the year.

It is also obvious that if the public were to particularly appreciate the new phone and sales skyrocket, incredibly positive operating results will be reported in the next budget and the price will leap forward again, but the movement will be given by the cash produced, not by the news of the 'iPhone.

So, if you want to invest in a company's project, be careful that this is not already priced by the market, because you may not find the earnings you are looking for until the actual results are published.

Timing of investments

When you invest in the stock market, it is not only important to understand which stocks to bet on, but also when to buy them. In fact, the market is not always efficient in pricing a stock.

It is possible that the market is distracted and underestimating the business potential, resulting in a low share price. It is much more common than you might think.

But, in the long run, the market is supposed to give a fair price to all stocks, it's just a matter of time.

Therefore, the timing of the investment (i.e. the decision of when to open a position) is very important.

Money is sovereign

There is an old saying that is very popular among stock market traders: cash is king.

Money is sovereign: a company that grinds money will most likely be a company to bet on, while a company in constant loss does not seem an attractive investment to me.

An example? Tesla.

For years Tesla has never brought a dollar of profit to its investors, yet the cost of a share has far exceeded $ 700.

This is due to future expectations of what Tesla may become, or, in the opposite view, pure speculation.

There are therefore two types of different companies:

- Valuable companies are those that produce money

- Companies with good growth potential are firms, often relatively young, that record operating losses for a medium to long period of time due to the large investments required to start their business (in fact some fail, so be careful)

What is the attractiveness of companies belonging to this latter category?

If a company with a winning idea but in constant loss starts making money, rest assured it will make a bang.

Best titles: parameters to check

To understand which stocks are the best, my suggestion is to identify stocks of companies with excellent fundamental values, that is, capable of producing large balance sheets and with a fair amount of cash flows.

In other words, focus on the value of companies.

Some of the key indicators of corporate profitability are:

EBITDA: is an important measure of the potential cash flow arising from the company's operating cycle. The higher this number, the better.

PE: is the price/earnings per share ratio and is used to determine the relative value of a company's shares, or if they are expensive. The PE of the action you are interested in should be compared with that of its competitors: for example, in the case within a certain sector the value of the PE is on average around 15, while the PE of the action you observe is 30, the title is considered overrated. If instead the value is 10, it could be a good deal for tomorrow.

EPS: report profits to total outstanding shares. Again, the higher they are, the better.

ROI/ROE: they are simply measures of the return on investment. Again, the higher the value, the better the indicator.

Costs: especially of an operational nature, are obviously viewed negatively by investors. Structured companies that need huge capital and personnel to guarantee their production activities seem to suffer consistently, on financial lists, from the lack of flexibility.

The reading of these values is even more relevant when compared with previous periods.

Furthermore, it is very useful to compare the results of the indicators with those of the competitors of the company in which you are considering investing, so as to have an idea of the company's strength compared to the competition.

However, as reported in Tesla's example, it must be kept in mind that large investors today seem to be heavily focused on business growth. The parameters shown in the list are undoubtedly crucial, but there is the risk, if not supplemented by growth prospects, that they can only provide a partial picture of the goodness of a stock.

Therefore, we pay particular attention to the growth rate, which indicates precisely the annual growth of the company. The measure relies on the ROE and the portion of profits not distributed to shareholders in the form of a dividend, so that it can be reinvested in the company's business lines.

I would like to clarify how the stock market trend is consolidating more and more towards positive evaluations of companies operating in the future and projected towards innovative sectors.

Worst stocks

I would also keep away from all companies that are not able to produce a profit of one euro, especially if consolidated within a business that is not innovative at all and therefore without room for growth.

A fortiori, I would avoid companies that only know how to post losses on their balance sheets.

Conversely, you could use contracts for difference (CFDs) to short sell these companies: short selling is a bit like betting against a company, so that if it goes wrong on the stock market, you can make money.

Unfortunately, I will not name companies that I think are poor (to say the least) because I don't want to be sued.

How to learn to invest in the stock market

There is no magic formula to learn how to operate on the stock market: the only way is to get information, study and experiment.

To learn how to invest in the stock market, start reading finance journals, studying business valuation principles, and using a trading simulator.

Focus primarily on fundamental analysis and pursue stock value.

With fundamental analysis you can be able to evaluate if a company is solid or not, if it is expensive or cheap, if it is profitable for its investors or if it is a slot machine.

Speculation passes, new trends and new fashions will go on the market (Bitcoin, Beyond Meat, etc.), but the value and growth remain.

As far as technical analysis is concerned, some indicators are certainly useful, especially for the timing of an investment (when to enter and when to exit), but I would not decide what to bet on just looking at technical analysis.

I suggest you initially focus on volumes, trend-lines (resistances and supports) and moving averages.

Finally, it is possible to experiment directly on the field thanks to completely free online trading simulators, which allow you to invest in the stock market without putting your capital at risk.

CHAPTER FIVE
STRATEGIES

High-frequency

High Frequency Trading: the secrets of HFT

High Frequency Trading, or HFT, are very high speed trading algorithms, with execution times that are measured in infinitesimal fractions of a second.

What they are and how they operate

Perhaps not everyone knows that, for some years now, those responsible for investment choices - or perhaps it is better to say for trading choices - of the majority of financial giants are no longer (only) men, but also algorithms. The latter have now taken hold so much that in some markets it is estimated that more than half of trading takes place with automatic systems. With peaks that in some cases travel on even much higher percentages.

Algorithmic trading systems delegate to a machine the choice, execution and management of purchase orders. Within algorithmic trading there is a sub-category known by the acronym HFT (High Frequency Trading), which identifies very high-speed trading systems, with execution times that are measured in infinitesimal fractions of a second.

Based on the execution latency and position maintenance, high frequency automatic trading differs significantly from traditional long-term investing and algorithmic trading.

To minimize latency (i.e. the time to send orders) co-location (i.e. proximity to the servers of the exchanges of the machines that send the orders) is essential. So much that in the first months of diffusion of these systems there was a real rush in search of the properties closest to the data processing centers of the stock exchanges around the world, to grab the best locations for the execution of these algorithms.

HFT systems are very popular in the stock market but are also applied to a maximum extent on other assets, such as options, bonds, derivatives and commodities. The duration of the transactions implemented by the HFTs can be very short. The purpose of these algorithms is to profit on very low margins but for a very high number of operations. Only in this way can these systems be profitable. Usually these systems pass a large number of orders to the market (typically in execute immediately or cancel format) but only a very small percentage of them are actually executed. The algorithm then remains in position for a very short time, even a few millionths of a second. At the end of the day, all positions are always closed.

There are numerous techniques used by High Frequency Trading algorithms to operate. Among the most used are:

- arbitrage that exploits discrepancies in the price of a security listed on different stock exchanges also through the analysis of the different degree of liquidity of the markets in question,

- arbitrage between ETFs and its underlying,

- statistical arbitrage, through which correlations between different asset classes are used,

- the exploitation of particular macroeconomic news, through the association of trading strategies with one or more particular keywords present in press releases,

- "order flow detection" techniques, i.e. the identification and exploitation of order blocks,

- "smoking" techniques that plan to entice other operators with proposals then modified at more favorable prices,

- "spoofing" techniques, which involve placing and canceling orders to trick traders into thinking that a certain trend phase has started

- "layering" techniques, with the insertion of a hidden buy order and a clearly visible sell order,

- "pinging" techniques, with the insertion of small purchase proposals to discover the behavior of other traders.

HFT systems have some positive aspects. They usually lower the spreads between bid and ask (i.e. between the best buy and sell proposals), increase the liquidity of an instrument (consequently of a market) and improve the so-called price discovery, i.e. the determination of the price of a financial instrument starting from the information available on that asset. However, they are not exempt from problems, such as the one - of a software nature - which in 2012 caused the collapse (after losses of half a billion dollars) of Knight Capital

353

or what in May 2012 led to an anomalous trend of the Dow Jones: due to of these high-frequency automatic trading systems, the index, in about ten minutes, went from 10,650 to 9,872 points, before returning to 10,232 points.

It is no coincidence that the supervisory authorities (and in the US even the FBI) have long been committed to monitoring the activities of high-frequency trading algorithms. However, according to staunch critics, the war on HFTs clashes with their ability to create trading volumes. And high turnover means high commissions ...

Momentum

Momentum trading is a strategy that uses the force of price movements to open a position, be it long or short. Let's discover some of the main indicators used to trade with this strategy.

Momentum trading is a strategy that takes into account only the price trend to decide whether to buy or sell a particular market. The idea behind the strategy is that if there is a strong enough force behind a certain price movement, then this market will continue to move in the same direction.

When the prices of a market are rising, they often attract the attention of traders and investors, giving an even stronger push to the current movement. This effect lasts until a large number of sellers arrive on the market and find current prices too high. At this point the price rise stops and the market changes direction.

Those who trade with this strategy therefore do not care

about the fundamentals of the underlying market or its long-term growth prospects. Rather, traders who take advantage of this strategy try to identify how strong the market trend is before deciding whether to open a position or not.

It should be noted that those who operate with momentum do not necessarily intend to sell on the highs or buy on the lows. Rather it focuses on the central part of the trend, the strongest one, exploiting the market sentiment and the so-called herd effect, or the tendency of operators to follow the 'mass'.

There are three key factors in identifying the Momentum:

Volume

Volatility

Time frame

Volume

Volume represents the amount of an asset traded in a given time frame. Pay attention, the volume does not therefore represent the number of transactions carried out, but the number of units traded - therefore, if three operators buy one security each, it is equivalent to an investor who buys three. The volume in this case is in fact 3 traded securities.

Volume is of vital importance for traders as it allows you to quickly enter and exit positions. A market with a large number of buyers and sellers is called a liquid market, as it is easier to trade an asset. Conversely, a market with a low number of buyers and sellers is considered illiquid and selling or buying the underlying is rather difficult.

Volatility

Volatility is the degree of fluctuation in the price of an asset. If a market is highly volatile, it means that there are large price swings, while a market with low volatility is relatively stable.

If the markets are volatile, traders can take advantage of short-term price rises and falls. It is important to remember to prepare an adequate risk management strategy to protect the operations from adverse market movements by inserting stop losses.

Time frame

Momentum strategies are usually focused on short-term market movements, although the duration of a trade may depend on the strength of the underlying trend. This makes this strategy suitable both for scalpers, i.e. those who operate on time frames ranging from a few seconds to a maximum of one hour, and for investors who have longer investment horizons.

How to start trading momentum

There are several steps to follow to make a strategy of this type. First of all:

- Identify the market of your interest

- Develop a trading strategy based on technical indicators

- Practice using a risk-free demo account

- Start practicing on live markets

The best momentum indicators

As already mentioned, momentum trading is based solely on the movement of prices. This is why most traders rely primarily on technical analysis and indicators.

In this regard, the most important momentum indicators include:

The momentum

Relative Strength Index (RSI)

Other oscillators, such as Stochastic, CCI, etc.

In general, all oscillators are good momentum indicators. We specify that oscillators fall within a particular category of indicators that analyze situations of overbought (excess demand) or oversold (excess supply).

Momentum

As the name implies, it is undoubtedly the most important indicator for this strategy. The operation is extremely simple: it takes the most recent closing price and compares it with the closing price of n previous periods. Obviously, the choice of the number of previous periods is arbitrary, even if usually on trading platforms there are often default values of 10, 12 or 14.

The oscillator is made up of a single line that moves around the center line of zero. The value of the indicator line gives traders an idea of the strength of the underlying trend. Obviously it will take on a positive value when the difference between the last close and that of n previous candles is positive. If the indicator line crosses the zero line from the bottom, then it means that the price is rising and has exceeded the closing levels of n periods ago. It could therefore be a potentially bullish sign. Conversely, if the indicator crosses zero from above, the sales are strengthening and the signal is potentially bearish.

Although some traders use the indicator to enter and exit positions, most traders use it to confirm if there is a trend in place.

Relative Strength Index (RSI)

The Relative Strength Index (RSI) is an indicator that moves from 0 to 100 and provides overbought and oversold signals depending on its value. If it rises above 70 the market is overbought, while if it falls below 30 it is oversold. Like the Momentum indicator, it is plotted on a separate chart and falls under the oscillators.

When using the RSI, it is important to note the overbought and oversold signal does not necessarily mean that the trend will change. It could also represent a simple pause in the current trend, before it regains strength.

Sometimes this indicator is also used to see if there are any divergences in the market, i.e. phases in which prices rise to new highs (fall to new lows) while the RSI does not reach the previous highs (lows).

Summary

Momentum trading is the strategy that allows you to buy and sell an asset based on the recent price trend.

Traders will open a position to take advantage of a strengthening trend and close the position when it starts to lose strength.

Momentum trading is based on volume, volatility and time frame.

The strategy does not involve studies on long-term fundamental or growth, rather it looks at short-term price action.

The best known indicators for momentum trading are the Momentum oscillators, the RSI and the Stochastic.

Pre-market and after-market

Not everyone knows that it is possible to carry out stock trading activities even outside the normal market session.

The period in which you can execute operations on the stock market before the opening of continuous trading is called pre-market, while the corresponding time frame after closing is called after-market.

The times of these two intervals depend on the exchange on which we wish to operate and on the conditions defined by the broker we have chosen to carry out our financial transactions.

If we intend to operate in these sessions, it is useful first to carefully evaluate the constraints imposed by the financial intermediary, so that we can plan our operations without surprises.

Although the methods of entering orders are the same as on the daytime exchange, market conditions are different and exchanges, in the pre-market and after-market, present both undoubted advantages and risks.

The main advantage of operating outside the institutional market is the fact that companies almost always disclose their economic results, such as earnings data, before or after the close of trading, so many operators are interested in seizing the opportunity to intervene immediately on the news.

It should be emphasized that this type of operation requires a lot of speed and coldness, so it is not suitable for everyone, but if you can follow the right direction you can get great satisfaction.

Another advantage is represented by the fact of being able to observe the performance of a stock during the pre-market and therefore, make an operational decision when the market opens, when volumes increase quickly.

In the face of these earnings opportunities, there are of course risks to be taken into consideration which, in the pre-market and in the after-market, have particular characteristics.

The first risk to consider is the lack of liquidity:

In fact, for many shares, in these two market sessions, the trading volumes are much lower than the regular trading hours, this can make it more difficult to complete our operation.

Higher spreads:

The scarcity of volumes can result in a larger

difference between bid and ask, so order execution will be more difficult or you may risk getting a less advantageous price.

Possible increase in volatility:

In this context, higher price fluctuations may be encountered than in continuous trading. This situation could also be an advantage, but you need to be able to manage sudden movements in prices.

During the pre and after-market, you have to deal with many professionals from large institutions.

They operate a lot during these hours and, as we know, they have access to much more information than small traders, also having a very high technological power.

In conclusion, the activities before and after the opening of continuous quotations represent excellent earning opportunities, but it is necessary to carefully study this type of market before operating as it presents some pitfalls that should not be underestimated.

CHAPTER SIX
SUCCESSFUL TRADE

How to create an efficient trading plan

What is a trading plan ?

A trading plan is a project or a set of guidelines that helps you outline your trading activity. This tool can be particularly useful for planning and implementing a negotiation strategy.

There is no absolute model to follow to get a perfect trading plan (each trader is unique and different styles suit different people), but there are universally accepted elements to be taken into consideration when drawing up a personal plan.

The trading plan can also be compared to a business plan. You would never start a business without a valid project: why starting a commercial activity without a trading plan?

General rules of the trading plan

Even if it is true that there is no absolute model to refer to in order to draw up a perfect trading plan, there are still some general rules that can help you in most cases.

1. Put it in writing. You should physically write down (or type in) your reasons for trading and the main goals you hope to achieve. This will help you to organize your thoughts, and solidify your plan.

2. Record your progress. Develop a clear and concise

method for recording your trading activities.

When planning a long-term strategy it is essential to be able to see past and present investments, both from a learning perspective and keeping track of the markets you trade in or are exposed to.

3. Check your financial situation. Capital management is another crucial element of the trading plan. You need a plan to manage your investments, especially your risk exposure.

Main questions about trading plan

Here are some important questions to consider when drafting your trading plan:

What is your motivation for trading?

What is your risk appetite?

How much time can you dedicate to trading?

What is your level of knowledge?

When creating a trading plan, the answers to these questions must be taken into account. Only by knowing our goals and capabilities will we be able to build the trading plan that best suits our characteristics.

Why using a trading plan? Here are all the benefits

The trading plan can be a valuable aid in many situations:

A. Configure facilities to better manage risk

What does the term high or low risk mean to you? By

quantifying it in advance, you can apply a scientific approach to assess whether a particular trade is too risky. Your risk scale for the size of the trade could be as follows:

Low risk: 1-2% of the total fee

Medium risk: 2-5% of the total share

High risk: More than 5% of the total share

Highly reckless: Over 20% of the total share

For example: With an account of $ 10,000, a 3% risk equals $ 300 on a single transaction (average risk).

Another way to consider risk is to set a risk/reward ratio. The risk is represented by the loss of a trade or when the market takes the stop loss, the return is instead the gain of an transaction or when the market moves in the direction favorable to us and reaches the target. Usually in an efficient trading plan the risk/reward ratio is equal to 1/2 or 1 / 3. Risk 1 to earn 2. Risk 1 to earn 3. In these cases, even with a 50% probability of success of my trading strategies will still have a positive balance.

B. Establish entry and exit strategies in advance

In many, if not most cases, being able to optimize your income and expenses is the most stressful part of the whole transaction.

Nowadays, there is often the risk of basing a decision on an emotional response rather than a strategic one. For this reason, it can be extremely useful to establish clear criteria and rules to be followed for the management of income and expenditure.

For example, you can use charts to monitor market trends and decide to initiate a trade only when particular patterns emerge. Alternatively, when considering closing a position, you can set profit/loss limits to adhere to as the position evolves.

It can be very helpful to have a set of guidelines established by you in a rational environment, away from the pressure of an ongoing transaction.

C. Stay focused and optimize decision making

Financial markets can move very quickly and it is at these times that you may feel overwhelmed and more prone to making hasty decisions.

A trading plan is a vital reference point in these situations, as many decisions are made in advance, before being faced with inevitable problems. Act on your plan rather than making decisions on the spot.

A trading plan can help keep the excitement out of trading. Some people may attribute profits to emotions or instinct, but long-term success will almost always be based on a carefully thought out and worked out strategy in advance.

D. Continuously evaluate transactions and manage money

A trading plan often includes a trading ledger or diary, which you can use to track all executed trades and make a note of their success or failure.

A trading log is an excellent tool that allows you to have a clear view of the big picture. In one image you can encapsulate your trading history and identify the successes and mistakes made along the way.

Honesty and self-awareness are important traits, but constant trading evaluation is one of the best ways to avoid repeating mistakes and to remember things that worked in the past.

E. Simplify trading and maintain discipline

A trading strategy can continually remind you of the goals you have achieved and the limits you have set for yourself.

A written plan is very useful for maintaining your trading discipline - it is increasingly difficult to deviate from the original plan when you always have it in front of your eyes. Keep it on your desk or hang it on the wall if needed.

Who needs a trading plan?

The synthetic answer to this question is: everyone. From newbies to professionals, no one can say they can really do without a trading plan.

Your experience will undoubtedly influence the extent to which you use and benefit from a trading plan, but using a trading plan according to your needs is undoubtedly in your best interest.

You decide how to use the trading plan, but in the next section we have highlighted some essential tips on how to create it. You can also see examples of a trading plan and log.

How to make a trading plan?

The 9 basic steps to build your trading plan is a tool that you shape by adapting it to your personal trading style. You are free to include any items you find useful in the plan, but by following these steps you will be sure that you have included all the essentials.

1. Know your trader skills

First of all, you need to complete the following sentence: 'I want to be a successful trader because...'

Secondly, you need to honestly assess your strengths and weaknesses, not only with regard to trading, but also with respect to any personal traits that may affect the way you trade.

2. Define and understand your trading goals

Defining trading goals is one of the most important steps in developing a trading plan. It is also the stage that many people overlook.

You must try to be very precise and scrupulous in terms of both profit and timing. Only by defining and quantifying your goals will you be able to assess the extent to which you have achieved them.

Many trading plans suggest that you identify your goals on a daily, weekly, monthly, semi-annual, yearly, or lifetime basis.

It may seem silly or impossible to set daily trading goals or set a goal to be pursued over a lifetime. But, more than the actual result, it is the thinking behind these goals that is important and beneficial.

3. Decide which types of trading you are interested in

You have several trading options on the financial markets. Some people prefer to stick to one method, others have successfully integrated different types of trading into the same plan.

Whatever path you decide to take, it is essential that you understand the options available to you and make the decision, as part of your trading plan, to stick to a particular system.

Of course, you can change your trading plan as your trader skills increase, but what you should avoid is trying a new type of trading on a whim, without trying to figure out if it suits your trading style. Only change your trading plan when you are almost certain that it will be more efficient for your trading.

4. Identify your markets and trading times

Besides knowing what types of trading you are interested in, you should also identify the markets that are best for you.

A first consideration is your level of preparation on particular markets (stocks, commodities, indices, foreign currencies) and the factors that drive them. The more you know, and the more interested you are in the subject, the more you will pay attention.

Likewise, you should consider the opening hours of these markets and evaluate your ability to offer them adequate attention during trading hours.

5. Establish your personal trading system

A trading system will apply a set of rules to turn trading into an automated process. You will have to decide if you prefer automatic (or algorithmic) trading where you choose a trading system and let this guide all your decisions, or discretionary, where you make decisions on a case-by-case basis.

6. Know how much you are willing to risk

Risk management is the most important aspect of a trading plan. There are many techniques for managing risk, from position sizing strategies to risk minimization tactics.

From the perspective of the trading plan it is important to consider money management, in order to adapt to your trading style and stick to it regardless of the trading conditions.

The following questions should be asked:

What percentage of my account am I ready to risk in each trade?

How many positions am I ready to manage at the same time?

What is the maximum exposure of the account that I am ready to accept?

How much risk do I want to take for each position?

7. Decide how you want to manage your open positions

This aspect of the trading plan concerns the management of

open positions. This is the situation where you are most exposed to emotional reactions - you see the market go down and you want to reduce your losses, or the market is frozen and you are tempted to hold the position even longer.

In these emotionally charged situations it is essential to already have a strategy to appeal to. The advice is always to trust your trading plan strategies. Only by being disciplined will you see results in the long run.

8. Plan to store your trading data

It is surprising how often people overlook this aspect of the trading plan, especially considering that it can be a very valuable learning tool. Regularly updating the document containing all of your previous transactions, including the details that made them successful or not, can be a valuable lesson for the future. Having a trading agenda is essential.

A simple spreadsheet is the only record you need to keep, but a comments section is very useful. Include everything from the ease with which you followed your strategy, and what worked and what didn't, to what you felt on a given day or hour.

You will be pleasantly surprised at how simple it is to identify successful trends and repeat them in the future.

9. Test your system

You can test the system of your choice by comparing it with historical data to determine if it would hold up to recent market movements. You can do this manually or choose one of the many systems provided by certain financial service providers.

Set your personal goals

What are the factors to consider before investing? The purposes of your trading must be clear and above all they must show us the amount of time we intend to dedicate to our investment.

Time and performance are the two key factors when it comes to understanding your goals and evaluating how to act. Without having carefully weighed what you want to achieve, it will be difficult to obtain good returns.

Imagine you have a garden to take care of, which you want to see grow over time. You don't know what will happen tomorrow, in a few months or in a few years, but your goal is to make it a well-kept garden in every respect.

The garden metaphor is one of the most used to explain how an investment works, what its variables are, what it depends on, and what its main goals are.

Here are some tips to understand how to calculate your investment goals and how to avoid mistakes.

Trading Goals: Time and Return

The two key factors determining the investment are time and yield.

These two elements, of course, are proportional. The performance, in fact, depends on the time we have chosen.

First of all, consider the timing, since you will have to choose the right tool based on it. Investing in CFDs has different timing than investing in mutual funds.

Space-time is therefore the first factor to be calculated as a preliminary element.

We will then move on to understand what is the return you want to achieve, in order to have a clear trading strategy. The return you want to get from your investment must also be related to the timing.

Trading goals: short, medium and long term investments

First of all, investments are divided into three different typologies: there are short-term investments, medium-term investments and long-term investments.

For short-term investments we mean an investment load not exceeding 12/18 months and are usually adopted to invest a certain part of liquidity that can be available in the short term.

The ideal financial instruments for short-term investments are represented by Bots, 12/18 month CCTs, 12/18 month BTPs, AAA government bonds belonging to the Eurozone in order to avoid exchange rate risks.

Short-term investing is also an ideal tactical solution for weighing other investment strategies.

On the other hand, as regards medium/long-term investments, it is necessary to pay due attention to all financial instruments and to have in-depth knowledge on the subject, especially for long-term investments. In fact, it is highly advisable to get the assistance of a professional in the sector.

Medium/long-term investments are useful for achieving certain objectives, such as increasing one's capital, maintaining purchasing power unchanged over time, protecting it from real inflation, or guaranteeing a substantial income for a supplementary pension.

Investment objectives: here are the main ones

The main objectives of the investment include the following:

- Accumulation, if you want to invest to increase your assets to be bequeathed to our years;

- Decumulus, to be connected with the pension position, which however allows us to constantly maintain our standard of living;

- Flow objectives, to obtain a periodic income starting from a certain time, in order to maintain a constant standard of living, even in difficult times ;

- Capital objectives, to increase your capital over time, aimed for example at planning large expenses in the future.

Everyone has its own precise purposes, but usually these are the goals that are taken into consideration the most and which are adopted to design their trading strategy.

Trading objectives: expected return

The expected return represents the relationship between the expected result and the invested capital. The expected return can be listed in the following types:

- Physiological return: aimed at safeguarding purchasing power, commensurate with the expected inflation rate;

- Minimum return: usually obtained with short-term government bonds, generally at zero risk;

- Return higher than the free risk rate: determined by a higher level of risk, the return is higher but in comparison with an equally higher level of risk.

Trading objectives: some useful advice

No joking with the investment, it is necessary to have in-depth knowledge of the subject or to have acquired some experience, or even be supported by a professional.

Here are some tips to follow:

- Identify your needs;

- Do not make hasty judgments and always consider the predetermined time factor;

- Understand if you are more inclined to a greater risk appetite or if you are more prudent;

- Constantly maintain a relationship with your consultant based on clarity and transparency.

How does intraday trading differ from classic trading?

One of the main differences between intraday trading and regular trading is time. In intraday, the trader is required to close the position the same day before the market closes, regardless of the profit or loss. In classic trading, the trader can choose to keep the position open for even longer than one day and in any case there is no time limit for closing the operation.

Come in and out at the right time

A great idea is to trade following an intraday trend. This offers the potential for low-risk entry points, while providing high earning potential if the trend continues. To identify these patterns, I invite you to read the related article "How to exploit market trends with a trading strategy with the stochastic".

To identify when to quit, two conditions can be observed; the first is when you have reached the target, the second is when you have reached the maximum loss limit below which you do not want to go (stop loss).

Always have a stop loss level set

Having a stop loss set is one of the basic rules of intraday trading. The stop loss is the exit level and the tool for capital protection in case your trend or expectations do not come true. On the other hand, if the predictions are correct, you should have set different price targets in which to profit from the trade.

The historical returns factor

We all believe that "history repeats itself". While this cannot be said with 100% certainty, financial markets usually follow their own historical path as well. Therefore, the goal should be to find a strategy that preserves capital and at the same time offers returns at a controlled risk.

You can choose to start trading after analyzing the trend of a specific asset and understanding its characteristics. Also, remember to choose the liquid asset that has a high average daily volume which will guarantee numerous opportunities.

Don't be impulsive

Traders often feel discouraged if their trading strategy doesn't work as hoped. Beginners should use historical analysis to find opportunities and build simple trading strategies.

A trader, before entering the market, should have a well-defined level of profit and stop loss and should not let impulsive nature take control of the trading activity. If you've devised an entry-and-exit strategy that best aligns with your needs, don't change it impulsively. Successful trading requires a strong ability to control personal emotions.

Start small

Some good exchanges could boost your confidence, and if that happens, don't get carried away by your strong ego. Don't be aggressive with your trades early on, focus on up to 1-2 assets to get started. Over time, the volume and size of the operation should increase.

Start small will allow you to make smaller mistakes and increase your familiarity with how the market works so you don't make the same mistakes twice. Gradually increase the trading volume as your experience and risk appetite increases.

Keep calm

Since intraday trading requires you to be hyper-vigilant about the market, it certainly brings anxiety with it. However, don't let emotions get the better of you. Decisions should be based on logic and a set strategy. Emotions such as fear, greed, etc. they should be kept at bay.

Alternatives to intraday trading

As mentioned above, intraday trading is very profitable but carries a high degree of risk.

The most common alternative to intraday trading is Swing trading. Swing trading is the trading technique that allows you to open a position on a certain market, short or long, and close it in a few days, capturing the sentiment that governs the trend of prices and the consequent expected price fluctuation.

This investment method is halfway between intraday trading and buy and hold: in a nutshell, swing trading means taking a position in line with the main trend of the underlying, keeping it for a few days.

Risk management

Money Management, Risk Management, Position Sizing, Bet Sizing... no matter what you call it, the important thing is to know it!

When you lose money, you find yourself with less capital to work with and to recover the loss you need to achieve a much higher percentage performance than the one you just lost.

Losing money is in fact negative in itself, but even worse is losing so much money that it definitively jeopardizes the chances of continuing as an investor. It is therefore of fundamental importance to adopt constant behavior by adopting capital protection techniques, which must in no way be disregarded.

Over the last few years there has been a proliferation of people who tried to invest their money independently, without consulting professionals , often using the online trading services offered by any banking institution or broker.

Few traders and managers, however, have developed the necessary disciplinary skills and have a clear understanding of money management strategies.

During the "speculative bubble" talking about strategies to limit risk was practically useless as all the markets were rising dramatically. In recent years, however, due to the well-known movements that are not always easily predictable (price actions), the importance of money management and risk management techniques has once again been realized.

Money Management, in simple terms, tells you how many contracts (or shares, or assets) you can work on at a certain time considering certain portfolio and risk parameters.

It is practically impossible to earn money without the correct use of Money Management techniques.

Money Management is a defensive concept; it allows you to stay on the market in a way that you won't be excluded from it. For example, it tells you if you have enough new money to invest in new positions. Money management should not be confused with the stop loss.

Statistics confirm that 90% of traders lose money, 5% reach break-even and only 5% manage to make money. Often, the losing trader could be part of that 10% that at least reaches break-even if only he were able to correctly size his trades.

Money management is risk management

Proper risk management is the difference between winning and losing trading. Operating correctly on the market is 90% made up of money and portfolio management; this is a fact that most people cannot or do not want to understand.

Once you have the correct Money Management, discipline and psychology complete the figure of the good investor.

Money Management serves to optimize the use of capital

Few people manage to see their wallet as a whole. Even fewer investors/managers are able to take the step from a defensive or reactive view of risk (in which they measure the risk to avoid losses: the risk suffered, i.e. the stop loss.) Towards an aggressive and proactive view in which the risks are actively managed for a more efficient use of capital.

Money management "basic guide"

It must be clear to those who are about to operate on the markets that the fundamental point to keep in mind is the protection and safeguarding of their capital. Only if you manage not to decrease the efficiency of your capital can you hope to stay on the market long enough to be able to continue operating. If you are convinced of this, if you consider it much more important than desperately looking for a gain, caught in the frenzy that is very similar to the one that assails the gamblers, then you are on the right track.

First of all, pay close attention to the drawdown, understood as "the amount of money that can be lost in trading, expressed in terms of percentage of the total available capital" (drawdown is the difference between a peak and a valley in an equity line graph).

The trading system or operating technique that you intend to adopt, or that you have used up to now, must have a maximum drawdown that does not affect the efficiency of your capital. Let's look at some guiding elements.

Tips for simple risk management

- risk a percentage of 2% of the available capital for each operation;

- avoid the use of "financial leverage" (or at least ensure that the borrowed capital does not represent a high percentage of your cash availability);

- invest a maximum of 20% of the capital present in the portfolio;

- for every dollar risked, propose to earn two or three.

For example, if you trade with $ 5,000, setting a stop loss at 3% ($ 150 risk) the target should be at least $ 300 / $ 450. In other words, the risk/reward ratio must be at least 1: 2 or better 1: 3;

- before opening a position, always evaluate the volatility of the market (on which it is also possible to calibrate the stop loss);

- monetize at least part of the profits made;

- the higher the operation, the lower the risk level must be;

- never increase or mediate a losing position;

- if you do not have the technique, avoid pyramiding (increase of the investment in a winning position);

- do not proceed with "mental" stops, but with sell orders actually placed.

A recommendation above all: when you run into a consecutive series of losing operations, it is better to stop the activity and re-evaluate your operating methodology. The legendary William D. Gann wrote, over fifty years ago:

Money management can be applied using a variety of techniques and strategies. From the simplest, linked to "common sense" to the more complex ones consisting of the application of mathematical models.

For most traders it may be sufficient to apply the rules of "common sense" to be able to survive for a long time and profitably to their trading system and the market.

The main rules for proper risk management

Don't be under-capitalized

It is important to have adequate capital for the instrument (future or equity) on which we are going to operate and not to take excessive risks. These two principles help you survive long enough to be able to thrive. There are numerous examples of traders with small capital that were quickly "eliminated" at the beginning of their career.

This concept can be exposed by analyzing a mechanical trading system (Trading System). Let's assume the system has an all-time high drawdown (for example over 5 years) of $ 10,000. Open a trading account with $ 10,000 that is the maximum drawdown and start trading following the signals that the Trading System produces. Let's assume that after a short time you begin to suffer a series of consecutive stop-losses that bring you $ 2,000 in your account. Now its efficiency has greatly diminished and even if the system starts producing good signals again, your portfolio is no longer in a position to work to follow them. Let's say you reset the initial $ 10,000 at this point and the system runs into a maximum drawdown. You are out of the game.

Your "failure" does not depend on the Trading System you were using, but depends exclusively on not having been adequately capitalized to follow the signals that your system generates in the long term.

You and your trading account should be prepared for a drawdown of at least double what a back-testing of your Trading System tells you (and for profits, take into account half of those indicated by back-testing). In the above example, if the all-time high drawdown was $ 10,000, you should have a starting account of at least 20,000 or more.

Risk, in a single transaction, should represent only a small percentage of the available capital, preferably no more than 2% of your portfolio.

You can build up fortunes in the long run even by trading only 2-3 contracts at a time.

The important thing is to survive long enough to continue working on the market, without being "wiped out".

<u>Use real stop orders</u>

Enter them immediately after taking a position on the market. "Mental" stop-losses don't work! Keep the maximum drawdown low (20-25%).

<u>Limit the risk of your entire portfolio to a maximum of 20%</u>

In other words, if you were to suffer stop-loss at the same time in all the positions you had taken, make sure that 80% of the starting capital still remains.

<u>Maintain a reward/risk ratio (= return/risk) at a minimum of 2: 1 and preferably 3: 1 or more</u>

If you risk 1 point try to have a target of at least 2, better 3 points.

<u>Be realistic about the actual risks required to participate in</u>

the market for a certain instrument

For example, do not underestimate the risk of an overnight position in a very volatile security or on a leveraged instrument such as in the Standard & Poor's futures market ($ 250 per point for the main contract, $ 50 per point for the minimum).

Study the volatility of the market on which you are about to operate and adjust the size of the position (position sizing) to the conditions of the volatility itself

Take smaller positions in highly volatile markets. Be aware that volatility is cyclical.

Understand the correlation between different markets and your positions

If you are "long" on heating oil, crude oil and gas, you don't actually have 3 different positions! This is because these markets are highly correlated, you actually have a position in the energy sector with three times the risk of just one position. It would be the same as having three positions in crude oil, or three in heating oil.

Never add positions to positions that are at a loss (average down)

If you find yourself on the wrong side, against the market, admit it quickly and close the position. Your ego is often detrimental to proper trading.

Try to block at least part of the profits you are making

If you are lucky enough to take a substantial move in a short time, liquidate at least part of the position. This rule is especially valid for short-term trading where large gains are few.

The more active you are, the more trades you make and the lower the risks for each trade should be

If you make dozens of trades a day you can't afford to risk 3% on each trade - a bad day could "blow you away" (if, for example, you suffer 10-15 stop-losses in a row your capital would lose efficiency). Long-term traders, those who make 5-7 trades per year, can risk more on each trade (say 3-5% per trade). Regardless of how active you are in the market, however, limit your portfolio risk to 20%.

Apply the pyramiding technique correctly

Only add positions to profitable positions and make sure that the largest position is that of the first trade. For example, if you normally take portfolio positions of 1000 shares per stock, make sure you buy 600 with the first trade. Then add 300 (if the first trade becomes profitable) and finally another 100 if the stock moves further in the direction you want. Moreover, if you pyramide, be sure that the total risk of the position follows the rules previously indicated (for example, 2% in the whole operation, total portfolio risk not exceeding 20%, etc.)

Take advantage of the position when it is in your favor

Once the profit you are making in the operation has exceeded the figure that corresponded to your initial risk, close a part of the position and bring the stop-loss to the value of the breakeven.

Get to know the market you are operating in

This rule is especially valid in the derivatives market (options, futures).

When you have suffered a series of consecutive losses, stop and re-evaluate the market and your working methodology

The market will always be there waiting for you. Gann summarizes the concept in his book "How to make profits in commodities", published more than 50 years ago:

Consider the psychological impact of losing money

Contrary to many other rules discussed here, the psychological impact is difficult to quantify. Each individual reacts differently. You have to ask yourself honestly, "What could happen if I lose xxx $? Would it have a material impact on my lifestyle? And what about my family or my psychological state? You should learn to accept the consequences of suffering a series of consecutive stop-losses. Emotionally, you should be fully aware of the risks you are taking.

Avoid making "hope" your strategy

The main point is to understand that money management practically consists in understanding that it is necessary to study the risk that the investment entails in order to be able to risk only a small percentage on each operation, keeping the total exposure within reasonable margins. The above list is not completely exhaustive, but it should help avoid most problems.

Those who survive long enough on the markets to become successful traders are not just students of trading methodologies and disciplined applicants of such methodologies; they are also students of the risks associated with their techniques.

Glossary of survival and rules of operation

1. Do not commit more than 10% of the capital in a single trade

2. Do not have more than 5 trading operations open at the same time (= max 50% on the capital)

3. Always use an appropriate stop loss and do not move or remove it once placed

4. Identify a goal, both for each individual operation and for all your trading activity

5. If the trend turns out to be favorable, insert and adjust a stop profit level

6. Let profits run and cut losses

7. Do not allow a profit to turn into a loss

8. Do not open a trade if it conflicts with the trend

9. If in doubt it is better to close and, if in doubt, it is better not to open

10. Never mediate a losing trade: wait or close

11. Regarding the cyclicality of the markets: looking for opportunities in both directions

12. Establish risk/return ratios for trading operations of at least 2: 1

13. After a loss do not increase the percentage, but decrease it until you have recovered

14. Pyramiding only on very clear and very strong trends

15. Trade only on liquid markets/securities

16. Do not operate on options, warrants or derivatives if you do not fully understand the mechanisms and risks

17. Do not buy or sell just because the price is low or high

18. Never follow the advice of the "well informed", especially relatives, friends or bank tellers

Rules of conduct

1. Always follow the rules of operation

2. Be disciplined, disciplined and still disciplined

3. Think autonomously, independently and stick to your guidelines. Do not follow the crowd!

4. Understanding and mastering emotions, especially uncertainty, fear and greed

5. Keep it simple: complexity breeds confusion

6. Remain humble: too much confidence lead to the worst

losses

7. Be patient: knowing how to wait for the right opportunities is one of the trader's greatest skills

8. Have the strength to admit a mistake and close even if at a loss

9. Do not operate if you are not calm and physically fit

10. Do the analysis and/or study your own closed market strategies

11. Maintain a perspective - also in terms of operating weight - between short, medium and long trends

12. Be objective: having the courage to face the reality of the market

13. Have the strength to maintain a position or a strategy against everything and everyone

14. Be flexible and ready to change strategy quickly if the technical situation changes

15. Do not close out of impatience, but above all do not open out of anxiety about losing an opportunity

16. Diversify in terms of both markets and stocks

17. Refrain from trading after large gains or large losses

18. Remember that the market is a machine for disappointing, but it is always right

Trading indicators

Beginner traders can use some trading indicators, available for free, which help to improve immediately the performance obtained on the financial markets with trading activity. The proposed indicators are very simple to use and therefore are particularly suitable even for beginners.

How are the best indicators for trading made? Here are some key features of the best indicators:

Works well

It is easy to use

It is free

They work well

The first point on our list is truly the most important. In fact, having a trading indicator that is free, easy to use and makes you lose money is certainly not advisable.

What does it mean that a trading indicator works? It means that it is possible to obtain good results when trading online by following the indications of the indicator.

In short, the best indicators simply tell us whether we should trade up or down and the prediction comes true in most cases. No trading indicator is able to correctly predict the market in 100% of the cases: it is mathematically impossible. However, the best indicators manage to provide accurate predictions almost always.

They are easy

Doing complicated mathematical calculations to get the

indicator, perhaps without even the support of a software, is a real madness. Usually you are wrong, especially if you have little experience. A complex trading indicator to use is never good, not even for the most experienced and seasoned wolf of the markets, let alone for a beginner.

The best trading indicators are therefore very simple to use: the perfect indicator for a beginner should automatically provide the suggestion to go up or down.

They are free

Spending a fortune to pay for a subscription to trading indicators services is not very convenient, especially if the trading volumes are not high. In short, if I start trading online with a capital of $ 100, it makes no sense to pay $ 1000 a month for a professional trading indicators service. If, on the other hand, I have a millionaire capital, then yes, I can afford to invest more. However, novice traders usually start with $ 100 or $ 200, certainly not millions.

1 - MACD (Moving Average Convergence Divergence)

The MACD indicator is one of the most used in the field of technical analysis. It is considered by industry insiders as an essential resource due to the fact that it can provide a truly impressive amount of market data.

The MACD consists of a series of elements that interact with each other and each one is able to generate trading signals. In particular, when using this indicator it is necessary to pay attention to the movements of the so-called MACD line and the Signal Line. The intersection between these two lines can offer trading signals.

A further element to consider is the MACD histogram which is able to show the market volumes, a very important factor that speaks about how much participation there is on a given asset at a certain time.

2 - Simple Moving Average

Known in English as the "Simple Moving Average", the moving average is the basic indicator of all trading activity both online and offline. Anyone involved in financial markets cannot fail to know the moving average and all the potential it can express during the investment phase.

The moving average represents an "average" of the price. Once calculated on the basis of data entered directly by the trader, it is expressed through a function that is displayed directly on the price chart.

The Moving Average is a trading indicator, which means that it is used by traders in order to identify the current trend, trying to understand its changes. It can be used alone or accompanied by other moving averages calculated differently.

3 - Pivot Point Indicator

A very special trading indicator are the so-called Pivot Points, with French pronunciation. The indicator in question is used because it serves to find the so-called "key points of the market". These are particular price areas that are always held in high consideration by the market.

Around the Pivot Points the market tends to behave as if it is in proximity to supports and resistances (another fundamental indicator in the field of online trading). For this reason, the study and use of Pivot Points can provide generally very interesting and reliable trading signals for traders who are able to grasp capture them.

4 - Supports and Resistors

Other indicators that you really cannot do without in the negotiation phase are the supports and resistances. They represent actually a graphic indicator, consequently the trader has to draw the supports and resistances on the price chart himself in order to take them into account and predict the next market developments.

Supports and resistances are limit areas of the price that the market cannot overcome respectively on the downside or the upside. Based on the strength and duration of a support or resistance, it is also possible to determine the reliability of the trading signals generated by the break of one of these price levels.

Plotting supports and resistances is simple: just note which are certain price quotas that have not been exceeded increasing or decreasing after several attempts by the market. There it will be necessary to trace some half-lines that indicate the pivotal point to be examined.

5 - Trend Lines

Very similar to supports and resistances are the trend lines. In any trading activity, it is essential to identify the current market trend. In other words, a trader must understand if the price is in a bullish or bearish phase of the price and act accordingly.

Thanks to the trend lines it is possible to immediately identify which phase the market is in, but also to understand if there are signs of a trend reversal or if the trend is still stable.

Each trend is made up of a succession of highs and lows that increase or decrease depending on the case. When this condition does not exist, we can speak of a market in lateral phase or not in trend. The breakdown of these dynamic supports and resistances marks a good time to enter the market.

6 - RSI oscillator

As you have understood now that we have talked about indicators of all kinds, in the analysis phase it is always important to identify the limit areas of the market. If there is an indicator capable of doing this, it is the RSI oscillator.

The RSI is precisely an oscillator, this means that it will not be displayed directly on the price chart, but below it because here its oscillation between the values of zero and 100 is configured. Based on where the RSI will be, it will be possible to understand the market phase.

In particular, the RSI is useful for identifying the overbought and oversold phases. We are talking about market excesses where buyers or sellers have prevailed for too long and too strongly. The RSI is able to show a similar situation by swinging between the above values.

Recognizing when a market is overbought or oversold is crucial because it helps to understand what the next wisest move to take in market trading will be.

7 - Bollinger bands

Another fundamental indicator for online trading are the so-called Bollinger Bands, an indicator named after their discoverer and inventor John Bollinger. These are a trend indicator that is based just on the simple moving average like many other trading indicators.

The bands get their name from the fact that they are 3 curves that move along with the price and constantly wrap around it. The crucial phases in the observation of this indicator come when we observe the price approaching the upper or lower band, here the trading signals are generated.

8 - ADX

The ADX is also a trend indicator and is used to measure the strength of the trend. It was invented by Welles Wilder to obtain information on the trends of commodities, but is now permanently used for the analysis of other markets such as Forex where it has also proved to be very effective.

The indicator is made up of two variables + DI and - DI. By observing these elements it is possible to understand the strength of the current trend and its direction both in a bullish and bearish sense. With these data in hand, the trader is able to understand if it is convenient for him to invest up or down and make the purchase of the correct market position.

CHAPTER SEVEN
10 MISTAKES TO AVOID

Making mistakes is part of the learning process when it comes to trading. Traders generally buy and sell stocks more frequently and hold positions for much shorter periods than traditional investors. This frequent trading and shorter holding periods can lead to mistakes that could quickly wipe out a new trader's invested capital.

While traders of all ages are guilty of the following mistakes from time to time, the novice trader should be especially careful not to make these types of mistakes.

1. No trading plan

Experienced traders enter trading with a well-defined plan. They know their exact entry and exit points, the amount of capital to invest in the trade, and the maximum loss they are willing to take. Beginner traders may not have a trading plan in place before starting trading; and even if they have a plan, they may be more inclined to abandon it than experienced traders would be if things were not going well. Or they may reverse course altogether, for example, going short after buying a stock initially because its price is falling, only to end up getting whipsawed.

Pursuing performance against rebalancing

Many investors choose asset classes, strategies, managers and funds based on recent strong performance. The feeling that "I'm missing out on big returns" has probably led to worse investment decisions than any other single factor. If a particular asset class, strategy or fund has done very well for three or four years, we know one thing for sure: we should have invested three or four years ago. Now, however, the particular cycle that led to this great performance may be near its end. Smart money is moving, and stupid money is pouring out. Stick to the investment plan and rebalance, which is the exact opposite of the performance chase.

What is rebalancing?

Rebalancing is the process of returning the portfolio to its target asset allocation as outlined in the investment plan. Rebalancing is difficult because it forces you to sell the asset class that performs well and buys more of your worst performing asset classes. This type of countered action is not easy for many investors. Also, rebalancing isn't profitable to the point where it pays off spectacularly (think about U.S. stocks in the late 1990s) and underperforming assets start to take off.

Such a portfolio that allows market returns to move, ensures that asset classes are overweight at market peaks and underweight at market lows - a formula for poor performance. The solution? A rigorous and constant rebalancing.

Don't consider your risk aversion

Don't lose sight of your risk tolerance or your ability to take risks. If you're the type of investor who can't handle the volatility and ups and downs associated with the stock market, perhaps it would be better to invest in the blue-chip stock of an established company rather than the volatile stock of a start-up.

Remember that the expected return carries a risk. If an investment offers very attractive returns, look at its risk profile as well and see how much money you could lose if things go wrong. And don't invest more than you can afford to lose.

A time horizon that is too short or non-existent

Additionally, do not invest without a time horizon in mind. If your goal is to accumulate money to buy a home, it may be more than a medium-term time horizon. If, instead, you are putting your money into the market with the goal of financing a child's college education, it is more of a long-term investment. You will need to find investments that fit your time horizon.

If you've been saving for retirement for 30 years, what the stock market does this year or next shouldn't be your biggest concern. Even if you are about to retire at 70, your life expectancy is probably between 15 and 20 years. If you plan to leave some assets to your heirs, then your time horizon is even longer. Of course, if you are saving for your daughter's college education and she is a secondary school, then your time horizon is appropriately short and your asset allocation should reflect this fact. In general, however, most investors are too focused on the short term.

2. Do not use Stop-Loss orders

If you are not using stop-loss is a clear sign that you do not have a trading plan. Stop-loss orders are generally limited before the losses become substantial. Although there is a risk that a stop order on long positions may be implemented at levels well below those specified if security gaps are reduced, the benefits of such orders outweigh this risk. Often a trader also makes another fairly common mistake, when he cancels a stop order on a loss-making trade just before it can be triggered, because he believes that the security could immediately reverse the course and allow the trade to succeed again.

3. Leaving support for losses

One of the hallmarks of successful traders is their ability to quickly take a small loss if a trade fails and move on to the next trading idea. On the other hand, unsuccessful traders can get paralyzed if a trade goes against them. Rather than acting quickly to make up for a loss, they may remain in a losing position in hopes that the trade will eventually resolve. A losing trade can tie uptrading capital for a long time and can result in increasing losses and severe capital drain.

4. Calculation of the average

Brokerage on a long position in blue-chip stocks may work for an investor who has a long investment horizon, but it can be fraught with danger for a trader who is trading volatile and riskier stocks. It is well known that many of the biggest trading losses in history occurred because a trader continued to add a losing position, and was eventually forced to cut the entire position when the magnitude of the loss became unsustainable. Traders are also below conservative investors and tend to average, as security is advancing rather than decreasing. This is an equally risky move that is another common mistake made by a novice trader.

The importance of accepting losses

Too often investors do not accept the simple fact that they are human beings and prone to making mistakes, just like big investors do. If you have made a purchase of shares in a hurry or one of your long-standing large earnings has suddenly taken a turn for the worse, the best thing you can do is accept it. One of the worst things a trader can do is to let his pride take priority over his portfolio and to hold on to an investment at a loss. Or even worse, buy more shares of the stock, since it is now much cheaper.

This is a very common mistake and those who make it do so by comparing the current stock price with the stock's 52-week high. Many people who use this gauge assume that a lapsed stock price represents a good buy. But the fact that a company's stock price increased 30% last year won't help it make more money this year. That's why it pays to analyze why a stock has fallen.

Understanding the fundamentals and false buy signals

Determination of fundamentals, the resignation of a chief executive officer (CEO), or increased competition are all possible reasons for a lower share price; but these same reasons also provide good clues to suspect that the stock may not rise anytime soon. A company may be worth less today but for fundamental reasons. It is important to always have a critical eye, because a low share price could be a false purchase signal.

Be careful to buy shares that look like just a bargain. In many cases, there is a strong underlying reason for a fall in prices. Do your homework and analyze the prospects of a stock before investing in it. You want to invest in companies that will experience sustained growth in the future.

Remember that a company's future operating performance has nothing to do with the price at which you bought its shares. When there is a sharp drop in the price of your shares, try to determine the reasons for the change and see if the company is a good investment for the future. If it is not, transfer your money to a company with better prospects.

5. Too much margin

Margin - the use of borrowed money to buy stocks - can help you earn more, but it can also exaggerate your losses, which makes it potentially detrimental. The worst thing you can do as a new investor is getting carried away by what looks like free money. If you use margin and your investment doesn't go as planned, you eventually find yourself in big debt for nothing. Ask yourself if you want to buy a stocks with your credit card. Sure, you wouldn't. Excessive use of margin is essentially the same thing, albeit probably at a lower interest rate.

Additionally, using margin requires you to monitor positions much more closely due to the exaggerated gains and losses that accompany small moves in the price. If you don't have the time or knowledge to keep an eye on and make decisions about your positions, and their values go down, your brokerage firm will sell your stock to recoup any accumulated losses.

Since you are a novice investor, use the margin sparingly, if possible, and only if you understand all its aspects and dangers. It can force you to sell all your positions downwards, where you should be in the market for the big breakthrough.

<u>Learn about leverage</u>

According to a well-known investment cliché, leverage is a double-edged sword because it can increase returns on profitable trades and exacerbate losses if trades are lost. Beginner traders may be dazzled by the degree of leverage they hold, especially in forex (FX), but they may soon find that excessive leverage can destroy trading capital in a flash. Attention: if you use a leverage ratio of 50: 1, which is not difficult to find in retail forex trading, a negative move of 2% is enough to wipe out the capital. Brokers must tell traders that more than three-quarters of traders lose money due to the complexity of the market and the negative side of leverage.

6. Follow the flock of sheep blindly

Another common mistake of new entrants is that they blindly follow the pack; as such, they may end up paying too much for hot stocks or they may start short positions in stocks that have already plummeted and may be on the verge of reversing. While experienced traders follow the saying the trend is your friend, they are used to doing business when they are too crowded. New traders, however, can remain in a trading position long after the smart currency has exited it. Beginning traders may also not be sure to take a contrarian approach when required.

Remember: don't put all your eggs in one basket

Diversification is one way to avoid overexposure to any investment. Having a portfolio consisting of multiple investments protects you if one of them loses money. It also helps protect against volatility and extreme price movements in any investment.

Many studies have shown that most managers and mutual funds underperform their benchmarks. In the long run, low-cost index funds typically perform in the top second quartile or above 65% -75% of actively managed funds. Despite all the evidence in favor of indexation, the desire to invest with active managers remains strong. John Bogle, the founder of Vanguard, says it's because: "Hope is eternal, indexing is a little boring, it flies in the face the American way [that]" I can do better ".

Index all or a large portion (70% -80%) of your traditional investment classes. If you can't resist the excitement of pursuing the next great performer, then set aside about 20% - 30% of each asset class for active managers. This could satisfy your desire to pursue outperformance without devastating your portfolio.

7. Do your homework

New traders are often guilty of not doing their homework or not conducting proper research before they start trading. Doing your homework is critical because novice traders don't have the knowledge of seasonal trends or data release times and trading patterns that experts have. For a person who has recently started trading the impulse to trade often exceeds the need to undertake some research, but this can ultimately result in an expensive lesson.

It is a mistake not to research an investment that interests you. Research helps you understand a financial instrument and know what you are in. If you are investing in stocks, for example, do some research about the company and its business plans. Do not act on the premise that markets are efficient and you cannot make money by identifying good investments. Even if this is not an easy task and every other investor has access to the same information you have, it is possible to identify good investments by doing the research.

Don't buy relying on unfounded advice

It is very likely that many people make this mistake at one time or another in their careers as investors. You may hear your relatives or friends talking about a stock they have heard about buying, making skyrocketing profits or releasing a revolutionary new product soon. Even if these things are true, it does not necessarily mean that the stock is "the next big thing" and that you should rush to your online brokerage account to place a purchase order.

Other unfounded suggestions come from television and social media investment professionals who often claim a specific stock as if it were a must buy, but in reality, it's just the flavor of the day. These stock market tips often don't pop up and go straight down after you buy them. Remember, buying media advice is often founded on nothing more than a speculative bet.

This is not to say that you should stop at every stock market tip. If one really gets your attention, the first thing to do is to consider the source. The next thing is to do your homework so that you know what you are buying and why. For example, buying a tech stock with proprietary technology should be based on whether it is the right investment for you, not just what a mutual fund manager said in a media interview.

The next time you're tempted to buy based on a suggestion, don't do it until you have all the data and are comfortable with the company. Ideally, get a second opinion from other impartial investors or financial advisors.

Do not pay too much attention to financial media

Often there is almost nothing in financial news that can help you achieve your goals. There are few newsletters that can provide you with anything of value. Even if there are, how do you identify them in advance?

If someone had useful stock market advice, trading tips or a secret formula to earn a lot of money, would they send it on TV or sell it for $49 a month? No. They would keep their mouths shut, make millions and wouldn't need to sell a newsletter to make a living. The solution? Spend less time watching financial programs on TV and reading newsletters and spend more time creating and sticking to your investment plan.

Face the big picture when buying a stock

For a long-term investor, one of the most important, but often overlooked, things to do is qualitative analysis, or look at the big picture. Bothering one of the best investors, Peter Lynch, once said he found the best investments by looking at his children's toys and the trends they would face. The brand name is also very valuable. Think about how almost everyone in the world knows Coca-Cola; the financial value of the name alone is therefore measured in billions of dollars. Whether it's iPhone or Big Mac, no one can stand in the way of real life.

So pouring budgets or trying to identify buying and selling opportunities with complex technical analysis can work for a long time, but if the world is changing against your company, sooner or later you will lose. Remember that in the late 1980s, a typewriter company could have outperformed any company in its industry, but once personal computers started to become commonplace, a typewriter investor of that era would have done well to assess the big picture and wander around.

Evaluating a company from a qualitative point of view is as important as looking at its sales and earnings. Qualitative analysis is one of the easiest and most effective strategies to evaluate a potential investment.

8. Don't trade on multiple markets

Beginner traders may tend to float from market to market, i.e. from stocks to options, currencies, commodity futures and so on. Operating in many markets can be a great distraction and can prevent the novice trader from gaining the necessary experience to excel in a market.

9. Don't forget about taxes

Keep the tax consequences in mind before investing. You will get a tax deduction on some investments such as municipal bonds. Before investing, look at what your return will be after adjusting your taxes, taking into account the investment, tax bracket and investment time horizon.

Do not pay more than necessary for trading and brokerage fees. By keeping your investment and not trading frequently, you will save on brokerage costs. Finally, look for a broker who does not charge excessive commissions, so that you can maintain a higher return on your investment.

10. The danger of Hubris

Trading is a very demanding occupation, but the "beginner's luck" experienced by some novice traders can lead them to believe that trading is the proverbial road to fast riches. Such overconfidence is dangerous as it breeds complacency and encourages excessive risk-taking that could culminate in a commercial disaster.

It is easy to see from numerous studies that most managers will often fail to achieve their benchmarks. It is not easy to select the managers who outperform in advance. We also know that very few people can profit from time to market in the long term. So why do many investors trust their ability to time the market and/or select the best performing managers? Loyalty guru Peter Lynch once observed: "There are no market timers in the Forbes 400.

Inexperienced day trading

If you insist on becoming an active trader, think twice before trading every day. Day trading can be a dangerous game and should only be attempted by experienced investors. Surely a successful trader, as well as working smart, can gain an advantage by having access to special equipment that is less easily available to the average trader. Did you know that the average daily workstation (with software) can cost tens of thousands of dollars? You will also need a significant amount of trading money to maintain an efficient day trading strategy.

The need for speed is the main reason why you cannot effectively start day trading with the extra $5,000 in your bank account. However, online broker systems are often not fast enough to serve the real day trader; literally, cents per share can make the difference between a profitable trade and a loser. Most brokers recommend that investors take daily trading courses before they start.

Unless you have experience, a platform, and access to fast order execution, think twice before trading daily. If you are not very good at managing risk and stress, there are better options for an investor who is looking to create wealth.

Underestimate your abilities

Some investors, however, tend to believe that they will never excel in investing because they believe that the success of the stock market is reserved only for sophisticated investors. This perception has no truth. While commission fund sellers will probably tell you otherwise, most professional fund managers don't even vote, and the vast majority have underperformed the broad market. With a little time devoted to learning and research, investors can become well equipped to control their portfolios and investment decisions while still being profitable. Remember, many investments stick to common sense and rationality.

Individual investors, for their part, do not have to face the liquidity challenges and overheads of large institutional investors. Any small investor with a sound investment strategy has an equally good chance of beating the market, if not better than so-called investment gurus. Do not assume that you will not be able to successfully participate in the financial markets just because you have a day job.

Conclusions

If you have the money to invest and you can avoid these beginner mistakes, you could charge for your investments; and getting a good return on your investments could bring you closer to your financial goals.

With the tendency of the stock market to produce high gains (and losses), there is no shortage of bad advice and irrational decisions.

Remember, if you are trying to make a big win by betting your money according to your instincts, try a casino. Be proud of your investment decisions and, in the long term, your portfolio will grow to reflect the strength of your actions.

CHAPTER EIGHT
FIVE GOOD REASON
TO DAY TRADING

Online trading has seen an increase in popularity in recent years, a growth also due to the increasingly accessible, simple and usable trading platforms even on smartphones and tablets.

More and more people are starting to trade in their free time with the aim of earning a little more every day. Trading can be the tool to get a second income, or in many cases even as a main activity, a living from trading is possible.

1) Become a financially independent trader

Going on your own at 50 is certainly more difficult than at 30 rather than 20, but with a little study, patience and great passion, I can tell you that it can be done. The road to economic independence can be reached even at 60, but it must be strongly desired. What to say, better to know that there are possibilities to do it, and we will go to see them in this article, than to get depressed and feel sorry for yourself without doing anything constructive. Before starting, I wanted to make a talk about passion. Here we are going to talk about financial markets and how to exploit them, a subject that for many of you may at first glance be boring, but when you understand that it is possible to create a respectable economic position at any age, understanding how to exploit the financial markets, I guarantee that the passion comes.

Being independent is a bit everyone's dream and online trading, being to all effects an entrepreneurial activity, allows you to set up on your own and manage your business independently. An independent trader is an entrepreneur who has decided to start his own business by investing in the financial markets.

Online trading is a high-risk business, it is true, but not less than any other business. Every entrepreneur when opening any business must take into account that there are risks. The important thing is to know how to manage these risks and in online trading this is possible and it is the fundamental aspect to learn when deciding to trade online.

Generally many kids who stop studying early or who have finished their studies and try their hand at online trading fail for the simple fact that they consider trading an easy way to make money. In trading, actually, if you're not careful it's so easy to make money but it's even easier to lose it. The approach is fundamental. I repeat, it must be an entrepreneurial approach.

Before opening any business, you always look at what are the expenses and what may be the possible earnings to see it is really worth coming across this experience. An entrepreneur who decides to open a shop must start investing by buying goods in order to resell them and must estimate that part of the goods will not be sold with great probability. Therefore he must estimate that the earnings he will have to obtain from the sale will also have to take charge of the unsold to be profitable. There is also the risk that the unsold may be greater than expected and therefore you can go at a loss. But a true entrepreneur does not stop and optimizes investments in order to make sure that the earnings exceed the expenses and thus grow with his business.

So it must be in trading. You analyze the markets, you see where you can have good margins and where any losses can be contained and you start investing. You can close your investment at any time. It is not certain that every investment must necessarily close in profit. To earn, you also need to know when it is the right time to exit a trade and focus your attention on other assets, on other markets that can be more profitable at that precise moment.

How do you do it? You have to study. The markets are analyzed and based on their trend, the learned trading strategies are applied which, like a dress, must be sewn on each asset. As traders, we must adapt to the markets and follow their curves. We must never make the mistake of thinking that it is the market that must adapt to our strategies, otherwise we will be screwed.

2) Work wherever you want

Working from home, or wherever you want, is the choice that day after day is made by many people who, rather than getting up early in the morning to go to an office every single day of their life, choosing comfort and saving their physical energy.

In fact, nowadays, the web offers various opportunities to

earn money online while comfortably seated on the armchair at home in total relaxation.

From home you have the possibility to manage your work in the way you prefer, because you will establish the best hours to work from home in a completely autonomous way and you can choose when to take a day off without being accountable to anyone.

Among the activities that allow you to work independently is online trading. Who decides to become a trader must know that it is a real profession.

Therefore, to trade it is necessary to study a lot and practice as well. If you want to make a profit, you absolutely cannot improvise as a trader, but you need to put the different trading strategies into practice.

3) The benefits of diversifying investments

When trading online we recommend that you diversify your investments across a range of different markets in order to minimize your risk exposure.

If you decide to export heavily and the market moves strongly against you, your potential losses could be huge. However, by differentiating your exposure across multiple open positions, you reduce the impact that a large market event can significantly impact your overall profit margins.

When trading online you can easily control and manage your investments to build a diversified portfolio that offers consistent returns.

4) Opportunity at any time

Markets can move quickly in both directions, there are opportunities at any time of the day or night; thanks to modern and reliable mobile trading platforms it will be easier to trade at the best time. Choose a broker that has a mobile application that allows you to manage your account via smartphone, tablet or PC.

5) Money always safe and secure

If you choose to start trading, choose a broker that is reliable, regulated, whose funds are safe and secure.

This is sometimes a difficult choice as it is not possible to know everything and the search is sometimes complicated and long.

CHAPTER NINE
WHY DO MOST ASPIRING TRADERS FAIL?

You may not have believed that an online trading book could tell you this much...but here's the truth: it has been estimated that 90% of aspiring traders will blow their capital up within the first year of business. This data could create dismay in traders or potential interested parties; but go ahead with the reading to understand how this is possible.

The question that arises is: why does this happen? Is trading so difficult that only a select few can succeed? The answer is no; everyone can potentially be good traders but under specific conditions.

Here is the classic story of many improvised traders: maybe it can happen that the first trades are lucky. We think we have already understood everything and we begin to increase the size of the positions. At some point comes a large unexpected loss that halves your capital. The impromptu trader tries to recover everything immediately. However, things no longer work as they did in the beginning and the capital continues to decrease until it is inexorably zero.

This is a stereotypical scenario but not very far from reality. The problem is that very often beginners throw themselves into the market with large sums of money, in a hurry to make substantial profits without really knowing what they are doing.

There are many other profitable professions in the world: lawyer, banker, doctor, etc. However, these professions require several years of study and practice before obtaining an important economic return. So why should trading be any different? Trading is a profession like any other. It can be carried out not as a main occupation (to have an extra income compared to a "classic job"); in any case, however, it is necessary to study and acquire specific knowledge. Fortunately, becoming a successful trader can take a lot less than the path it takes to become a doctor or an engineer. A lot of study and a lot of practice, however, are the same fundamental requirements to be a good trader.

Don't be in a hurry: the market continually offers good opportunities. In the world of trading, the saying "every left over is lost" is the most wrong thing that can exist. It is good to know first what you are doing: practice trading using a demo account and, only after you are confident enough in your strategy and skills, you can think about using part of your capital.

When starting with real money it is important to start with caution by opening small positions. The key point is not to win very quickly, but to stay in the game long enough to really know how to move and really start earning.

There are three basic concepts that an aspiring trader must absolutely know before starting. They are very simple concepts that we have decided to summarize in a formula to always keep in mind.

1. Strict method:

It is important to choose a strategy that is suitable for your trading style (we will talk about this in the following articles) and to stick to the strategy without inventing. Trading is a systematic business; trusting an intuition can lead to some lucky wins but it doesn't work in the long run.

2. Money management:

Managing your capital is essential. The key to trading success is to keep your capital whatever happens. We will go into more detail in this topic but it is essential to understand the right balance between maximizing profit and keeping risk under control. Only good money management will allow you to make the success of your trading strategy bear fruit.

3. Cold Mind:

Trading psychology is an underestimated aspect but it is very important. When there is money at stake, stress increases, compromising our lucidity in making decisions. There is a tendency to close profitable positions early to make a quick profit. On the contrary, we tend to leave losing positions open for too long in the hope of being able to recover. This causes winnings to be less than losses and in the long run this destroys the trader's capital. Trading psychology is important to be able to implement your strategy without greed or fear. The good trader learns to trust his system after the "defeats"; in the same way he knows how not to get too carried away even after many "victories".

CHAPTER TEN
THE BEST TRADERS
IN THE WORLD

Getting to know who the best traders in the world are can not only satisfy your curiosity, but if you are working or approaching the online trading sector it can be an option to have points of reference from which to draw inspiration and learn.

Of course, no novice trader can think of joining the best professionals in the world, nevertheless having the opportunity to learn from the best traders can be very useful.

Who are the best traders in the world?

Being among the best traders does not necessarily correspond to being the richest.

In fact, the best are those who have managed to make history, not only for the earnings obtained, but also for the great skills demonstrated.

It goes without saying, however, that often the two lines correspond, and mostly they are investors who have made their way through their methods.

For this reason, among the best traders in the world there are investors who are often mentioned on TV or in newspapers, and not necessarily only in the financial sector.

The best traders in the world are:

Warren Buffett

Also known as the Oracle of Omaha, Warren Buffett is a true legend.

Only a single person can own as many as seven investment funds since the 1960s.

The creation of the Berkshire Hathaway fund, the fund with which Buffett has stakes everywhere, is certainly what made him go down in history.

Warren Buffett's input has always been to invest in companies that are understated and that have especially long-term potential.

Buffett is rated as the best trader of all time.

Among the most important investments made by Buffet there is necessarily the one made in Coca-Cola.

George Soros

He is also on the list of the best traders in the world.

Shares represent one of the best known, appreciated and always used investments by savers.

Today the name of Soros is also and above all recognized for events that not only concern finance but also politics and society.

Soros' success is all based on the Soros Fund Management

investment fund, a fund dedicated to speculation on upcoming bursts of financial bubbles.

In practice, it was through this fund that Soros made stratospheric gains by betting, for example, on the collapse of the pound in 1992, the collapse of our Lira and the fall in price of the Swiss Franc.

However, Soros' speculations have not always translated into earnings, but today his financial assets are calculated above 19 billion dollars, which also makes him fall into the category of the richest traders in the world.

James Simons

James Simons is certainly one of the most talented and capable traders to enter the history of online trading, although not among the richest.

The reason that led him to be among the best is characteristic.

Simons, in fact, was one of the first investors to adopt mathematics to finance.

His investment fund is all about mathematical models.

But Simons is also part of the history of the best traders in the world for having predicted the subprime mortgage crisis and for having used short positions on stocks at the right time.

John Paulson

John Paulson is the Founder of the Paulson & Co.

With his nickname, The Sultan of Subprime, Paulson made it

into the books of trading history.

In fact, Paulson was the trading genius who most of all managed to anticipate the subprime crisis.

Thanks to short selling, in the middle of the subprime crisis, Paulson was able to multiply the capital of his funds by up to 2500 percent.

<u>Steven Cohen</u>

Also called the lord of the hundred thousand dollars a day, Steven Cohen must necessarily be included among the best traders in the world.

In fact, this trader's earnings when he worked as a broker at Gruntal & Co.

Short selling of shares is the secret of its success.

It was thanks to the gains made through shorts that Cohen was able to enter the top ten of traders.

The richest traders in the world

As we have mentioned, the best are not always necessarily the richest.

In fact, among those we have indicated among the richest there is only George Soros.

According to the latest data, in addition to Soros, the richest traders in the world are:

Martin Schwartz

Day trading professor Martin Schwartz made his fortune as quickly as it was surprising.

According to some estimates, Schwartz is now able to earn around seventy thousand dollars every day.

A large part of his success is linked to his proverbial ability to use futures.

Stanley Druckenmiller

While having no background in the world of finance, Drockenmiller was able to earn something like $ 3.5 billion during his career.

This investor has managed to become one of the richest traders in the world using a methodology focused on the concept of top down.

A shrewd and scrupulous study of the economic environment and of the famous reference context within which he used to insert the most classic technical analysis.

Alexander Elder

Alexander Elder is not only one of the richest traders in the world but he is also one of the most followed by all investors.

With so many books and interventions, Elder's advice is considered very valid by most traders around the world.

Elder is identified as one of the greatest experts in technical analysis and market psychology.

Larry Hite

Larry Hite's name is linked to the development of the most important trading community in the world.

Larry Hite is very productive in training.

Larry's advice, like Elder's, is also found to be very useful and has a huge following from industry users around the world.

CHAPTER ELEVEN
THE STRATEGIES
OF THE GREATS

Warren Buffett's strategies

In-depth description of Warren Buffett's strategies, which will make you invest in the stock market with criteria, imitating the choices of a character who dominated the market in the new millennium.

If you have no idea who we are talking about, we advise you to pay close attention to the premise on the companies that have made Warren Buffett known, with the aim of making you understand how precious the tips on the approach to investments in the stock market can be provided by such a industry expert.

According to many, he is the largest value investor ever. According to Forbes he was the richest man in the world in 2007 and 2008 and is currently firmly in the top ten. In short, here's who Warren Buffett is and why everyone should follow the advice offered by the Omaha economist. Born 85 years ago, still today without rivals at its height when it comes to finding the most appropriate way to invest in the stock market and earn impressive figures.

Even if we talk about charity, Buffet has proved to be a great man that many should take as an example, having donated a whopping 37 billion dollars to the populations of the Third World and pledging to allocate 83% of his total wealth to the

Bill & Melinda Gates Foundation.

Warren Buffett's ten strategies

Investing in the stock market in the best way, here are the ten strategies that Warren Buffett uses when dealing with important decisions. Widespread a few years ago, they still occupy a very important role even today for investors who choose the most modern trading routes to make their money grow.

1. Invest based on your knowledge

If you don't know a market well, Warren Buffett advises you to change your lens and not get carried away by the desire to try always and in any case. Even if you are based on successful forecasting methods, the most appropriate choice is always to refer to personal knowledge brands, such as companies whose information is known through their work.

2. Yes to long-term investments

Warren Buffett does not pay attention to what happens in the short term, but rather advises users to thoroughly study the trends relating to at least the last ten years, before making a long-term investment where he even recommends holding the position forever, if possible, just as he did with the Coca-Cola shares he has owned for 27 years.

3. Here are the factors to keep an eye on

Before reserving part of your capital for the shares of a

particular company, it is necessary to understand if you can really rely on it without taking too many risks and with an excellent probability of profit. The factors are low debt amounts, a good balance sheet and a sufficiently high price-to-earnings ratio.

4. Approximate management? No thanks

If you have a great opportunity to take home securities at bargain prices, but on the other hand the company that issues them does not reveal real management amounts (keeping vague), the right choice according to Warren Buffett's strategies is changing direction and not risking bankruptcy.

5. Buy at the right time

As Buffet teaches, who in the past has made great deals buying companies in a recession (Bank of America is one of them) it is good to find the right time to make purchases as well as for sales. If others are greedy you need to be afraid, if others are afraid you need greed, says the economist, describing his experience with a sort of proverb.

6. Don't buy everything right away

If following the previous advice you have decided to invest in the stock market considering the shares of a particular company that you consider advantageous, do not immediately rush into the purchase of all the securities by exhausting your available capital. This is because the unexpected is always around the corner and a right intuition could turn into an incredible loss. Warren Buffett teaches that the right method is to invest some of the money in the initial phase, and then analyze the trend and gradually proceed with new purchases in case everything goes as planned.

7. Cash always available

Warren Buffett believes cash reserves are very important in any case, both if we win, and if instead we have to face unpleasant losses, hypotheses always to be considered. In the first case, liquidity would give us the opportunity to increase our investments in a stock (in this regard, we connect to the sixth advice), while in the second it would avoid total disaster if our shares were to take a bad turn.

8. Admit your mistakes

When it comes to investments, it is always hard to admit to yourself that you were wrong to make a prediction and that therefore it is time to look towards new horizons learning from the past. Even Warren Buffett, who we reiterate as one of the richest men in the world, admits he made glaring oversights, such as when he sold Disney shares before a noticeable rise.

9. Also consider foreign securities

Although Buffet admits that investing in the stock market by basing his attention on stocks he knows is the best choice, he adds that the right strategy is to keep an eye on foreign stocks as well. This is because sometimes they can yield more than the internal ones or even compensate for the losses of the latter.

10. Calculate the weight of the tax on profits

The capital gain, that is the capital gain or in simple terms what you go to earn from the difference between the sale and purchase price of a stock, is subject to annoying taxes that limit profits. For this reason, before closing a position in your favor, it is good to calculate how much you are going to earn by removing the amount due to the tax authorities, in order to understand if it is really convenient to close the position. Of course, avoiding commissions will also be an important aspect.

Investing in the stock market like George Soros

Who is George Soros?

George Soros understood how the game works and not just the stock markets but the economy in general. He is ten steps ahead of the others and this explains the results that have always made people talk about himself.

Investing in the stock market is one of the many ways in which "the rich" manage to grow their capital year after year. They defend it from the erosive force of inflation and George Soros has used this and many other tricks to build a boundless empire of wealth.

Soros protected himself from inflation like this

To realize the incessant "hard work" that inflation does on our savings, I'll give you an example.

If inflation is 2.5 percent annually, the purchasing power of your money decreases by the same percentage every year. So if for example this year you buy a pound of platinum for $ 1000, the following year the same pound of platinum will cost you $ 1025. The figures are invented but they give the idea.

The solution to beat inflation

The only solution to this phenomenon is to find a way to make your money grow with a force greater than the one of inflation.

One of these methods is investing in the stock market with a method that guarantees, I repeat, guarantees, the constant increase of your capital over time.

To do this you have to strictly block the losses and let the profits run.

I said strictly since this is a golden rule. This rule is trivialized by most but it is fundamental. This is because if, for example, you force yourself to block your losses at 7 percent and to collect profits only when your stock reaches at least 30 percent, the differential between these two percentages will mathematically guarantee you the increase in capital in the long term.

George Soros made Easy

By taking advantage of the strength of compound interest, your money can be multiplied easily. This force according to Einstein is the most miraculous force of nature. This phrase is well known to Soros and has always been applied by him without exception. We will see our savings increase at a rate comparable to that at which mice reproduce. This is realized by reinvesting the profits made in order to obtain a more and more robust capital.

As the amount of capital invested increases, the speed at which it grows multiplies.

This is another explanation of the immense wealth accumulated by Soros.

This method even works if we assume that we randomly choose the securities we want to invest in. But rest assured that Soros doesn't do that. In fact it will work much more if we respect certain investment criteria. This happens when we use certain (trivial but very effective) tools that can make us find certain titles in a short time and with minimum effort. These are the stocks that can maximize the yield of this strategy.

How does this strategy work?

This Soros taught, but it was not at all easy to understand because the simple is always masked by the complicated.

It is necessary to choose stocks with excellent fundamentals, that is guided by a management that knows how to make money go well. Over the years, these stocks have seen excellent returns on investment in terms of capital gains and perhaps even dividends distributed to shareholders.

Only a trainer other than the classic ones, able to explain these concepts to you in a very simple way as it should be explained to a child, will clarify how all the premises I have just described can be applied in practice.

It is necessary to carry out a rigorous analysis but know that not all rigorous analyzes must necessarily be complicated: rigorous analyzes are such because they are conducted with simple effective criteria and in a very careful way, not because they are complicated to put into practice.

This analysis allows you to compare certain fundamental variables with each other (i.e. that describe the economic characteristics of the Company) in a specific market context and have a fairly precise idea of the financial health conditions of the company you are at a "glance" examining (a more detailed analysis can be obtained by reading the financial statements carefully).

Soros teaches us the importance of the Safety Margin

You need to look for a safety margin that is realized only when you are able to buy a security at a price well below its intrinsic value.

In other words, it is like knowing that a pair of Roberto Cavalli shoes are worth about $ 200 (for how they are made, for the material they choose and for the image impact they give you), you know that they are normally available on the market for more than $ 400 and you can buy them in an outlet for $ 150: you got a great deal right from the start.

In this case it can be said that you bought with an excellent safety margin.

You have a kind of insurance that guarantees you even in the worst market conditions that your stock will hardly go below the price at which you bought it.

You will also know that since the average market price is

around $ 400 with peaks even at $ 500, sooner or later the market (made up of a sometimes very bizarre relationship between supply and demand) will recognize the intrinsic value of that security.

The stop loss

When the stock reaches the maximum price that the market can give it, it is time to take home some of the gains made.

For example, we could collect only the gain made and continue to trust that stock while strictly respecting the Stop Loss at minus 7% (remember that stocks that grow very often continue to grow without stopping).

Then the moment will come when for a stock you invest in, the Stop Loss will be positioned above the price at which you bought it: from this moment on for this stock you will no longer be able to lose, because even if it loses 7%, you will sell at a price higher than the price at which you bought it.

The stop loss is dynamic

This happens because the stop loss is dynamic and is raised as the stock grows in price. In fact, if you imagine buying a stock at 37 dollars and 45 cents, you will initially set a stop loss at 32.55 dollars.

If the stock goes from $ 35 to $ 45, the minus 7 percent stop loss will go from $ 32.55 to $ 41.85 and even if the stock price falls to this level triggering your stop loss, you would still sell for profit, since the price at which you sell (the stop loss in fact) is higher than the price at which you bought it.

You may think that it is not easy to choose stocks that have a good chance of passing this test and giving high returns on your investment: in general it is so because if for example we consider the size of the American market the work you should do to study one for oneself among one all titles is truly monstrous.

But there are tools called Stock Screener which are software that extract you from the "great sea" of the American market (for example and not only) the stocks that reflect certain characteristics you are looking for.

You simply have to specify what characteristics the title you are looking for has and the Stock Screener will return the title or titles that meet the requirements you specify: a bit like agencies for lonely hearts do.

So let's imagine you have the name of the stock you intend to invest in: it's a stock that has a good safety margin and high growth potential.

Soros buys stocks only when the time is right

I understood from Soros that to buy stocks it is always better to wait for the right moment.

This is because the market sometimes makes fluctuations that can penalize the stock you have chosen in the short term (days or months) even if it has excellent characteristics and potential.

This happens because the market has psychological characteristics being made up of people like you, who are in the throes of euphoria on some days and in depression on others.

The study of a stock chart: Soros docet!

Studying the stock chart will help you decide the most profitable time to avoid these short-term penalties.

What I have described to you is the method that real investors follow, those who earn on the stock market constantly and continuously. I have shared these secrets in this course.

Remember that to aim for maximum results you must also take care of your psychology, that's how: you too can join this group if you want to learn how to manage your money autonomously through Investments in Shares but if you still think that Investments in the Stock Exchange are similar to the lottery game and you expect to have results without committing a minimum, then this "adventure" is not for you.

If, on the other hand, you are willing to dedicate yourself to this discipline because you don't like the idea of letting your money rot in the bank or entrust it to people you don't even know, then for you this article can represent the beginning of a path that can give you great satisfaction, both financially and personally.

CONCLUSION

If you are reading the conclusion, it means that you have reached the end of the book.

I hope it was a pleasant reading and the content was interesting.

Hope all of this has served to improve your way of trading intraday, but not only that!

I have also tried to help you understand how important it is to have a trading plan, or understand what your goals are or how to best manage risk.

I also hope with this book you will discover the method to make your trading more profitable, but above all, that you will learn the tools to try to safeguard your capital.

As I always say, trading doesn't mean playing in the casino.

Trading has become their job for many, and for some, the possibility that has allowed them to significantly increase their standard of living.

But behind all this there is study, preparation, discipline, organization and above all, never improvisation.

I wish you every success in trading and in other types of business, have a good life!

CPSIA information can be obtained
at www.ICGtesting.com
Printed in the USA
LVHW011308221220
674886LV00001B/60